Beginnings of the Cold War Arms Race

The Truman Administration and the U.S. Arms Build-Up

RAYMOND P. OJSERKIS

Westport, Connecticut
London

Library of Congress Cataloging-in-Publication Data

Ojserkis, Raymond P., 1969–
    Beginnings of the Cold War arms race : the Truman administration and the U.S. arms build-up / by Raymond P. Ojserkis.
        p.   cm.
    Includes bibliographical references and index.
    ISBN 0–275–98016–2 (alk. paper)
        1. United States—Military policy.   2. Military readiness—United States—History—20th century.   3. Arms race—History—20th century.   4. United States—Foreign relations—1945–1953.   5. Cold War.   I. Title.
    UA23.O43 2003
    355'.033573'09044—dc21   2003044215

British Library Cataloguing in Publication Data is available.

Library of Congress Catalog Card Number: 2003044215
ISBN: 0–275–98016–2

First published in 2003

Praeger Publishers, 88 Post Road West, Westport, CT 06881

An imprint of Greenwood Publishing Group, Inc.
www.praeger.com
Printed in the United States of America

∞™

The paper used in this book complies with the Permanent Paper Standard issued by the National Information Standards Organization (Z39.48–1984).

10   9   8   7   6   5   4   3   2   1

Contents

Preface and Acknowledgments		vii
Abbreviations Used in Notes		ix
Introduction		1
1	Demobilization	5
2	Consolidation	13
3	Reconsideration	47
4	Transformation	85
5	Globalization	107
6	Actualization	129
Conclusions		153
Notes		161
Bibliography		215
Index		231

Preface and Acknowledgments

The Cold War arms race did not begin when the Cold War began. Convinced of the deterrent power of the American atomic monopoly, the Soviet leadership's lack of desire for war, the need for economy in the federal budget, and the importance of avoiding waste in the military, the Truman administration continued to demobilize U.S. forces even as the Cold War grew ever more competitive, in 1945, 1946, and 1947. Only with the beginning of the Korean War, on June 25, 1950, did the Truman administration shift its stance on military preparedness. From that time, the administration swung to an opposite extreme, almost tripling military budgets, deploying large combat-ready forces to those areas of Europe and East Asia where the American-led bloc bordered the realms of Soviet and Chinese influence, expanding the strategic air fleet, and augmenting the nation's nuclear weapons production programs. This reversal was not a simple case of remobilizing for the Korean War: it was a remobilization for the Cold War. Truman administration officials explicitly stated that the arms build-up was meant to create and maintain both conventional and nuclear parity with the USSR worldwide even after the expected cessation of hostilities in Korea. The expenses incurred by the expansion of programs, forces, and obligations ensured that, as a proportion of national income, military funding, despite some slight downturns in the 1950s, would remain at wartime levels until the 1970s. U.S. combat-force deployments outside of the Western Hemisphere would last into the twenty-first century.

This book relates, in a generally chronological fashion, the events leading up to the arms build-up, and the build-up itself. In doing so, it also assesses the causes and effects of the build-up. In particular, it attempts to answer seven critical questions: Did the United States and its European allies come to find themselves in a position of relative weakness, vis-à-vis the Soviet Union, in terms of conventional power, by 1950, as Western leaders then believed? Why were certain officials within the Truman administration unsuccessful in their efforts to initiate an arms build-up, before the start of the Korean War, even though they managed to gain Truman's signature on a National Security Council document calling for expanded military budgets? Why, in the first days after the start of the Korean War, was the Truman administration convinced of the need for an arms build-up and deployment of global scope and indefinite duration, even though the conflict in Korea was not expected to last long? How did the Truman administration incorporate such radical policy shifts into the budgets, and finance them so rapidly? Why was the administration successful in its efforts to win congressional support for troop deployments to Europe, even though the war was in East Asia? To what extent did the Truman administration's arms build-up of 1950–51 initiate the Cold War arms race, especially in terms of conventional forces? Was the decision to initiate the arms build-up a sound one?

In researching this book, I read government documents in archives and presidential libraries, the memoirs and diaries of relevant individuals, and the work of historians who blazed a trail in this field. These documents are listed in the bibliography following the text. I should also especially thank Professor David Stevenson, of the London School of Economics and Political Science, for his close and helpful supervision of this work through many stages; Professors MacGregor Knox and Robert Boyce, also of the London School of Economics and Political Science, for reviewing parts of the text; Randy Sowell and Liz Safly, for helping orient me amid the vast holdings of the Truman Library; Dr. Donald Steury, of the Center for the Study of Intelligence, for reading an early draft and providing valuable commentary and background information; Jim Dunton of Praeger Publishers, for helping arrange publication; Alissa Gafford, for copyediting early portions at of the book; and the team at Impressions Book and Journal Services, Inc. for organizing the production of the manuscript. Lastly, I would like to thank my late father, Richard, my mother, Rosa, my brother, Nelson, and his wife, Deborah, for general support.

Abbreviations Used
in Notes

The U.S. Army Center of Military History	ACMH
The Basil Liddell Hart Center	BLHC
The Churchill Archives	CA
Central Intelligence Agency, Historical Office	CIAH
Congressional Service Quarterly	CSQ
The Dwight D. Eisenhower Presidential Library	DDEL
The Franklin D. Roosevelt Presidential Library	FDRL
Foreign Relations of the United States	FRUS
The Harry S. Truman Presidential Library	HSTL
The U.S. National Archives & Records Administration	NARA
Office of the Secretary of Defense, History Office	OSDH
The Papers of Dwight David Eisenhower	PDDE
The Public Record Office of the United Kingdom	PRO

Introduction

Charles Bohlen, a career U.S. Foreign Service officer specializing in Soviet affairs, described the scope and scale of the American arms build-up during the Korean War (1950–53) by saying:

Before Korea, the United States had only one commitment of a political or military nature outside the Western Hemisphere. This was the North Atlantic Treaty. Our bases in Germany and Japan were regarded as temporary, to be given up when the occupation ended. True, as a hangover from pre-war days, we felt it necessary to retain bases in the Philippines, but there was no pledge on their use. The only places we had military facilities were in England, where we had transit privileges, and Saudi Arabia, where we had an airfield. As a result of our overinterpretation of Communism's goal [during the Korean War], we had by 1955 about 450 bases in thirty-six countries, and we were linked by political and military pacts with some twenty countries outside of Latin America. It was the Korean War and not World War II that made us a world military-political power.[1]

This extension of American power entailed a renewed use of conscription, a reintroduction of World War II-style price and wage controls, and a near tripling of U.S. military budgets in a two-year period. The funds covered everything from new combat divisions to new navy super carriers to the construction of the largest nuclear weapons plants yet built. The motivation was the fear that unless the United States engaged in a militarized containment of Soviet power, the Korean War could be a prelude to a much wider conflict with the USSR.

The arms build-up began immediately after June 25, 1950, the start of the Korean War. Although many other events (such as the Turkish Straits and Iranian crises of 1946, the Greek civil war that began after the end of World War II, the Berlin blockade of 1948–49, the Soviet detonation of an atomic weapon and the collapse of Chinese nationalist resistance in mainland China in 1949, and the signing of the Sino-Soviet Treaty of Mutual Assistance in February 1950) contributed to tension between the Soviet Union and the United States, it was only after the start of the Korean War that the Truman administration embarked on an arms build-up designed to reverse the perceived Soviet lead in conventional forces. Such action was in direct contrast to President Harry Truman's policies from V-J Day right up to May 1950. It contravened his decision to demobilize forces as rapidly as possible after the war, as well as the National Security Council's decision in February 1948 to "work towards the earliest withdrawal of all occupation forces from Germany."[2] The arms build-up was also in direct contrast to Truman's decision to submit the lowest proposed American military budget of the post-1945 era to Congress in May 1950, a month before the beginning of the Korean War, while asking the Department of Defense if its budget could be further cut by a half-billion dollars.

The need to build forces throughout the anti-Soviet world became so critical during 1950–51 that the United States reversed its policies on the demilitarized status of Germany and Japan. Other radical changes included the decisions to fund a globally deployed American military on an indefinite basis, reintroduce conscription, and create a domestic air defense system against enemy penetration.[3]

Almost all such decisions were made in the first three months of the Korean campaign. Later events, such as the start of the Chinese conquest of Tibet in October 1950, the Chinese entry into the Korean War, the introduction of Soviet pilots in that war, the beginning of a negotiated settlement in Korea, the successful testing of thermonuclear weapons by both the United States and the USSR, the election of President Dwight Eisenhower, and the death of Soviet dictator Josef Stalin, had an impact on American arms spending. However, their impact was not revolutionary: the general scope of American commitments had been set in the summer of 1950. The Truman administration, and the other Cold War administrations that followed until the 1970s, only altered the scale or expense gradually, and could never seriously reconsider the deployments decided upon in 1950.

The military commitments made during the Korean War were global. In Korea, American troops returned in 1950, after having withdrawn in 1949, and have stayed to the present day. In the Arctic, the United States embarked on the creation of a new radar system, the Distant Early Warning (DEW) line, to protect against Soviet attacks. In the air, the United States built the Strategic Air Command (SAC) into a potent force of several hundred thousand personnel, with bombers in the air at all times to retaliate in the event of a nuclear strike upon the United States or its treaty allies. At sea, the United States began patrolling the Straits of Taiwan, becoming militarily involved in the Chinese Civil War for the first time. Under the seas, the United States launched its first nuclear-powered submarines. In Germany, where the American occupation units had previously been unarmored, without air power, and involved primarily in denazification and maintaining public order, the North Atlantic Treaty signatories began building that paper alliance into an effective armed force, creating the North Atlantic Treaty Organization (NATO), with a multilateral command structure, a Supreme Allied Commander for Europe (SACEUR) in charge of field operations, four American divisions, and increased commitments from other member states.[4]

Without the Korean War, or an incident similar to it, it is doubtful that America would have engaged in an arms build-up or deployed its forces around the globe. Although Truman would later claim, in an official address to Congress asking for military funds, that the decision to ask for an increased military budget "should have—and, though no doubt in smaller measure, would have—been taken" even in the absence of the Korean War, the evidence suggests otherwise.[5] As we shall see, Truman was attempting to trim the military budget right up to the day the war began. Truman may have been closer to expressing his real feelings on the impact of the Korean War in a January 1953 discussion with a journalist, during which he discussed Stalin's decision to allow the North Koreans to invade South Korea: "It's the greatest error he made in his whole career. If he hadn't made that mistake, we'd have done what we did after World War I: completely disarmed. And it would have been a cinch for him to take over the European nations, one by one." But the beginning of the Korean War had dramatically changed matters: "It caused the rearmament of ourselves and our Allies. It brought about the North Atlantic Treaty [sic]. It brought about the various Pacific alliances. It hurried up the signing of the Japanese Peace Treaty. It caused Greece and Turkey to be brought quickly into the North Atlantic Alliance."[6]

The defense policy changes of 1950–51 had long-lasting repercussions. The new deployments of forces in Germany and Korea would survive not only the end of the Korean War, but also the end of the Cold War. The military agreements with Japan, Australia, and New Zealand are still legally binding, and the NATO military structure is not only alive at the beginning of the twenty-first century, but also preparing to expand.

CHAPTER 1

Demobilization

AMERICAN AND WESTERN EUROPEAN MILITARY PREPAREDNESS, 1945 TO EARLY 1948

The American, British, and French forces acting under Eisenhower's supreme command in the days leading up to V-E Day in May 1945 were formidable. In terms of air and sea power, they were more effective than any other force in the world, and on land had shown that they could drive from the English Channel to the center of Germany. But by 1948, the Americans, British, and French, not to mention allies such as the Netherlands, had little military power in Europe. In the United States, a large national debt and a high political priority on returning to a traditional version of peacetime, one with little need for large arms budgets, led to a swift and significant demobilization. For Britain and France, a high priority on funding economic reconstruction and the draining effect of colonial conflicts in Asia prevented the maintenance of sizable and effective forces in Europe. On both sides of the North Atlantic, confidence in the deterrent effect of the United States's atomic monopoly, and tardiness in concluding that the USSR was a substantial rival, contributed to the general rush to demobilize. With Germany and Italy demilitarized, there was little military force in Europe west of the Soviet occupation sector in Germany by the end of 1947.

In the United States, the prospect of a peacetime mobilization appeared unlikely to most Americans in the aftermath of World War II. Despite the intense acrimony that divided the governments in Moscow and Washington by, at latest, early 1946, it was by no means apparent that a cold war (the term was coined that year) would entail an extensive worldwide build-up of troops and weaponry. Following previous practices, but in contrast to practices after future wars in Korea and Vietnam, the United States demobilized its conventional forces to such an extent that there were hardly any American combat forces outside the United States.

Many, if not most, Americans had been opposed to America's military participation in World War II until the attack on Pearl Harbor and the German declaration of war on the United States. During the war, most Americans hoped for a quick resolution and a return to the old ways of small armies and relatively little military action outside the Western Hemisphere. Although isolationist sentiment, especially in its most strident forms, was on the decline, Americans still almost universally assumed that army and naval forces would return home after the war and that there was no need for permanent military deployments abroad.

By the November 1944 elections, both of the major parties, reading the polls, tried to make electoral gains by claiming that their party would demobilize the fastest.[1] The Roosevelt administration began decreasing munitions production during 1944[2] and made plans to slow warship construction.[3] President Franklin Roosevelt informed Harold Smith, director of the Bureau of the Budget, that after the war he wanted to give a higher priority to cutting the national debt than to spending on foreign policy or tax relief.[4]

Truman, on assuming the presidency in April 1945, was similarly inclined toward a rapid postwar demobilization. In his September 6, 1945, message to Congress, at 16,000 words the longest address ever delivered by a president to the legislatures, Truman barely mentioned foreign policy, despite the fact that only four days earlier General Douglas MacArthur had hosted the formal surrender of Japan in Tokyo Bay.[5] The message represented the end of the war in American politics. The goal was a return to normalcy: an ending of the unpopular shortages of the war years, and an effort to use the boom in production that the war had created (national income had doubled from 1939 to 1945) to boost the domestic standard of living and pay off the immense war debt, which was more massive relative to the size of the American economy than at any time in U.S. history before or since (almost double the amount, as a percentage of gross national product, than at present).

Truman, looking over a world in which the governments that composed the Axis alliance had been replaced by occupying military forces, confident that the American atomic monopoly would maintain U.S. security in the future, and under intense public pressure to bring the troops home and restore a sense of normalcy,[6] ordered immediate demobilization and the withdrawal of almost all American soldiers overseas. In one month, the Pentagon cancelled $15 billion in contracts,[7] and by the end of the year, the Department of Defense canceled more than $21 billion in contracts with aircraft manufacturers alone.[8]

Truman did not face significant congressional opposition over demobilization. Sensing war weariness in the public, the Democrats, forming the majority in both legislatures, were eager to demobilize and end the unpopular wartime conscription. The Republicans, who would gain the majority in both houses of Congress in the 1946 midterm elections, came into office on an election platform of reining in government expenditure. A substantial minority of congressional Republicans also maintained the pre-World War II prejudice against high levels of military spending. Even had they wished to do so, the Republicans were in a poor position to make major changes, considering they had won a tiny majority of seats on a minority of votes and faced a hostile executive branch.[9] By the time they opened the Eighty-first Congress in January 1947, the demobilization of the military had already taken place, and the Republicans made no effort to revise it.

Demilitarization took only two years. The military budget fell from $81.6 billion in fiscal year 1945 (July 1944–June 1945) to $44.7 billion in fiscal year 1946 to $13.1 billion in fiscal year 1947,[10] with Truman envisioning a time when defense spending might level off at $6 to $7 billion annually.[11] As a percentage of gross national product, military spending dropped from 38.5 percent in fiscal year 1945 to 5.7 percent in fiscal year 1947.[12] The decline in personnel was even steeper, as detailed in the chart below.

Between V-E Day and November 2, 1945, nearly 2.5 million troops returned to the United States.[13]

The result was a U.S. military that lacked sufficient conventional power to carry out some of the political commitments the Truman administration wished to uphold. When there was a crisis in March 1946 concerning Soviet unwillingness to withdraw, as promised, from the northern regions

Table 1.1
Decrease in U.S. Military Personnel after World War II

Decrease in U.S. Military Personnel after World War II		
	Personnel in 1945	Personnel in 1948
Army	8,266,373*	530,000
Navy	3,380,817	419,347
Marine Corps	474,680	84,988

*The 1945 army figure includes 2,200,000 personnel in the Army Air Corps, which became an independent service, the United States Air Force, in 1947.

of Iran, Secretary of State Jimmy Byrnes felt that the U.S. armed forces were already too weak to play a role.[14] By 1948, the army had less than half the number of troops in uniform that it had at the time of Pearl Harbor.[15]

Between February 1945 and 1948, the number of navy aircraft carriers fell from 90 (almost 60 of which were purpose-built) to 11.[16] From the end of the war until early 1948, air power was cut from a total of 218 groups (each consisting of either 30 bombers or 75 fighters) to 38.[17] Despite the focus on strategic bombing, which we shall consider later, the 2.2 million personnel in the Army Air Corps of 1945 were reduced to 411,277 in the Air Force by June 30, 1950.[18] The number of civilians in military aircraft production decreased from 2,101,600 in November 1943 to 138,700 in February 1946, and the number of airframe plants in operation dropped from 66 to 16 in 1945 alone.[19]

The pace was so rapid that Truman would later claim that it was not demobilization, "it was disintegration."[20] Perhaps an even more apt analogy was General Alfred Wedemeyer's claim that the nation had "fought the war like a football game, after which the winner leaves the field and celebrates."[21]

Although American forces did remain as occupation troops in Japan, Germany, and Austria, these units were stripped of most armor and air power and assigned only maintenance of public order and denazification duties. Only the desire to fulfill these commitments prevented the United States from completely withdrawing its forces from theaters of operations in 1945, as it had in the few years following World War I.

There were no large British or French forces in Europe to compensate for the withdrawal of American forces. In the chaotic first two years after World War II, the pressing question on the minds of most Western European policymakers was how to survive the economic collapse the war had created, rather than how to maintain or build effective fighting forces.

The war had led to marked declines in the standard of living and the volume of economic output. Many cities had been pulverized by aerial bombardments, which wrecked manufacturing centers, disabled transportation networks, ruined communications systems, rendered central business districts unusable, and left countless families homeless. Dams and dikes had been destroyed, causing immense flooding. In the chaos after the collapse of Axis governments and occupation regimes, currencies were ruined and order difficult to maintain. Businesses that survived the war often found it difficult to reestablish peace-time business relationships and reconvert to the production or sale of peace-time goods. As soon as officials accomplished the challenging task of reorganizing governments in the formerly occupied nations, they turned their energies toward the call for economic recovery.

Defense, in the strictly military sense of the word, was relatively neglected, since economic recovery was considered the primary defense against Soviet-inspired Communism. The Council of European Economic Cooperation (CEEC), created to oversee the distribution of aid from the European Recovery Program (better known as the Marshall Plan), focused on industry and commerce, rather than military aid. Military expenditures were low.

What money France had for her armed forces went to resuming control of the empire, especially in Indochina, which the Japanese had occupied, and where, from 1946, the French were fighting the Vietminh.

The Dutch were slow in concluding that the Soviet Union was the greatest threat to their independence, rather than Germany. Only after the failure of the London Conference of 1947 to create a new unified and demilitarized Germany did the Dutch, perceiving that it was Soviet intransigence that prevented a settlement, conclude that security against the USSR was necessary.[22] But economic difficulties, stemming mostly from the destruction caused by fighting in Holland in 1944–45, made military funding scarce.

British policy, as reflected in the 1947 Future Defence Policy Paper, was based on the assumption that defense of the British Isles, control of the Middle East, and maintenance of sea communications were the highest defense priorities of the nation. Having borrowed heavily to fight World War II, and having domestic spending programs of vast size, Britain had a debt that was 2.7 times the gross national product,[23] making any contribution of armed forces to Central Europe financially difficult.

In the unlikely event that a war with the Soviet Union would arise,[24] Britain was to abandon Europe and fight Communism in the Asian parts of the empire, particularly the Middle East, and through the use of strategic bombing.[25] The British War Office assumed that the Soviet Army would be able to occupy Germany, the Low Countries, and France in two months, and would then embark on attacks on the oil-rich Middle East.[26]

The assessment was based not only on Western military weakness, but also on Soviet military power, which was significant.

SOVIET MILITARY PREPAREDNESS, 1945–47

Conflicting factors affected Soviet military preparedness after World War II. Driving military spending and troop levels up were the vast scope of the goals of Soviet foreign policy, substantial disagreements with the other World War II victors, a political culture in the Kremlin that viewed foreign powers with suspicion and that sought protection through military force, insecurity over perceived Western technological superiority, the desire for internal security, and awareness of the American atomic monopoly. Driving military spending and troop levels down were the American demobilization, the perception of war weariness in the United States, and the very substantial demands of economic reconstruction.

The Soviet leadership had multiple foreign policy goals and sought to achieve as many as reasonably possible without jeopardizing the Communist Party's power. In probable order of importance, the Soviets sought: the USSR's 1941 frontiers (with the further addition of East Prussia); friendly governments near their borders (especially in Poland and Romania, which had border disputes with the USSR); a neutralized, reparations-paying Germany; Western recognition of these changes; cooperation with the West based on these accomplished facts; and the extension of Soviet power outside the areas dominated by the Red Army, perhaps through the use of Communist factions abroad.[27] They achieved the first goal in 1944–45 by reconsolidating Estonia, Latvia, and Lithuania into the USSR and redrawing the national boundaries of Poland, Romania, Germany, and the USSR, forcibly moving parts of the concerned populations in the process. This action caused considerable unease in the West, with the United States and Britain refusing, in July 1945, to recognize the new western boundary of Poland. The other Soviet goals proved harder to achieve and led to even greater tension with the other World War II victors. In particular, the decision to install governments in Poland and Romania that were malleable to Soviet aims, rather than accepting American interpretations of democratic self-determination, increased the political distrust between Moscow and Washington.

A wide variety of other disagreements existed as well, many stemming from Soviet distaste for the American vision of a postwar world dominated by relatively free trade (with currencies pegged to the dollar) and elected governments. Disagreements on the governance of occupied Germany, the Anglo-American prohibition of Soviet involvement in occupied Japan and Italy, the ongoing struggles between Communist and conservative forces in China and Greece, and Soviet meddling in Iranian and Turkish affairs all increased the friction between the West and the USSR. At the Potsdam Conference of July–August 1945, the major victors in the European theater of war had agreed on the denazification of Germany and the need to finish off Japan, but could not agree on issues independent of their mutual antagonism toward the Axis powers. The status of governments in eastern Europe was covered in language that was open to much interpretation. The failure to produce more fruitful results was a foreshadowing of how the Grand Alliance would crumble once the war was fully over. After the surrender of Japan, the decline in relations between the Soviets and the Anglo-American coalition became precipitous. By February 1946, Stalin, in a radio address, began preparing the Soviet populace for the possibility of a future war with the capitalist powers.[28]

The Soviet willingness to accept high levels of distrust in their relations with the United States may have stemmed, in part, from a predilection to assume that foreign relations, particularly with capitalist powers, were unlikely to ever be based on mutual understanding and commitment. The best that could be hoped for would be wary cooperation for a limited duration on issues of mutual interest. Russian and Soviet history had produced a political legacy of anxiety regarding foreign intrigues and a view of national security that was highly dependent upon the occupation of territory. Such history, combined with insecurity over internal weaknesses and Stalin's conspiratorial personality, led the Soviets to operate under the premise that conventional military operations of unspecific scope were a significant possibility.

The Kremlin was acutely aware that the Soviet Union was years behind the West in industrial technology and that it would be some time before the Soviets could create their own atomic weapons. This insecurity did not, however, lead to decreased military spending. On the contrary, it led to a greater drive to compensate with quantities of goods and troops, and quality of military operations. The Soviets continued to grant primacy to the military in acquiring materials and workers, both for production of conventional war materials and for the atomic research program that was vastly expanded after the bombing of Hiroshima. Stalin told his confidants that the USSR needed at least three more five-year plans to prepare for "all contingencies,"[29] and that he wasn't content to demobilize extensively before then. The populace was made to understand that they could not expect a consumer economy soon.

In addition to the international tension, the Soviets had internal security issues. The Soviets were fighting approximately 50,000 to 200,000 Ukrainian members of anti-Soviet paramilitary organizations in 1947,[30] and they also admitted losing tens of thousands of troops against Lithuanian partisans.[31]

Knowledge of the American demobilization moderated Soviet urges to maintain significant military forces. The Soviet leadership had access to information on many details of American and Western European military preparedness. Much of the information was public information in the West, easily attained by Soviet foreign ministry personnel. There were also spies, the foremost being Donald Maclean, the first secretary of the British embassy in Washington, who gave the Soviet intelligence services a wealth of data, including detailed reports on the month-by-month changes in American forces at every U.S. base, domestic and foreign,[32] and information on political talks among Western leaders. A host of other material from a variety of American, Australian, British, and other sources was added to Maclean's information.[33] The Soviets knew that, in the immediate postwar era, the United States had only a tiny nuclear arsenal (fewer than six bombs in March 1946), and that the British still had none.[34]

The Soviets also had perhaps the greatest need for economic reconstruction of any of the World War II combatants. The war with Nazi Germany had been extraordinary in its scope, harshness, duration, and damage. Within the USSR, 1,710 towns had been annihilated; 70,000 villages

burned to the ground; 32,000 factories rendered unusable; 65,000 kilometers of railroad track destroyed; 90,000 road bridges wrecked; 100,000
collective farms laid to waste; 70 million livestock animals killed; 1,000
coal pits made unusable; 3,000 oil wells destroyed; and 25 million people
left homeless.[35]

However, despite the necessities of reconstruction and Soviet knowledge of American demobilization, Soviet military budgets did not have
to sink as far as the American ones before they reached a point at which
the factors driving costs up were at least equal to those driving them
down.

The Soviets seem to have concluded, in the 1945–47 period, that there
was sufficient need for forces, and that the USSR's security needs and
political aims afforded it only a partial demobilization.[36] Millions of troops
were decommissioned, but the armed forces were not cut to an extent that
would jeopardize the Soviet preponderance of force in central Europe (we
will examine this force in Chapter 2).

The Soviet military leadership protected the critical armored and air
elements, as well as the core of the infantry, from the brunt of the cuts.
Where possible, the Soviet staff decommissioned service members too old
for normal service as well as obsolete units, such as cavalry,[37] but tank
units and the fleet were unaffected by the initial demobilization.[38] Many
divisions at full strength were maintained on forward deployment in central Europe, and, as we will see in a later chapter, the decrease in Soviet
manpower was at least partially offset by improvements in Soviet military
technology and techniques, which made the smaller force more mobile
and advanced.

CHAPTER 2

Consolidation

THE STABILIZATION OF AMERICAN MILITARY PREPAREDNESS

By 1948, American military spending had tumbled so far that the Truman administration was forced to decide where the floor would be on military spending. Analysts set about creating a more comprehensive strategy for matching American military means and ends, linking goals, limits, and requirements.[1] As with any military budgeting, political desires, competing demands for funds by other sectors of government and society, current capabilities, and the existing military balance all affected the decision-making process.

Opposing forces affected spending. The American monopoly on nuclear weapons, the American military's emphasis on strategic bombing (which was relatively cheaper than the conventional armed services), the priority placed on paying off the federal debt, a president who assumed that the military leadership would squander funds, the seeming remoteness of a major war, and the American tradition of small peacetime military budgets drove costs down. On the other hand, the maintenance of occupation forces in defeated Germany and Japan, the use of American military personnel to help train Allied armies, the maintenance of a bomber force capable of posing a nuclear deterrent, the new postwar internationalism that permeated American political culture, and, most importantly, the continuing disagreements on postwar settlement issues with the Soviet Union drove costs up.[2] In the 1945–47 period, the factors driving costs down outweighed those driving costs up, but by 1948, an equilibrium between the opposing forces had been reached. The new level of military spending, which hovered around five percent of the gross national product in the June 1948–June 1950 period, was, relative to national income, far in excess of 1930s prewar budgets, but far short of most of the Cold War military budgets after 1950.

Among the factors keeping military spending down, the atomic monopoly was perhaps the most important. In the wake of Japan's surrender, shortly after the atomic attacks on Hiroshima and Nagasaki, American military strategists saw nuclear weapons as war-winners, and favored using them early and often in the event of a war with the USSR. On August 30, 1945, just days after Japan's unofficial surrender, and before the formal surrender in Tokyo Bay, the U.S. Army Air Force[3] delivered a manuscript to American forces in the Pacific detailing the number of atomic bombs needed to destroy each of the major Soviet cities, and the bases useful to carry out such a plan.[4] Atomic bombing became a main axiom of all U.S. contingency plans, such as BROILER, TROJAN, HALF-MOON, and FLEETWOOD, for a possible conflict with the Soviet Union in the late 1940s.[5] Bombers were to fly from bases in the United Kingdom, Okinawa, and the Middle East, and from aircraft carriers. BROILER designated targets in 24 Soviet cities[6], and TROJAN designated industrial targets in 70 Soviet cities. U.S. strategists in this era greatly preferred strategic bombing of major Soviet command, production, and transportation centers to tactical bombing of Soviet military forces in the field. The plan was to win a war primarily through atomic bombing, rather than use the weapons in a way that might enable a ground army to slog its way to a victory.

The reliance on atomic weapons resulted in, and was also a result of, the low American military spending on conventional arms. Omar Bradley, the army chief of staff, would later claim that "the Army of 1948 could not fight its way out of a paper bag"[7] after its budget cuts. As we shall see in a later section, U.S. military planners did not expect that the existing French, American, and British armies would be able to make a determined stand on the European mainland in the initial stages of a war with the USSR. If the atomic attacks on the USSR failed to induce a quick Soviet surrender, it would take many months for the United States to remobilize its forces in sufficient number to challenge the Soviets in continental Europe.

Besides atomic weapons, another major factor militating against any growth in defense budgets was the emphasis on debt reduction, particularly by the president. Although Truman could sometimes talk as if he fervently believed in the reality of a Soviet military threat, saying, for instance, after the March 1948 Soviet-sponsored coup in Czechoslovakia, that "we are faced with exactly the same situation with which Britain and France were faced in 1938–39 with Hitler," his actions suggest that he believed that large debt was the greater threat to national health. In contrast to his predecessor in the Oval Office, and in disagreement with at least one of his chairmen of the Council of Economic Advisers, Leon Keyserling,[8] Truman valued balanced budgets. The New Deal and, more importantly, World War II, had created more than $250 billion of federal government debt, which Truman was convinced had to be slashed to relieve the economy of onerous interest payments. Although economists and liberal advisers in the administration often lobbied for government-stimulated demand and easy money, tenets of the American version of Keynesian economics that were the guiding ideas of the moderate left at that time, Truman was absolutely opposed to the ideas of fiscal and monetary management that had become influential since the first term of Franklin Roosevelt. As a local official in Missouri and later as a U.S. senator, Truman had aimed to cut deficits through careful control of expenditure.[9] He had even made a name for himself doing so,[10] and was disinclined, as president, to accept new ideas about deficit-financed spending that he did not fully understand. As Alonzo Hamby, perhaps the most thorough of Truman's biographers, has written, "Truman . . . never fully accepted Keynesian economics of any variety. His ideas on budgetary management had been formulated during ten generally grim years of local government administration in which raising funds through debt had been a difficult process and the goal had always been to balance income with outgo."[11] It was Truman's opinion that "during World War II, we borrowed too much and did not tax ourselves enough. We must not run our present defense effort on that kind of financial basis."[12] Truman was unimpressed by his advisers' promises about running an economy at full employment through borrowing. When Keyserling wrote to Truman to try to persuade him to engage in deficit-financed stimulus, Truman responded by writing "Leon, you are the greatest persuader I ever knew, but nobody can convince me that the Government can spend a dollar that its not got. I'm just a country boy."[13] His first chairman of the Council of Economic Advisers, Edwin Nourse, later commented that "he was figure-minded and he relied very strongly on Jim Webb, who was Director of the [Bureau of] the Budget. You see they had a set of figures which we developed into economic indicators and that was the one thing where Mr. Truman made his most effective contact with the work of the Council. He had a leather-bound, short version of economic indicators each quarter . . . and he said 'Yeah, I keep this here all the time, and when people come in and talk to me about this, I say 'Here are the figures' and I pull that out.' But he didn't say, 'Here's the reasoning about these matters the Council of Economic Advisers has given me.' That was beyond his intellectual ken."[14]

Following his own instincts toward politics and policy, Truman labored carefully on each budget, feeling that the budgeting of expenditure was at the heart of good government. Truman would later write in his memoirs that "the federal budget was one of my more serious hobbies."[15] His budgeting was successful. He became president in April 1945, and thus had little impact on fiscal year 1945 (July 1944–June 1945) budget. That year, the federal government's deficit was $20.7 billion and the federal government's debt was $258.7 billion.[16] From July 1, 1946, until June 30, 1952, the federal government collected slightly more revenue than it spent,[17] and by fiscal year 1950, immediately before the start of the Korean War, the federal government's debt had been reduced to $256.1 billion. This constituted a decrease in ratio of federal debt to gross national product from 122.1 percent in fiscal year 1945 to 89.9 percent in fiscal year 1950. Per capita debt in this period fell from $1,849 to $1,688.[18] By eliminating the deficits, the bulk of which consisted of military spending, Truman had allowed the peacetime economy to reduce the debt to more manageable levels.

Taxation played a role in cutting the debt. Truman often suggested increases to stay in the black. However, he had difficulties with Congress on this issue. In 1948, the Republican-majority Congress passed a tax reduction bill over Truman's veto, and in 1952, the Democratic-majority Congress failed to pass a Truman taxation plan to fund the Korean War on a "pay as you go" basis, as Truman referred to it.[19] So spending cuts played a much more significant role.

The military was the obvious target to raid for funds. At the end of World War II, it absorbed 85.7 percent of the budget.[20] Combined with international programs, the military absorbed more than half of the budget in the late 1940s, and approximately half of the remainder was for fixed charges that could not be easily reduced, such as interest on the federal debt and the payment of pensions.[21] Much of the rest was domestic spending of high value to critical constituencies. In particular, Truman was loath to trim the Fair Deal programs[22] that were the most important source of the Democrats' popularity among their core voters: the urban poor, organized labor, ethnic groups, and blue-collar workers.

Truman had little compunction in cutting military spending, given his distrust of the American professional officer corps, especially in regard to money. His experiences in World War I convinced him that the officer ranks were composed of "ornamental and useless fops" who "can't see beyond the ends of their noses" and were incapable of getting value for money. "No military man knows anything at all about money. All they know how to do is spend it, and they don't give a damn whether they're getting their money's worth or not . . . I've known a good many who feel that the more money they spend, the more important they are."[23] In one World War I letter, Truman claimed that he wished he had a seat on the Senate Military Affairs Committee, so that he could set the brass straight. The president took offense at officers who continually complained about lack of funds and refused to rely on the military's estimates of either needs or costs. As an amateur military historian,[24] Truman felt he was knowledgeable enough to set the limits.

Confident that the United States would have time to build its forces before the outbreak of any hostilities, he said, "Our friends the Russkies understand only one language—how many divisions have you, actual or potential."[25] He was sure that the U.S. industrial strength provided those potential divisions. Truman's Munitions Board approved a mobilization plan that operated on the assumption that there would be a lengthy period between the start of a mobilization and a declaration of war.[26] The president was not to be convinced of any more immediate threat by anyone from the Pentagon. Told by Secretary of Defense James Forrestal that the administration should review its budget ceilings, Truman snapped, "The proper thing for you to do is to get the Army, Navy, and Air people together, and establish a program within the budget limits which have been allowed. It seems to me that is your responsibility."[27]

Truman's confidence may have been buoyed by the conviction, held by many in Washington in early 1948, that a war with the Soviets was very unlikely, and that it was possible to win the Cold War without going on a permanent war footing. The fact that the conflicts in Greece and Iran were resolved in a manner acceptable to the administration probably led Truman to believe he could rely on aid programs that were inexpensive, relative to standing armies. Communist factions in these nations had been bloodily suppressed, with the United States supplying dated weaponry but not actively involving the U.S. military. While the Truman Doctrine speech of early 1947 included references to helping anti-Communist forces everywhere, this pledge was not necessarily intended to include American military action. The speech was made to help pass a specific military aid package for Greece and Turkey, and the example was not to become standard procedure, as can be seen from the later decision to terminate aid to the Nationalist Chinese government even as it was falling to Communist forces in 1949.

Truman's victory in the 1948 presidential elections, against an opponent, Thomas Dewey, who proposed a $5 billion per year increase in the military budget, seemed to signal that the public did not view military spending as a critical issue.[28] In Congress, the wartime tendency to avoid using foreign policy as a partisan weapon was still strong. Both parties had supported the administration on demobilization and on a series of containment policies in the eastern Mediterranean and central Europe. Arthur Vandenberg of Michigan and John Foster Dulles of New York, the two most outspoken and important Republican senators on foreign affairs issues, preferred working with the administration to challenging it.

The tendency toward low military budgets was also enhanced by the American tradition of maintaining low peacetime military budgets. Having achieved economic preponderance over its neighbors at an early age, the United States had survived (and even expanded, through a conquest of Native American territory) by relying on a full-time army that was tiny by European standards and on part-time state militias that were relatively inexpensive, given the size of the national economy. From the end of the Civil War in 1865 until the start of the Spanish-American War in 1898, the U.S. Army never had more than 50,000 troops, and often had fewer than 30,000.[29] Even between 1899 and 1933, when the United States was an imperial power in the Caribbean, Mexico, Central America, and the Philippines, the country maintained a standing army that was small in terms of the national population and the national income. The World War I intervention only changed this temporarily. From 1933 to 1939, this tendency to avoid European power politics and the large militaries, heavy taxation, and powerful national security organizations typical of garrison states had been augmented further through isolationist and pacifist trends. The Neutrality Acts, the Good Neighbor Policy, the plan to grant Philippine independence, and the growing sentiment that American entry into World War I had been an error of judgment (in an April 1937 Gallup poll, 71 percent of respondents felt it had been a mistake)[30] indicated a process that, had it not been cut short by concerns about Japan and Germany, seemed destined to redefine the limits of American military operations as the American national borders. In 1937, the United States had spent $1.032 billion on the military,[31] approximately 1.52 percent of national income.[32] This percentage was one of the lowest of any nation in the world. The public sentiment of the 1930s, a decade of relative economic hardship in American history, was focused on domestic reform. Neither the many supporters of the New Deal, nor its opponents, saw much political gain to be made in foreign policy while such a significant rethinking of the role of the state in domestic policy was taking place.

Given the traditionally low emphasis on military preparedness in American national politics, it is worth asking why funding levels in the late 1940s were not cut even further. Had either a regional power policy or isolationism been pursued in the post-World War II era, the military funding levels of 1948 would have been more than enough. Chester Bowles, the noted liberal writer and politician, suggested in 1948 that the military was in fact too powerful, consuming more in one year than the whole federal government had a decade earlier.[33] There was no immediate threat of invasion to the nation or the hemisphere by any power. If American interests had been defined in their pre–World War II sense, there would have been little need for a strong military. But several things kept American military budgets much higher proportional to national income in 1948 than they had been in 1937. Three were most important. The first was the decision to maintain military units in Germany and Japan for the purposes of occupation. The second was the necessity of maintaining strategic air capabilities, as seen by the production of atomic bombs and efforts to maintain base rights in the Azores, Greenland, Iceland, Labrador, Okinawa, the Philippines, Saudi Arabia, and elsewhere.[34] The third, which was a partial cause of the first two, was the desire to play a stabilizing role in European politics.

World War II changed the American political philosophy, perhaps more than it changed the politics of the other two major victors, Britain and the USSR. The shift was not merely one in presidential administration, with the customary changes that entailed. It was a deep change in political culture, resulting in more than two decades of support for an activist foreign policy. Given the failure of European collective security efforts to contain German expansionism at the start of World War II, and the subsequent difficulties in reaching a satisfactory postwar settlement with the Soviet Union, the American public became convinced that peacetime participation in European power politics, in the form of containment of Soviet power, was a necessary security precaution. It could not be assumed that Western Europe would be able to contain the USSR's political ambitions without American political, economic, and military support.

NUCLEAR RELIANCE CONSOLIDATED

In the spring and summer of 1948, some attempts were made, by U.S. defense strategists and by supporters of conscription, to lessen the American doctrinal emphasis on strategic nuclear bombing. Most of these planners sought to rebuild the more expensive conventional forces. But their efforts came to naught. By the end of the summer, the creed of strategic bombing was as strong as it had ever been.

Both of the traditional armed services disliked the reliance on nuclear weapons. The army favored a strategy of forward defense in Europe, in which it would play a leading role.[35] In the event of a war with the USSR in Europe, the army would attempt to fight the Soviet forces as far to the east as possible, retreating as slowly as events would allow until reinforcements could be transported from America. It was hoped that North Atlantic Treaty forces would not have to abandon the continent, and might even be able to prevent certain industrial centers in continental western Europe from falling into Soviet hands. The forward defense strategy was much more agreeable to treaty allies than a strategic bombing strategy, in part because a reliance on nuclear weapons meant that atomic bombs would be dropped in western Europe as the Americans tried to attack advancing Soviet troops.

Navy leaders agreed with the army's assertion that war plans needed a greater emphasis on conventional weapons and tactics. They wanted newer and larger aircraft carriers to play the dominant role carriers had against the Japanese fleet in the Pacific War. Additionally, the navy emphasized to budget planners that in the event of a war with the USSR, the navy would fight the Soviet submarine menace while funneling troops and material to Europe, and, perhaps, the Middle East. The navy defended itself against air force assertions that surface ships would soon be obsolete in an age of transoceanic bombers and nuclear weapons.

In the air force, strategic nuclear bombing was the dominant doctrine. The personality of the organization was shaped by its past as part of the army (the air force was only made independent in 1947). Since at least the era of Brigadier General Billy Mitchell in the 1920s, air warriors had been advocating strategic bombing, in which wars could be won by destroying the enemy's industrial base in air attacks. They chafed under the army's insistence on tactical bombing, in which air power was used to support ground forces by destroying targets in the army's immediate theater of operation.

The creation of the Strategic Air Command (SAC) in World War II had strengthened the strategic bombing lobby. The leaders of this corps went on to form the nucleus of the top air force staff, and they lobbied for heavy long-range bombers. Their influence could be seen in the relatively large budgets SAC received during a period of low military spending and in SAC's preeminent position within the air force command structure. SAC was directly responsible to the air force chief of staff, whereas the Tactical Air Command (TAC), as well as the Eastern Air Defense Force and the Western Air Defense Force, were under the Continental Air Command.[36]

Even though the damage surveys of 1945–46 showed that the strategic bombing in Europe had failed to break the back of German industry, air force generals claimed that the existence of atomic weapons now made strategic bombing the preeminent means of warfare, with ground troops necessary mainly to finish off the enemy and restore order after the raids.[37]

Since the air force had won control of atomic targeting during the period in which the Department of Defense was created, this meant that had a war with the Soviets occurred in the Truman era, nuclear weapons would have been used primarily against industrial conglomerations, as the air force desired, and not against enemy supply lines, command centers, and liquid fuel production, as the army wanted.

In 1948, the interservice bickering over the related issues of strategy and budgeting became so intense that the services publicly attacked each others' viability. The air force claimed that new atomic weaponry and long-range bombers had rendered the navy's carriers obsolete, and the navy countered by publicizing the faults of the air force's B-36 bomber project.[38] In order to increase its importance and funding in this era of strategic bombing, the navy decided to develop its own carrier-based bombers,[39] and sent members of Congress a map of the Soviet Union showing that the range of carrier-based bombers covered major centers in the USSR.[40] Both the navy and the air force hinted that the army plan was too expensive, given the quantities of armor, vehicles, artillery, antitank weapons, and manpower it required.

The older services failed to weaken the air force's strategic bombing program. In early March 1948, the Congressional Aviation Policy Board (a select committee with members from both houses) suggested alterations in the budgets to give the air force greater weight.[41]

Truman, ever interested in budgeting, disapproved of both the air force's call for more bomber groups and the traditional forces' attempts to augment their capacities. He managed, as we will see, to keep cutting budgets across the board, and, despite his administration's doctrinal emphasis on strategic bombing, would refuse to spend money Congress allotted to the air force in the fiscal year 1950 defense budget.

The president's only major interventions in the debate on military strategy in 1948 consisted of another effort to implement Universal Military Training (UMT), and, later, a conscription plan. Under Truman's UMT proposals, similar to ones that had been rejected by Congress in 1945 and 1947, all young male citizens would have to receive basic training and be commissioned into a reserve force.[42] Truman liked the plan because the army favored it, as it would lay the groundwork for any possible future mobilizations, and it was economical.

Even more important was its appeal to Truman's ideological prejudices. Truman lionized the ideal of citizen soldiers doing their public service. The plan would replace the standing military with the type of unit Truman had served with at the western front, and the power of the professional military establishment that Truman mocked would be curbed.

UMT even gained some popularity, with most polls showing that more than 65 percent of the public supported the idea.[43] With the full support of Secretary of State George Marshall,[44] whose years as an infantryman and a general had convinced him of the value of training and manpower, UMT was presented again to Congress.

Differences in strategic thinking doomed UMT. As can be seen from the budget debates, Congress had already been sold on strategic (and preferably nuclear) air power, and saw UMT as an attempt to prepare forces for an outdated version of attritional warfare that might never arise again. Congress was also probably taking into account the fact that UMT might prove less popular in reality than the polls showed. The 1948 UMT bill was defeated.[45]

A second and more politically palatable method of maintaining manpower was selective conscription. Although Truman had, in 1947, advocated allowing the draft to end, he asked for new authority to conscript men, but not the funds to implement the plan, on March 17, 1948, less than a month after the Communist coup in Czechoslovakia.[46] The new selective service plan would make 19- to 25-year-old men eligible for 21 months of service, and enable a maximum manpower level of more than 2 million.[47]

The package was passed, but the manpower ceiling was not reached before the Korean War because of the continuing effort to hold the line on military expenditure.

On the same day that Congress passed the Selective Service Act, June 24, 1948, the Soviets closed the roads and rail lines leading through their occupation sector of Germany, so that the British, French, and American occupation zones in Berlin would be cut off from the larger Anglo-French-American occupation sectors in the western part of Germany. Stalin, concerned that the British and Americans were rehabilitating their occupation sectors of Germany, seemed to have started the blockade in an attempt to force the allies to reopen negotiations on the future of Germany.

The days following the initiation of the Berlin blockade were some of the tensest moments of the Cold War. Truman was advised by Secretary of Defense James Forrestal and General Hoyt Vandenberg, chief of staff of the air force, to implement BROILER, attacking the USSR with atomic strikes.[48] He declined. Instead, the U.S. military began a three-part policy, beginning negotiations with the Soviets to reach an agreement on the issues of German sovereignty and currency (which failed to produce results),[49] effecting a Western counterblockade designed to harm the East German economy,[50] and airlifting millions of tons of goods into the city daily, with the provision that the United States was only to put BROILER into effect if the Soviets interfered with the airlift.[51] The United States publicly announced it was sending atomic-capable bombers to Britain.

It is unclear whether Truman thought that the U.S. military, after his budget cuts, approached war readiness. In retrospect, it did not. The U.S. stockpile of nuclear weapons was tiny, approximately 50 weapons.[52] The American B-29s didn't have the fuel capacity to fly to Moscow and return.[53] Only the B-36s, of which there were very few, could do so.[54] The United States was so unprepared that the bulk of the American force, consisting of three bomber groups of approximately 30 aircraft and more than 2,000 personnel apiece, did not arrive in the U.K. until July 1949, more than a year after the Berlin blockade had begun.[55] Nevertheless, the Soviets chose not to interfere with the airlift. The land blockade continued until May 1949, when Stalin terminated it in return for a four-power conference on Germany.[56]

The Berlin blockade spurred debate in America about the inadequacy of military preparation for a conflict, and then left the impression that hinting at strategic bombing could be sufficient to deter the Soviet Union from military action. One result was that the air force continued to win the battle of funds in Washington. Although total military spending remained fixed, the number of air force wings had been brought up to 48 after the Berlin blockade.[57] After the crisis began, air force personnel levels soon expanded to 850,000, although Truman would cut this down to 677,000 by the end of the year.[58] In April 1949, Truman, acting on Forrestal's recommendation, approved $31 million of funding to lengthen the runways at Abu Sueir, Egypt, so as to accommodate long-range bombers.[59] The military also sought air bases or landing rights at sites in Morocco, Algeria, and Libya to supplement the existing arrangements elsewhere.[60] Meanwhile, the older services continued to suffer. Not one new tank or naval vessel was purchased between 1946 and the start of the Korean War.[61] Although the Berlin blockade undoubtedly increased Cold War tensions and helped foster the environment in which the American arms build-up would later develop, it did not, in itself, lead to any large and long-term strengthening of the U.S. military.

THE IMPACT OF THE WESTERN UNION AND THE NORTH ATLANTIC TREATY ON WESTERN MILITARY POWER

The creation of the Western Union, by European states, and the North Atlantic Treaty, which also included North America, are often regarded as monumental events of the twentieth century. Former enemies formed alliances for containing Soviet power and worked toward that goal for four decades. These pacts are correctly regarded as important. However, a closer look indicates that their political importance was not immediately matched by a corresponding improvement in military preparedness. Despite the resounding ring of the rhetoric of these agreements, and despite some improvements in creating multilateral bodies on political and military issues, the signatory powers of these arrangements generally continued, on an individual basis, to weaken their military forces until June 1950. It is necessary to briefly explain this process here, and then treat the question of comparative Soviet-Western power in the next section.

Negotiations leading to collective security were initiated by Ernest Bevin, the British foreign secretary, who sought bilateral defense pacts with European nations as a means of countering Soviet power and, in the event Germany was to rearm, German power. He succeeded in gaining agreement on a bilateral pact with France, in the March 4, 1947, Treaty of Dunkirk. Paul Henri Spaak, the Belgian prime minister, informed the French and the British that he wanted to see the pact expanded to include other Western European nations.[62] In January 1948, Bevin responded with a plan for a multilateral security system involving Belgium, France, Luxembourg, the Netherlands, and the United Kingdom. The Benelux nations (as Belgium, the Netherlands, and Luxembourg were called after their 1946 agreement to have greater cooperation in economic and foreign policies) agreed to Bevin's proposals on February 19, 1948.[63] In the following days, a coup by the Communist Party in Czechoslovakia against the other members of the ruling coalition government, followed by the murder of

Czech leaders, convinced Bevin more than ever that the Soviets wanted "physical control . . . of the whole world island."[64] He was even concerned over a possible Soviet threat to Norway.[65] Negotiations for a defense union were sped up, and the Treaty of Brussels was signed on March 17, 1948, by France, the Benelux nations, and the United Kingdom. It pledged the signatories to mutually enforce their respective frontiers and created the Western Union, which was to have a committee of commanders-in-chief, first led by British Field Marshall Bernard Montgomery, in October 1948.[66] Further efforts to expand on the concept of collective defense led to the North Atlantic Treaty, signed April 4, 1949.[67]

However, collective security did not necessarily mean an increase in military power for Western nations. Factors preventing an arms build-up included the continuing existence of the American atomic monopoly, concerns over the impact of diverting resources from economic recovery, the seeming unlikelihood of war, and the feeling that without German commitment any attempt to match the Soviets division-for-division was futile.

In Britain, the only change was a slowing of demobilization, which involved an extension of the period of conscription by three months.[68] Total military spending as a portion of national income continued to fall, from 9.5 percent of the gross national product in 1947, to 7.7 percent in 1950.[69] In France, the comparable figures were 5.0 percent of the gross national product in 1947 and 4.9 percent in 1950.[70] Belgium was still weak, occupied Germany was still unarmed, and several important nations, such as Italy and the Scandinavian countries, remained outside the Western Union. The Netherlands was the only signatory to increase military funding during this period (the traditionally neutral Dutch government's decision to spend 5.1 percent of 1949 gross national product on defense was the highest such figure since 1815),[71] but even then, the Netherlands did not have a single standing division in Europe.[72] For France and the Netherlands, the colonial wars in Indochina and Indonesia absorbed a great deal of military strength. For the United States, as we shall see, military spending would reach its postwar nadir in fiscal year 1950 (July 1, 1949–June 30, 1950). These figures may not seem low by standards at the beginning of the twenty-first century, but as we will see in the next section, the perception by many in the United States and among its treaty allies was that the forces that could be afforded at these sums were insufficient to nullify the preponderant edge the Soviets had in conventional forces in Europe.

Although there was much discussion of the treaty's significance during its creation, particularly as it represented a reversal of American unwillingness to enter an entangling alliance with European states, the treaty merely formalized what already existed: an American commitment to use force should any European state become embroiled in a war with the Soviets or the Soviet allies.[73] As we have seen, American plans for such a war depended primarily on the use of strategic nuclear bombing of the Soviet Union. The treaty did nothing to change this, nor was it meant to. It was designed primarily to show both the Europeans and the Soviets that America had the political will to put such policies on paper, and that the isolationist forces in the United States, especially in the Senate, were not strong enough to defeat such a move. Secondarily, the treaty was signed to pave the way for future increases in American aid to Western Europe.[74]

The treaty warned the Soviets that the Western powers would not be split. American anticolonialism, and French, Belgian, and Dutch fear of Germany were of secondary importance to containing Soviet ambitions. The United States stopped linking military aid to the termination of certain colonial wars, such as the Dutch war in Indonesia,[75] and instead merely insisted, sometimes not very strongly, that military material given as aid be used solely in Europe.[76]

The Truman administration felt that this public display of solidarity with Western Europe, combined with the atomic monopoly, was enough to deter Soviet moves. Truman was willing to wage atomic war in the event of a war with the Soviets and was confident that the Soviets were aware of this plan. He placed a high premium on deterrence and did not feel that any increases in the size of the military budget would be necessary to back up the pact. At this time, he did not advocate a stronger American conventional military presence in Europe,[77] and his secretary of state, Dean Acheson, publicly ruled out the possibility of sending troops to Europe as part of the treaty.[78] Acheson would later work toward the goal of sending such troops, but this would not become administration policy until after the start of the Korean War.

U.S. military leaders, given what they perceived as a small budget with little sign of an increase in the immediate future, continued to plan on the assumption that Western conventional forces would be little more than a delaying force against the Soviets in the event of a war, perhaps not a speed bump the Soviets would roll over on their way to the Atlantic, but certainly not a challenge to the Soviet army. The British had similar assumptions. A directive for wartime planning stated that "because of the great geographic characteristics of Russia, and the great numerical superiority of her land forces, the only means of taking offensive action initially is by a strategic air offensive," which meant placing primary emphasis on holding the air bases in Britain, the Middle East, Pakistan, Japan, and sea areas near the USSR for use by carriers, while waiting for troops to arrive from the main support areas, which were the United States, Canada, Australia, New Zealand, the British areas of Africa, Argentina, and, if arrangements could be made, the Indian subcontinent.[79] The treaty did not create a supranational body that had the authority to coordinate military action. Although various planning groups were created under the North Atlantic

Council to recommend policies, including regional planning, there was not an integrated multinational military force.[80]

Support in Congress for military aid to Europe proved limited, and a radically new and improved European military would never have arisen without the Korean War. The Mutual Defense Assistance Program (MDAP), which came into law on October 6, 1949, and which might not have passed if not for the administration's public pronouncement on September 23 about the existence of the Soviet nuclear device,[81] was watered down by clauses designed to ensure that the new American military aid to Europe would be slow in coming and would reinforce existing U.S. military plans. The legislation had the specific provision that a new umbrella organization, run by the Department of Defense, the Department of State, and the Economic Cooperation Administration, would have to withhold aid from European states until they signed bilateral agreements, committing them to the U.S. strategic defense concept, based on American nuclear air strikes and an increased European military presence on the ground.[82] The only hint that the Americans might become more involved with conventional forces in the future was the similar insistence on gaining U.S. base rights and other operating rights as a quid pro quo for aid,[83] but there was little funding for the vast network of bases that the United States would begin using in the winter of 1950–51.

Many Europeans opposed the American insistence on signing these agreements,[84] and progress was slow. To compound matters, the American military leadership, including the Joint Chiefs of Staff, resented having to send war goods to Europe at a time when they felt the U.S. military was underfunded and did the minimum to help the program.[85]

The North Atlantic Treaty, just like the military aid to Greece and Turkey, the European Recovery Program, and the Military Defense Assistance Program, was not designed to facilitate the deployment of more American troops to Europe. Rather, like those other programs, it was designed, in part, to fulfill the role that an American standing army in Europe would have, and therefore was intended to prevent the emergence of such an army. The importance of the North Atlantic Treaty for the U.S. military, therefore, was not that it resulted in any enlargement of forces, but that it was a foundation that would later be used to erect the NATO force.

THE FISCAL YEAR 1950 AMERICAN DEFENSE BUDGET

The fiscal year 1950 (July 1, 1949–June 30, 1950) budget was not very different from the two budgets preceding it, either in the quantity of funds allocated or in the degree to which the total resulted from Truman's arbitrary imposition of ceilings. It is usually remembered only as one of the most problematic U.S. defense budgets ever made. Its preparation led to public bickering between the services over the appropriate importance to be assigned to strategic nuclear bombing and the use of more conventional means of combat. This strategic predicament, which was intrinsic to all post-1945 American defense budgets, was never, before or since, to result in as much public disagreement and controversy among the services, congressional committees, the president, and European allies as it would for this year.

The Department of Defense spent much of 1948 creating a fiscal year 1950 budget, and submitted it to the president. Forrestal asked for $16.9 billion for defense.[86] Truman, working with the Bureau of the Budget, slashed the sums mightily. On January 10, 1949, the president revealed his own proposed military budget for fiscal year 1950, for approximately $14.2 billion: $4.5 billion for the army, $4.35 billion for the navy, and $4.55 billion for the air force, with another $830 million set aside for related items, including an anticipated pay increase. He told Congress that this budget set a defense spending ceiling for "the foreseeable future."[87]

In Congress, there had been a change in the budgeting process. Formerly, each service had been judged in a separate subcommittee of the Appropriations Committee. Congress attempted to use a unified subcommittee for the first time with the fiscal year 1950 budget.[88] The services had to directly compete for funds at an earlier stage in the budgeting process, and resorted to publicly attacking each others' viability.

Ironically, it was Forrestal who had helped water down the National Defense Act when he was secretary of the navy, so that the service secretaries would remain powerful. Now, as secretary of defense, he had a rebellion on his hands that he had little power to stop, a rebellion which almost certainly contributed to his eventual resignation. After Forrestal's departure, the new secretary of defense, Louis Johnson, proved more determined to force his will upon the services, but, as we shall see, his cancellation of the construction of the USS *United States* led to much controversy and caused the debate on the budget to be increasingly conducted in the media. Through protest resignations and lobbying, navy admirals managed to persuade Congress to investigate Johnson's activities, but these actions did not get the super carrier built. Truman, roasted in the press for his inability to control his own Department of Defense, sought help in dampening the disputes and recruited Eisenhower, hoping that the retired general's reputation would enable him to act, with backing of the public and Congress, as an arbiter in the interservice disputes.

Eisenhower took the job of broker in January 1949, and accepted Truman's suggested overall budget sums.[89] He labored to convince the services to cooperate, meeting with the Joint Chiefs, Bradley (chairman), Hoyt Vandenberg (air force), Louis Denfeld (navy), and Alfred Gruenther (army), on a regular basis.[90]

Eisenhower requested that each service submit estimates on the mini-

mum funding necessary for their service, as well as the other two, to meet
the basic challenges for a campaign to defend Europe and the Middle East
in the event of a war with the Soviets. He then used the lowest estimates.[91]
The navy insisted that using limited funds to provide the air force with
the fifteen new air wings it requested to carry out strategic bombing was
wasteful, arguing that many of the bombers would be shot down by Soviet
interceptor aircraft in the event of a war, and questioning the goal of destroying centers of production in the USSR while allowing the Soviet army
to capture more efficient factories in western Europe. The air force insisted
that its land-based bombers were more efficient than any flown from the
aircraft carrier the navy was requesting.[92] Army studies tried to show that
efforts to halt a Soviet advance might not be futile, and sought to convince
the public, and Eisenhower, that the United States should not plan on
abandoning the European continent in the event of war.[93]

Eisenhower's task was made more difficult by Truman's insistence on
lowering the ceiling he had set on defense expenditure. The nation was,
from approximately mid-1948 until the summer of 1949, in recession. Industrial production dropped about 13 percent during this time.[94] Tax revenues were falling, and yet Truman felt the economic conditions dictated
that he avoid a planned tax increase. Something had to give. Truman did
not believe in deficit-spending to aid recovery, and besides, Nourse, his
chief economic adviser, was warning that if the administration failed to
cut federal government debt, the United States would have difficulty financing any future war.[95] Frank Pace, director of the Bureau of the Budget,
agreed.[96] Nor would Truman cut revenue at the political base of his administration, the Fair Deal. Federal domestic spending absorbed only 24
percent of the federal budget[97] and less than 5 percent of the gross national
product. Foreign aid totaled an enormous $6.5 billion, but the adminis-
tration would not reconsider American commitments to Europe and Japan.[98] So Truman, in June, lowered the arbitrary spending limit on the
military for fiscal year 1950 to approximately $13 billion.[99]

By July (after the fiscal year had already started), Eisenhower had
helped produce a budget within the $13 billion ceiling. In doing so, he
had produced new estimates of forces to meet a new strategic concept.
This concept was then fashioned into an emergency war plan, named
OFFTACKLE.[100] OFFTACKLE was a compromise, combining strategic nuclear bombing of 104 Soviet cities, plus extensive ground and naval operations.[101] Eisenhower's support for naval funding, to provide for the
domination of the western Mediterranean in the event of war, and for the
flexibility aircraft carriers provided, prevented the air force from getting
all the funding it desired. However, OFFTACKLE, like other war plans in
the time between demobilization and the Korean campaign, envisioned
extensive strategic atomic bombing.[102] OFFTACKLE called for protecting
the United Kingdom, controlling the western Mediterranean, retaining a

position in the Middle East, and using nuclear weapons to blunt any Soviet military advance into western Europe and to curtail Soviet production of war goods.[103]

OFFTACKLE presented the administration with two difficulties. First, it was incomplete. Eisenhower purposely did not make many specific determinations on which forces would be sent where. He wanted to grant American military leaders flexibility, especially since they would have little power at their disposal in the early stages of a war. Only in the event of combat with Soviet forces would American planners be able to gauge the relative strength of the fighting forces, and make subsequent decisions on whether to maintain a bridgehead in Europe. The limits Truman set on military spending made a force large enough to guarantee a stand at the Rhine impossible. This realization created the second problem. The plans could not be shown to European allies without giving them the impression that the United States was unprepared for a large conflict in Europe.[104] In discussions with North Atlantic Treaty allies, the Americans had to use information from the long-range war plan named DROPSHOT, produced simultaneously to OFFTACKLE, and based on a possible war in 1957.[105] The complaints from Europe also caused the administration to begin creating a medium-term defense plan, to be finished the next year.[106]

Meanwhile, the budget process went ahead, using the suggested OFFTACKLE force allocations. The budget was delayed in Congress until October, and when passed, had been altered by the pro-strategic bombing group in Congress to shift funds from the older forces' budgets to the air force. Truman, not convinced that the air force really needed so much extra money, and, as always, concerned over budgeting, gave orders that the extra amount (totaling $735.7 million) not be spent.[107] OFFTACKLE was approved by the Joint Chiefs of Staff in December.[108]

Defense expenditures for fiscal year 1950 totaled $13.496 billion,[109] representing approximately 4.7 percent of the gross national product. Military expenditures amounted to $11.9 billion, funds for the governance of occupied areas totaled $760 million, army civil expenditures were $720 million, and military aid to Greece and Turkey was $120 million.[110]

THE TRUMAN ADMINISTRATION'S PERCEPTIONS OF SOVIET MILITARY CAPABILITIES, 1948–50

In 1948, 1949, and early 1950, the Truman administration perceived the Soviet Union to be, relative to the Western powers, economically weak, militarily strong, and overtly hostile, but too cautious to risk a major war in the near future. There was a consensus within the administration that the Soviet army was capable of conquering Western Europe, but a consensus that there was a significant possibility of a general war with the

Soviet Union was slower in developing, not reaching a critical stage until the beginning of the Korean War in 1950.

There was ample evidence indicating that the Soviet economy was weak. Even the Soviet government's published statistics, which were thought to be generally exaggerated, revealed an economy far behind the West. Soviet diplomatic actions in the immediate postwar period indicated economic deficiencies, whether in the form of attempts to lobby for more favorable conditions for Lend-Lease payments, a large German reparations payment, Austrian oil,[111] or the transportation of basic infrastructure from conquered Eastern Europe to the Soviet Union. General Walter Bedell Smith, a future head of the Central Intelligence Agency, estimated that it would be another 10 to 15 years before the Soviets recovered from the last war.[112]

The CIA's Office of Research and Estimates (ORE) tried to appraise the Soviet Union in terms of war potential, looking at the industrial strength, technology, and possible bottlenecks to increased production. The ORE concluded that Soviet economic weaknesses gravely limited the ability of Moscow to fight a prolonged war with the North Atlantic Treaty nations.

In particular, American analysts felt that Soviet shortages of high octane fuel, spare machine parts, rolling stock, nonferrous metals, and finished steel would contribute to the country's inability to handle wartime needs.[113] Complicating these shortages, and, to an extent, causing them, were the Soviet deficiencies in properly trained technological personnel and managers.[114]

However, despite the nearly universal agreement among American analysts that the United States possessed economic superiority, it was believed that the Kremlin had, by diverting a substantially higher percentage of its limited resources to war-making capacities, more than offset its poverty and placed itself in a position of conventional military superiority. The Joint Chiefs of Staff (JCS) believed that the USSR had 175 divisions: 105 rifle (of which 40 were motorized), 35 mechanized, 25 armored, and 10 cavalry.[115] They were presumed to have a disposition that would enable them to attack Western interests at many points along the periphery of Soviet power (see Table 2.1).

Another, more alarmist, report, submitted to Truman by Major General Lauris Norstad, serving in the Operations and Planning Division of the War Department, claimed that the Soviets had 208 divisions, including 93 facing western Europe.[116] Norstad added that the Soviets had 15,500 operational aircraft.[117] The JCS believed that the Soviets could put 320 divisions in the field within 30 days of the start of mobilization, and that this amount could be increased to 470 divisions and 12 million troops after one year of mobilization.[118] The figure of 4,000,000 troops was cited in terms of Soviet military manpower.[119] That number did not include the 56

Table 2.1
Size and Location of Soviet Land Forces

Area	Divisions
Soviet-Occupied Europe	35
Western Frontier Military Districts	49
West Central Military Districts	20
Caucasus Military Districts	21
Middle Asia Military Districts	19
Far East (Including 4 in Manchuria)	31
TOTAL	175

Note: The USSR was divided into 21 military districts.
Source: BLHC, Records of the Joint Chiefs of Staff, Part 2.

divisions possessed by the Eastern European allies of the Soviet Union by February 1950.[120]

Soviet armored vehicles, heavy mortars, and towed antitank guns were considered superior to those in the West,[121] and the JCS declared that:

The postwar reorganization of the Soviet Army along modern mobile mechanized lines, plus a year-round intensive training schedule and generally successful efforts to reconstitute sagging morale, have imparted in the Soviet Army as a whole a combat efficiency in excess of that in any other existing army in the world today, at least for initial operations.[122]

It was believed that the Soviet air force had approximately 600,000 men[123] and that the Soviets had significant biological and chemical war-making capabilities,[124] a well-developed airborne force,[125] and military expenditures that were increasing by as much as 30 percent annually in 1948–49.[126]

The Joint Chiefs of Staff felt that "if war occurs, little or no warning will be received" because of the difficulty in gathering information from the other side of the Iron Curtain.[127] Cities in North America would not be immune from attack, since the Soviets, according to the JCS, could fly Tu-4 bombers on one-way atomic missions from the eastern tip of the USSR and from Murmansk.[128] The JCS felt that despite weaknesses in the surface fleet and in strategic mobility, an overreliance on rail transport, shoddy electronics and fire control devices, and its inexperienced Long Range Air Force, the Soviet military would have such a commanding edge in mass and preparedness that, in a war with the North Atlantic Treaty powers, it could undertake the following actions:

a. *Simultaneously [launch]*

    (1) A campaign against Western Europe

    (2) An aerial bombardment against the British Isles

    (3) Campaigns against the Near and Middle East

    (4) A campaign against Yugoslavia and Italy

    (5) Campaigns with limited objectives in the Far East

    (6) Attacks against Canada, the United States, and Alaska

    (7) A sea and air offensive against Allied sea communications

    (8) Subversive activity and sabotage against Allied interests in all parts of the world

b. *If necessary, [launch] a campaign against Norway and Sweden*

c. *If possible, [launch] a campaign to overrun the Iberian Peninsula and secure the Straits of Gibraltar*[129]

The possibility of such actions did not even take into account the activities of the Chinese communists. How successful would such campaigns be? The Joint Intelligence Committee at the American embassy in Moscow concluded that "the Soviet Army is probably capable of overrunning continental Europe with the exception of Spain and Portugal and of occupying strategic areas of the Near East."[130] The committee also concluded that the Soviets were working to achieve the logistical support necessary to maintain a hold on these territories once captured. We shall examine the accuracy of these reports in the next section.

The Red Army, after its bloody but successful sweep into central Europe in 1945, was bound to impress outside observers. German army generals who were interrogated by the Americans after the collapse of the Nazi regime had the highest regard for the Soviet soldier. In one poll by the U.S. army, former Wehrmacht generals indicated that the Soviet army had a much greater impact on the defeat of Germany than either the Western armies or the Western navies, and that only the Allied strategic bombing had been more important.[131] With the creation of logistical bases in the heart of central Europe, the Soviet position had improved since the war. By 1948, after the demobilization of the armies of Britain and the United States, the Soviet force had become an object of fear and awe.

In Europe, which was considered the most vital battlefield should there be a Soviet-American war, NATO had a small force relative to what the Truman administration believed the Soviets to have. Although Western nations may have had as many as 800,000 troops on the European continent in 1947–48,[132] most of these were conscripted forces without the armor or air power to win a general war. At the time of the signing of the North Atlantic Treaty, the signatory states possessed fewer than 20 divisions of troops worldwide,[133] and it should be assumed that the bulk of the quality European divisions were either fighting colonial wars in Indochina, Indonesia, Malaya, and elsewhere, or were dispersed to other distant locales, such as Hong Kong and the Middle East. The American force was stationed, for the most part, in the United States. The sum of all divisions in western Europe, American and other, was approximately 11 in the summer of 1950.[134] These figures should be compared with the force of more than 120 divisions that France, Britain, and Belgium had in the spring of 1940, when they were defeated by a swift German envelopment.

The United States had only 14 active divisions in May 1950, of which just one, the First Infantry, was in Europe (occupying Germany).[135] There were only 94,300 American military personnel in Europe.[136] These American personnel were primarily involved in denazification and the maintenance of law and order, and did not possess the armor or air power that would have made them capable of taking on a Soviet force. There were no American naval forces assigned to the western European region.[137] Most critically, some planners did not expect American air forces to control the air over Europe in the event of a war with the Soviets.[138]

The British forces in Germany, which consisted mostly of conscripts serving 18-month deployments, lacked an armored division and were almost entirely dependent on German civilians for transport.[139] Their commander, General Bernard Montgomery, considered them to be even less effective than the American troops.[140]

Montgomery also considered the French forces incompetent because of defects in structure and personnel at the commanding level and the country's brief draft service period.[141] The overall defense of Western Europe was, according to Montgomery, a "façade."[142]

Military planners in both the United States and the United Kingdom felt that a Soviet attack might be slowed, but not blunted, and made estimates of up to six weeks when predicting how long it would take before the Soviet armored divisions reached the Pyrenees. There was little chance of a quick American air or sea lift of troops to Europe in the event of a crisis, considering the shape of the American army as a whole. American war plans of 1948 envisioned a 10-month delay before a D-Day-style landing could be attempted,[143] and in 1950 the Joint Chiefs of Staff were so convinced that the Soviets could march across most of Europe in the event of a war that they planned to land the first troops to cross the Atlantic in northwest Africa.[144] Winston Churchill, as leader of the opposition in the British Parliament, summed up the prevailing view when he claimed, in 1948, and again in 1950, that "if it were not for the stocks of atomic bombs now in the trusteeship of the United States, there would be no means of stopping the subjugation of Western Europe by Communist machinations backed by Russian armies and enforced by political police."[145]

In Asia, things were little better. Army Chief of Staff General L. J. Collins informed the Secretaries of State and Defense, as well as the other members of the JCS, that American forces were spread so thin in Hokkaido that it would be easy for the Soviets to make an amphibious landing there.[146] The local forces defending the Turkish and Iranian borders with the USSR were no match for the Soviet army. In China, the anti-Communist Guomindang Party was losing its civil war with the Communists. Governments in the Philippines and South Korea seemed hard-pressed just preventing Communist takeovers in their own country.

For the United States, relying on atomic bombing of Soviet cities was a matter of course in the event of war. By the end of 1949, the American military had 250 atomic weapons, each one of a series of bombs that were developed from the Fat Man plutonium bomb used at Nagasaki,[147] with the newest of these weapons having an explosive capability five times that of the Hiroshima bomb.[148] However, the importance of this arsenal would, as we shall see, be increasingly questioned once the Soviets developed their own atomic weaponry.

Intentions are a much more difficult thing to judge than capabilities, and naturally there was much more disagreement about them. Pessimists, such as Foy Kohler, an official at the American embassy in Moscow, assumed maximum aims on the part of the Kremlin leadership, asserting that only the reality of the current situation restrained Moscow:

[My] conclusion that the Kremlin will not initiate war in the next several years does not mean any alteration in the springs of action of the Soviet state nor change in Communist belief in the inevitability of war between the Soviet Union and the capitalist West. In fact this belief must be considered the basis of Soviet plans and policies. The mechanism of the state is being canalized toward preparation for war expected to eventuate some years hence . . . the Soviets will not deliberately resort to war until they have in production advanced weapons of mass destruction . . . they will utilize the intervening time for intensification of scientific development.[149]

The belief that the Soviet Union was plotting an aggressive war against Europe was also sometimes cited, particularly by air force generals. But it wasn't the norm in the Truman administration.

Most executive branch analysts felt that the Soviets did not consider a military expansion of their sphere of influence to be Soviet policy. The ORE told Truman during the Berlin blockade of 1948 that the Soviets were not ready for war.[150] The embassy in Moscow sent back a report in April 1949 stressing that the Soviets would not resort to force in the near future,[151] with which the State Department's Policy Planning Staff agreed.[152] An ad hoc group consisting of the heads of U.S. intelligence agencies concluded in May 1949 that the Soviet Union would, most likely, "exercise some care to avoid an unintentional outbreak of hostilities with the United States."[153] The Joint Chiefs of Staff opined in February 1950 that "it is improbable that the Soviets would deliberately venture any military action which would involve them in an open war."[154] There were, at least compared to the year following the start of the Korean conflict on June 25, 1950, only a few analysts believing the worst about Soviet intentions. The president, except for a few statements made in anger (Truman was known for his blunt and emotional flare-ups), seems through his actions to have agreed with the more moderate group that war with the Soviets was not likely in the immediate future. Truman's efforts to keep military spending down and to focus on domestic social programs, as well as his unwillingness to reinstate wartime civil defense programs, do not suggest a real fear of war in the immediate future.

THE ACCURACY OF THE TRUMAN ADMINISTRATION'S PERCEPTIONS OF SOVIET MILITARY CAPABILITIES

There are two questions that must be answered in order to judge the accuracy of the Truman administration's perceptions of the Soviets: Were Soviet conventional military forces much stronger than those of the West between 1946 and 1950? Was the Soviet leadership considering military action in central Europe in the near future?

The answer to the first question is yes, and to the second is no. In 1948 and 1949, the Truman administration answered these questions correctly, although later, after the beginning of the Korean War, there was considerable speculation by a vocal minority of administration officials as to the answer to the second question.

The Soviet military, even after partial demobilization, was huge. Later estimates of its size range from 2.5 to 2.874 million troops in 1948,[155] deployed in 100 to 175 fully manned divisions.[156] These estimates place the number of combat aircraft in the 14,000 to 15,000 range in 1947, increasing to 18,000 to 19,000 in the mid-1950s.[157] The latter figure included about 1,000 jet fighters.[158] Qualitative improvements made to the armed forces since the war had offset much of the shrinkage in size.

Foremost was the improvement in the Soviet air force. Traditionally a technologically backward force by international standards, the Soviets engaged in a quantum leap in air technology in 1945–47 that made them world leaders. There was a revolution in air technology resulting from the development of the jet engine, and the Soviets were able to bypass years of propeller-powered development and start on the same footing as the West.

One factor was the acquisition of German knowledge. Approximately forty thousand German scientists were forcibly brought into the USSR in

1946 alone.[159] One historian, Alexander Boyd, has explained the way this affected the Soviet air force:

Two thirds of the German aircraft industry with its research and production facilities fell into Soviet hands . . . Most of the aircraft factories in Soviet-occupied areas were stripped of their presses—including two of the world's largest hydraulic presses which had been used to produce spars for the Ju88—and their machine tools as well as drawings, models, and equipment. The dismantling and transportation of the captured factories were supervised by special squads of engineers sent out from Soviet aircraft plants and train loads were sent east.[160]

German experts were rounded up and transported to centers in the Soviet Union that were exact replicas of the ones they had used in Germany, even down to the ashtrays and calendars.[161]

The Soviets did not stop with merely imitating German aircraft. They created some of the best jet fighters in the world. Foremost was the Mig-15, which went into service in late 1947. The Mig-15 was comparable to Western models in speed, with climbing and turning abilities that were, perhaps, better than those of American fighter aircraft, especially at high altitudes.[162] Although the first Mig-15 engines were purchased from the Rolls Royce Corporation of Britain, the plane was Soviet-designed and built.[163] Soviet efforts to create their own high-quality jet engines, under way since 1945, would enable them to imitate the Rolls Royce engine, and, by 1951, to have a fleet of fighter aircraft, 20 percent of them jet-powered.[164]

After the creation of the Long Range Air Force in April 1946,[165] the Soviets made rapid strides in improving their strategic bomber fleet, a relative weakness of the USSR in World War II. Many of the new long-range bombers were TU-4s, which had been created by copying a captured American B-29 four-engine bomber. The TU-4 was in mass production by 1948,[166] and more than 1,000 were built in the next six years.[167]

Rocketry was yet another area of improvement. Research probably improved as a result of the Red Army capture, in April and May of 1945, of the Peenemunde and Nordhausen rocket complexes, where the Germans had developed the V-2 rockets.[168] Soviet research on ballistic missiles began at this time.[169]

Although it would have been impossible to stop all aircraft carrying nuclear weapons from penetrating airspace over Soviet cities, the Soviet air force improved defenses dramatically through radar development, which began in 1945.[170] Sabotage operations by the MGB (Ministry for State Security, later renamed the KGB, or Committee for State Security) against American forward bases were also planned in the event of war.[171]

The trend toward new thinking was not limited to the air force. Whereas many of the leading innovators in the Red Army had been purged in the

1930s, during a time when lack of contact with the outside world was the most important career asset a Soviet military officer could possess, the initial Soviet setbacks in the war with Germany had made the Soviet leadership more willing to allow forward-thinking officers to study foreign ideas on doctrine and equipment.

The trend was toward creating a professional military establishment to replace the party-dominated old force. The changing of names in 1946, from Workers-Peasants Red Army to Soviet Army, symbolized this development.[172]

The inclination from 1941 on, though not admitted publicly by the Soviets, was to build the Soviet army around the same types of massed tank strikes that the Germans had used so successfully in the early stages of Operation Barbarossa. The Soviets specifically designed three types of divisions, each modeled after a Wehrmacht counterpart.[173] Armored divisions, modeled after Panzer divisions, were designed to break through enemy lines and use speed and firepower to envelop enemy troops.[174] Each armored division had approximately 240 tanks in addition to a small amount of infantry.[175] Mechanized divisions, modeled after Panzer Grenadier divisions,[176] had approximately 220 tanks plus a larger complement of infantry than the armored divisions.[177] The task for these divisions was to support armored thrusts, often by sealing off the flanks to prevent a counterattack from isolating the penetrating armored divisions. The third type of division was the rifle division, essentially an infantry division, but with its own tanks, unlike a British infantry division.[178] Further differentiation between traditional rifle divisions and new motorized rifle divisions existed in that trucks replaced horse-drawn transport methods.[179] By 1950, only half of ground forces transport was horse-drawn, whereas a Soviet rifle division of 1943–44 had used only 25 to 30 motor vehicles, but more than 600 horse-drawn wagons or carts and up to 2,000 horses.[180] The German army, in its successful 1940–41 blitzkriegs, had operated with far more reliance on horse transport than the Soviet army of 1950. In the event of a war with the West, the Soviets could have increased the speed of their conquests by taking advantage of the road networks in central and western Europe.

The tanks that the Soviets possessed were capable and reliable, the foremost being the T-34, the main battle tank of the Great Patriotic War against the Germans. Many of these were improved in the postwar modernization by the addition of greater armor and a stronger 85mm gun.[181] These tanks were supplemented by Joseph Stalin IIIs, which had 122mm guns, providing greater firepower than any Western tank.[182] The United States, in contrast, was still using the Sherman as its main battlefield tank. Events in Korea would show the Sherman to be inferior to the T-34.

Airborne landings, begun by parachuted troops and backed by massive airlifts of troops and material to captured airstrips, were already in practice by the time of the Manchurian campaign of 1945, and the Soviets focused on building up this capacity in the postwar period.[183] In 1946, the Soviets created the VTA (Military Transport Authority), which was subordinate to the airborne troops.[184]

The Soviets believed that, in areas close to their air bases and ports, they could control the sea lanes and launch amphibious landings, as they had in the Black Sea during World War II.[185] In the late 1940s, Stalin deployed the 14th Army to the Chukotka Peninsula to land in Alaska in the event of a war with the United States.[186]

An added dimension was research into chemical warfare. In the final stages of World War II, the Red Army had acquired German nerve gas plants at Breslau and Dyhernfurth.[187] By the end of 1945, the Soviets had already moved two nerve agent production plants to the Soviet interior and were supplying the Red Army with lethal chemicals.[188] In 1945, the Soviets had also captured a Japanese biological warfare facility in Manchuria, which the Japanese were in the process of destroying.[189] It is not known how much the Soviets learned from this find.

Soviet doctrine emphasized that these components, including air power, would have been used in combined operations to penetrate enemy lines, with follow-up by envelopments of enemy troops, similar to the German actions on the eastern front in the summer of 1941.

Troop morale seems, by most accounts, to have been high. Although the living conditions of many soldiers in the Soviet army were probably significantly worse than their counterparts in Western armies, the relative difference between civilian and military standards of living in the USSR was no greater than in the West. The enlisted men of the postwar era were almost all born after the Russian revolution and had been raised in the Communist system that inculcated the spirited propaganda of the regime. While serving abroad, they generally were not allowed contact with the locals, who might weaken their will, under penalty of demotion or worse.[190] The political officers attached to every sizable unit ensured that the security services exacted punishment upon those who questioned the system or attempted to desert. Obedience, by both civilians and military units, was enforced by the 700,000 troops of the MGB and MVD (Ministry of Internal Affairs).[191] The murdering of returned Soviet prisoners of war and the use of harsh punishment for those who disobeyed orders—which during World War II sometimes meant transfer to battalions used in the bloodiest of frontal assault and mine-clearing operations—almost certainly reduced the willingness of anyone in the Soviet armed forces to desert.[192]

By late 1949 and early 1950, Soviet power in central Europe was further enhanced by the strengthening of the Eastern European satellites.[193] The East German Alert Police, in reality an army, had 50,000 personnel by March 1950, and were being issued Soviet tanks.[194] After the introduction of conscription in 1949, the Polish army grew to 400,000 troops,[195] and by 1950 the Czechoslovakian army had 140,000 troops.[196] These Czech troops, and to a lesser extent, the other Soviet-bloc armies in Europe, relied on goods from the Skoda arms works, one of the largest military production complexes in the world.

Critiques of the Truman administration's fear of Soviet power cast doubt on the battle-readiness of the Soviet army in this era. Nikita Khrushchev would later claim that only one-third of the Red Army's divisions were anywhere near battle-ready, another third were semi-organized, and the rest were virtual shells.[197] But Khrushchev was not very specific about how ready a partially organized division was. Even if only one-third of the Soviet army divisions were battle-ready, the Soviets still had a large preponderance of power in the field, especially if those units closest to readiness were the ones in central Europe. By 1949, the Soviet forces in eastern Germany were undergoing large-unit field maneuvers as part of their training.[198]

Another factor mentioned by historians critiquing the Truman administration's estimation of Soviet fighting power is that Soviet divisions historically had fewer troops than Western divisions, a fact that was sometimes not acknowledged in reports on Soviet strength. During this era, a Soviet army division had approximately 10,000 men, half the number of men as a typical British division, and only a small proportion of the extra man power in the British division could be accounted for in its larger administrative support structure.[199] However, even if we divide these estimates in half to account for smaller division size, the Soviets maintain an advantage of between two and a half and eight times the overall manpower of Western armies in Europe, enough, it would seem, to successfully conduct an offensive. Improvements in mechanizing transport and adding armor (about 20 to 30 divisions were either armored divisions or mechanized divisions)[200] may have made the Soviet force of the late 1940s as powerful as the wartime Red Army, which began the war with 300 divisions and ended with approximately 500 divisions, each of which had considerably less manpower and less sophisticated weaponry than a postwar division.[201]

A third criticism sometimes made of the postwar Soviet army is that it had to devote a considerable portion of its efforts toward transporting capital equipment from the occupied territories to the Soviet Union to general cleaning and reconstruction projects, such as the clearance of wartime mines and the rebuilding of factories and farms.[202] This criticism, while important in the 1945–46 period, became less significant in later years. The Soviets successfully prosecuted the war against Nazi Germany, even with a very high proportion of troops involved in moving industrial infrastructure east of the Urals and building production centers for war goods. The proportion of Soviet troops involved in such activities in 1948–

49 was probably much lower. The Western occupation forces in Germany, which would have fought the Soviets in the event of a war, were themselves weakened by their various occupation tasks.

A fourth criticism of Soviet war-making capacities was that the Soviet navy was too weak to pose a threat, as shown by the World War II experience. This criticism is the most valid, as the Soviet navy during this era was, compared with Western ones, weak both in size and in strategy.[203] However, it does not invalidate the premise that the Soviets could have rolled across western Europe. The Soviets did not need to dominate the Atlantic during the few weeks it would take for the Red Army to drive to the English Channel, since it was highly unlikely that North America's productive capacity could be converted with sufficient rapidity to send war goods across the ocean in such a brief time. The Soviet navy was capable of doing all that was needed: the submarines and the fleets and flotillas[204] could achieve enough power in the Barents, Baltic, Black, Caspian, and Japan Seas to cast serious doubts in the minds of anyone considering offensive action against the Soviet Union.[205]

A fifth criticism of the postwar Soviet military was that its leaders were weak men put in power for political purposes. There is some basis for this claim: the ever-paranoid Stalin, fearing men who might threaten his rule, preferred to rely on cronies. In 1946, false charges were used to demote Marshal Georgi Zhukov and Admiral Nikolai Kuznetsov, the deputy minister of defense (Stalin was the minister of defense) and the commander of the navy, respectively. Zhukov had earned international respect as one of the leading generals in the world during the war. Stalin then resigned as minister of defense and promoted Nikolai Bulganin, a man whose qualifications for the position seem to have been mostly in the field of surviving the Byzantine world of Kremlin politics.

However, this criticism of the Soviet military can also be used against other nations. In both the United States and the United Kingdom, the Cabinet officers in charge of the armed forces at the time of the outbreak of the Korean War, Louis Johnson and Manny Shinwell, also possessed almost strictly political backgrounds. Furthermore, Stalin, as was his habit, kept certain demoted people whom he considered to have valuable skills alive so that they could be placed in power in time of need. Kuznetzov would be reinstated by Stalin in 1952, and Zhukov survived to become minister of defense in 1953, after Stalin's death.

In retrospect, Stalin was telling the truth when he claimed in January 1951, weeks before the first additional U.S. troops arrived in Europe that "No European army is capable of seriously opposing the Soviet Army,"[206] and the Truman administration was correct in agreeing. But the Truman administration also believed that in a long war, Soviet weaknesses in production, communications, weapons development, internal transport, and naval power would all lead to a gradual turning of the tide in favor of the North Americans and whichever European forces survived the initial Soviet onslaught.

Once more, the administration was correct. The Soviet economy was too weak for a long war against the West. From approximately 1929, it had been subjected to Stalinist planning, which achieved some gains in heavy industries, such as steel, but led to a lowering of the real wages of Soviet workers by 22 percent from 1928 to 1940.[207] Then the Soviet economy experienced the shock of an almost genocidal war with Nazi Germany. In 1947, the rebuilding Soviets claimed that they had managed to get back to 1940 levels of production,[208] but these were not impressive quantities relative to the United States. By 1948, Soviet workers' wages were only 59 percent of the 1928 level.[209] The Eastern European economies, wrecked by war and Soviet plundering, were in a state of chaos. As American intelligence interceptions of Soviet communications would reveal a few years later, the rail lines and rolling stock in East Germany that the Soviet military depended on were in substandard condition.[210]

In addition, the USSR was weakened by the continued fighting with various resistance groups, especially in the western Ukraine, where there was strong opposition to reimposition of control by Moscow. There was also a battle to reimpose control in the Baltic states, with one Lithuanian partisan group later claiming that the Soviets lost 100,000 men while fighting there from 1945 to 1952.[211] Stalin, afraid that those sections of the populace that had been exposed to foreign rule would have increased doubts about the validity of the Soviet system, began a fresh campaign of terror, sending millions of people to penal camps, often for the sole reason that the government believed that they had not been suitably active in countering the Nazis.[212] Such alleged disloyalty probably gave Stalin second thoughts about popular support for any new war.

The Eastern European allies, with whom Stalin was signing treaties of friendship, were still consolidating their power, and it could not be assumed that they would prove effective allies in a general war. In August 1944, the Romanian government under King Michael switched its allegiance from the Germans to the Soviets when such a move appeared in its best interest. How could the Soviets be sure that the Romanian Communists would not do the same in the event that Western troops ever entered the Balkans? Eastern European nations had forfeited, without their consent, much of their industrial plant to the Soviet Union, and the Soviets had created a trading order that forced Eastern European nations to pay heavily to support the occupying Soviet army, which was bound to stir feelings of resentment.

Despite the development of their jet fighters, the Soviets had good reason to fear Western strategic bombing, which, in the nuclear age, would be exponentially more destructive than the Western bombing of Germany had been in the last war. In April 1945, during the final month of World

War II in Europe, Allied soldiers noticed that the Soviets were constructing antiaircraft defenses in Austria, despite, or maybe because of, the fact that the German air force had been replaced by the U.S. Air Force and the British Royal Air Force in the skies over central Europe. In the postwar era, the Soviets mounted 85 or 88 mm antiaircraft guns around Budapest[213] and strengthened their internal air defenses.

On the matter of political intentions, the result of internal Truman administration policy debates seems to have been a victory for those who believed that the Soviet political leadership would not initiate a general war in Europe, except in the most dire circumstances.

The administration was correct in this belief. Despite the glaring examples of territorial expansion in Soviet history, and although the Soviet leadership appears to have not been in the least bit intimidated by America's nuclear weapons,[214] the USSR was not expecting war in the late 1940s.

The large Soviet military presence in Germany served several purposes. In the minds of the Soviet leadership, it enhanced Soviet influence over the nature of postwar Germany, and acted as an intimidating force that would make the American leadership recognize Soviet influence and pause before considering any efforts to change the regimes in Europe by force.

Stalin's comments to foreign notables, such as Winston Churchill and T. V. Soong, indicate that he sensed a rebuilt Germany could threaten the peace again in 15 or 20 years.[215] In the event of a failure to create a demilitarized and dependent Germany in cooperation with the other occupying powers, a large Soviet military presence could help prevent the formation of an independent, unified Germany. Stalin's fears of Western encirclement also emerged undiminished from the war. Memories of the Allied interventions of the early Bolshevik years, and the failure of the Western powers to accept a Soviet role in collective security in the 1930s, were sharpened by the extension of American aid to Greece and Turkey (the Soviet press spoke of a "Mediterranean military bloc");[216] the rehabilitations of former enemies Japan, Italy, and, eventually, Germany as pro-Western nations; and the American atomic monopoly. The passage of the American National Security Act of 1947, which led to the unification of the armed services and the formation of the National Security Council, was followed closely by Stalin, who ordered all available material on the act to be translated, considering it possible that the act was meant as preparation for war.[217]

In hindsight, the Soviet Union, despite possessing a very capable field army, had severe internal weaknesses that limited its potential to win a lengthy war. The Soviet leadership, at least partly for this reason, did not intend to involve itself in a war with the West. However, those in the West who feared a Soviet attack had understandable reasons for their anxiety. Since intentions can change rapidly, and military capabilities can only change slowly, it made sense to be concerned with the military imbalance in Europe.

A further complication was that Western intelligence on the Soviet Union was lacking. The Truman administration had to assume that assessments of Soviet capabilities were semieducated guesses and that assessments of Soviet intentions were even more speculative. The administration could not presume that intelligence services would give much advance notice if and when Moscow did begin final preparations for an offensive.

The German intelligence unit in the World War II eastern front, whose commander, Reinhard Gehlen, was now working in a similar capacity for the Americans, failed to predict the critical Soviet offensive of 1944.[218] The Japanese failed to predict Soviet offensives in Manchuria in the following year. The CIA, charged with the task of predicting Soviet behavior, had only been formed in 1947, and the quality of its work may have been shoddy in this era. General Walter Bedell Smith, who worked with CIA agents when he was ambassador to Moscow in the late 1940s and who reluctantly agreed to become CIA director in 1950, told his friend George Allen, ambassador to Yugoslavia, that regarding CIA personnel, "My experience in Moscow was not particularly reassuring."[219] Before beginning his term as agency director, he told another friend, "I expect the worst and know I won't be disappointed."[220]

The CIA did not insert its own agents into the Soviet Union until late 1949, when airdrops began as part of a spy operation code named RED-SOX.[221] The officer in charge of these air operations, Harry Rositzke, would later claim that they were partially compromised by Kim Philby, the MI6 liaison officer in Washington who was secretly giving information to the Soviet Union.[222] Many of the dropped men may have been turned into double agents by the Soviets, who used them to send back misinformation. Peer de Silva, who in 1951 became the chief of operations for the CIA's Soviet Bloc Division, later claimed that "a close review of our operational files led me to [believe] that practically every one of our parachuted agents was under Soviet control and was reporting back to us under duress. The KGB was writing their messages and feeding back information they wanted us to have which was either false, misleading or confusing. We therefore had almost no assets, in terms of agents, within the borders of the USSR or the Baltic states."[223] The dropping of agents proved so valueless that it was terminated in 1954.[224]

As for handling those Soviets and Eastern Europeans who fled to the West and offered to spy for America, the CIA, according to intelligence expert Angelo Codevilla, was so incompetent that the "communist security services were able to learn the identity of Western cross border agents even before they were dispatched."[225] These leaks were a result of the agency's habit of pooling its recruits together, which enabled those agents who were working for foreign security services to betray the rest. Furthermore, "the CIA never attempted to use [these] thousands of willing East European recruits as long-term penetrators of their societies, their governments, or their Communist parties," preferring to allow them only to give basic information on local troop formations, because the agency was too inflexible. In the CIA culture, "moles [could] be courted and handled only by 'classic' American officers posing as diplomats."[226] Codevilla believes that before 1952, the United States had no moles in the Soviet government.[227]

CIA estimates of Soviet aircraft production were guesses based on the square footage of known Soviet factories and occasional overflights of certain air bases,[228] neither of which were reliable means to gauge Soviet capabilities as a whole.

The CIA met with a little more success in Eastern Europe than it did in the USSR, but even these accomplishments were limited. Dr. Walter Linse, who directed an underground network of East Germans from Berlin, was kidnapped outside his apartment one day and driven into the Soviet sector, never to be seen again.[229] The CIA supported a Polish underground anti-Communist group named WIN (the Polish acronym for Freedom and Independence Movement), only to find that it was thoroughly penetrated, from 1947 on, by Polish security services, who turned the organization against the United States.[230]

As for cryptanalytic work, the Army Security Agency had notable success in the late 1940s in deciphering Soviet cables, but it too was short-lived because of the presence of Philby in the deciphering room.[231]

The CIA was not yet an impressively funded organization. The agency, which operated from shabby buildings that had been set up on the National Mall in Washington as temporary space for the government during World War II,[232] had a small staff and a limited number of field agents.[233]

The military intelligence services may have been little better. As late as November 1948, the Air Force Material Command's Intelligence Department estimated that "95% of the qualitative intelligence on Russian aircraft" came from the air attaché watching the annual May Day military shows in Moscow,[234] which says little on behalf of the air force's observation efforts. The overflights of Soviet territory by air force reconnaissance craft had just begun in the late 1940s and were nowhere near the sophisticated operations they would become during the mid to late 1950s.[235] The air force was trying to monitor Soviet radio traffic in this era,[236] but the Soviets generally did not transmit significant messages over the airwaves. During and preceding the Soviet offensives in the latter part of World War II, misinformation was transmitted by radio, and orders were given verbally.[237]

In fairness to the CIA and other intelligence agencies, the Soviet Union was a hard target for information acquisition. The primary method of acquiring military intelligence in the era before spy satellites was through the use of moles, and recruiting moles in the Soviet Union was difficult. The purges in the 1930s and 1940s had established in the minds of every Soviet official that contact with the West or Westerners was grounds for suspicion and might result in death. Soviet security agencies maintained networks of informers who related the affairs of their neighbors to the government on a constant basis. It was so unusual for American embassy staff to converse with Soviet citizens that when such meetings did occur, almost all of which were innocuous chance encounters of short duration at skating rinks, opera intermissions, or similarly mundane occasions, the embassy would send a memorandum back to Washington reporting the exchange.[238]

The enormous size of the USSR made it possible for the Soviets to spread their military and industrial facilities over an interior so large that American spy planes had a difficult time locating them. Even within the USSR, many of these locations were only known to top party or military officials. Secrecy was so strict that networks of defense cities were created in which children growing up could only meet children from other defense cities. Soviet citizens themselves had internal passports that limited their movement, and travel by foreigners within the USSR was extremely limited, with certain cities, such as Vladivostok, declared off limits to all non-Soviet citizens.[239] The press was also closely supervised by the government. Stalin himself is perhaps most famous for his extreme paranoia, in which he imagined that even his personal friends, their wives, his doctors, or his employees were, at any given moment, employed by foreign intelligence services. Partly as a result of this paranoia, the Soviet government may have paid more attention to the threat of spies that any other government in modern history.

The general lack of sound information on the Soviets would make it increasingly likely for the Truman administration to believe that they had to assume the worst about the USSR.

CHAPTER 3

Reconsideration

THE BEGINNING OF THE ACHESON-JOHNSON CONFLICT OVER ARMS POLICY

In 1948, while Secretary of Defense James Forrestal was proposing increases in his department's budget, Secretary of State George Marshall was agreeing with the president's decision to hold the line on military spending. By the next year, there was a role reversal. The new secretary of defense would be launching a cost-cutting drive while the new secretary of state would be pushing for enormously greater funds for the U.S. armed forces.

Forrestal's pleading for an arms build-up was ahead of its time and received little support. It is possible that this frustration, combined with an inability to prevent public bickering among the service chiefs and his fears that Truman was trying to oust him because of his disloyalty during the 1948 campaign, contributed to Forrestal's sense of crisis. Forrestal suffered a series of mental breakdowns and was replaced (he offered his resignation on March 2, 1949) shortly before committing suicide.

Forrestal's replacement was Louis Johnson, a World War I veteran, lawyer, and businessman from West Virginia, whose involvement with the Democratic Party had led to a position as assistant secretary of war from 1937 to 1940. He met Truman in the early 1930s during his work with the American Legion, of which Johnson had been a founder and a national president. Johnson had always been ambitious, going so far as to resign in 1940 when Roosevelt passed him over for the secretary of war post to appoint Henry Stimson.[1] Johnson became Truman's finance chairman during the 1948 presidential campaign, providing much of the funding from his own wallet. After Forrestal's demise, Truman rewarded Johnson's loyalty by naming him secretary of defense, a position for which Johnson had specifically campaigned, going to each state delegation during Truman's inauguration week and asking for their support.[2]

Johnson was tough and blunt, with self-confidence bordering on arrogance. He was exactly the opposite of the insecure Forrestal. Upon arrival at the Pentagon, Johnson jettisoned the army leadership from the best office space and moved himself and his staff in. His demeanor would lead to many confrontations with other cabinet members, especially after Secretary of Commerce Charles Sawyer discovered that Johnson was trying to meddle in his department's affairs.[3] He also clashed with the powerful Senator Brien McMahon of Connecticut, the chairman of the Joint [Congressional] Committee on Atomic Energy, when Johnson declined to share classified atomic information with the senator.[4] But this strength of will may have given Johnson the personality necessary to enforce discipline among the generals and admirals, some still smarting from the unification debate.

Johnson proved loyal to the president's aim of reducing military costs. His confidence, and the backing of Truman, allowed him to take such actions even as sections of the military and the foreign policy establishment tried to oppose him at every turn.[5] His ability to produce change was strengthened by new legislation, passed in 1949, that made the secretary of defense much more effective, rectifying some of the difficulties in leadership that Forrestal had encountered.[6] He was so adamant in trimming what he termed fat from the defense establishment that Deputy Secretary of Defense Stephen Early prophesized that Johnson would become famous as the Secretary of the Economy.[7]

The new secretary of defense's political outlook meshed perfectly with his designated task of slashing budgets. He had little fear that the Soviet threat existed, and does not seem to have favored American participation in NATO, telling a Daughters of the American Revolution meeting in 1948 that "military alliances are not in the tradition of the United States," a statement he was later forced to retract, but probably not with much relish.[8] Defending his cost-cutting, he declared that excessive spending would cripple the economy. He was also of the opinion that no amount of spending on arms could ever guarantee protection against Soviet nuclear attack.[9]

Greater reliance on nuclear weapons, which were relatively cheap (they had more bang for the buck, in Pentagon terminology), and massive cuts in more conventional military programs were the essence of Johnson's program. Within a month of taking office, he cancelled the $100 million construction order for the 65,000-ton supercarrier USS *United States*, whose keel had already been laid in a Norfolk, Virginia, naval shipyard. Johnson instead began ordering the relatively inexpensive B-36 bomber,[10] which could deliver nuclear weapons to enemy territory less expensively than the navy hoped to do with carrier-based bombers. More atomic bombs were ordered from the Atomic Energy Commission (AEC).[11]

The navy reacted by launching a public protest, asserting that surface fleets were still vital in the nuclear age, questioning the desirability of primary reliance on atomic bombing as a means of defense, and asserting that if the United States was to use A-bombs, some should be dropped from navy bombers flying from aircraft carriers.[12] The House Armed Services Committee investigated the matter, holding unification and strategy hearings in which the services argued their case.[13] Congressman Charles Van Zandt, a Navy veteran acting on information from an assistant to the under secretary of the navy, accused Johnson of collusion with the Convair Corporation, manufacturer of the B-36, in his decisions. He alleged that Johnson, having been a director of the Atlas Corporation, which owned a large portion of the Convair, was profiting from his decisions.[14] The navy and its friends also challenged the B-36's viability, claiming that it would be an easy target for enemy interceptors, with Admiral Arthur Radford calling the airplane a "billion dollar blunder."[15] Admiral Louis Denfeld, chief of naval operations, resigned at the end of October 1949 as part of the campaign against Johnson, but it was to no avail. The B-36 program went forward.

The public bickering highlighted what would be a recurring problem for Johnson: a lack of understanding between himself and much of the military leadership. The Pentagon was, by the end of 1949, only nine months after Johnson was sworn in, already marked by high levels of distrust toward the secretary. Members of the Joint Chiefs of Staff challenged Johnson's budgeting programs publicly, without mentioning his name, and four service secretaries, Kenneth C. Royall and Gordon Gray of the army, John L. Sullivan of the navy, and Stuart Symington of the air force, resigned during Johnson's first year, probably because of the difficult environment of Johnson's Pentagon.[16] A perception existed within the armed forces that Johnson placed personal political considerations above national security requirements. He was accused of trying to gain the 1952 Democratic nomination for president, for which his cost-cutting was allegedly a publicity tool.[17]

The most important opponent of Johnson's fiscal austerity programs, and the man who would remain in office long enough to see both Johnson's firing and a tripling of defense budgets, was the new secretary of state, Dean Acheson.[18] In 1949 and early 1950, much of the policy debate over American defense budgets took the character of a personal duel between the two secretaries. Acheson began a lobbying campaign to increase American military budgets, only to be countered at every turn by Johnson.

Acheson was a well-connected lawyer (he was friends with Roosevelt's personal assistant, Averell Harriman, and Supreme Court Justice Felix Frankfurter) who had served for a short time as a White House counsel in the Roosevelt administration before resigning over what he considered a question of ethics. He had come back to government service during World War II, served as assistant secretary of state under Marshall, and, like Johnson, had remained steadfastly loyal to Truman during the 1948 election, when many Democrats, wrongly convinced of the inevitability of a Dewey victory, had offered either lukewarm support to the administration or deserted it altogether. He took command of the department on January 20, 1949, and successfully lobbied Truman for wide responsibilities, including formulation of German policy upon the end of the military governorship, greater direction of foreign aid programs, and recognition of the State Department's superiority over the National Security Council.[19] Acheson was familiar with the constant bureaucratic fighting in Washington and was determined to be assertive in foreign policy formulation. He did not consider military budgeting to be beyond his jurisdiction.

Acheson agreed with the State Department evaluation that "the Soviet Union will not deliberately resort to military action in the immediate future,"[20] but felt that the United States needed greater military spending if it was to be the international champion of liberal democracy that he wished it to be.

Acheson saw the Cold War, to some extent, in civilizationist terms. Some biographers have suggested that his Anglophilia and Europhilia led him to perceive the confrontations with the USSR as a conflict between East and West. He wanted to strengthen Germany and Europe for a crusade against Soviet Communism. As Acheson would later write:

The threat to Western Europe seemed to me singularly like that which Islam had posed centuries before, with its combination of ideological zeal and fighting power. Then it had taken the same combination to meet it: Germanic power in the east and Frankish in Spain, both energized by a great outburst of military power and social organization in Europe. This time it would need the added power and energy of America, for the drama was now played on a world stage.[21]

Acheson felt that American diplomacy was impotent because of the lack of conventional military power, especially in Europe. He felt that persuasion and compromise would only work when backed by strength. He was a proponent of traditional international power politics. If the power of a state or alliance was equal to or greater than that of potential adversaries, the state could either forcibly achieve its aims or threaten other states into concessions. This belief was best illuminated in his insistence that the United States had to operate from "situations of strength."[22] He declared that the initiative in international affairs would belong to whoever was willing to back up their desires with power and a willingness to use it. He wanted to show that the United States could not be intimidated and that it would pursue firm policies in Berlin, Indochina, and the eastern Mediterranean (a notable exception was China). He especially wanted to make the North Atlantic Treaty alliance a militarily competent force. As Paul Nitze, soon to become the State Department director of policy planning, would later write, the alliance was, at this time, "viewed as a North American political commitment to the defense of Europe rather than as a framework for a military organization."[23] Although there was a permanent alliance staff, there was no supreme commander of NATO forces with the authority to order units of various nationalities into action. The treaty was not backed up with enough American forces, according to Acheson, and its provisions still granted Congress ultimate control over an American formal entry into war, allowing both the Soviets and the Western Europeans to question the American commitment to European affairs. Acheson had sarcastically noted during the celebrations in Washington at the signing of the treaty that the band's choice of the song, "I've Got Plenty of Nothing," was appropriate.[24] Acheson, along with much of the State Department staff, believed that the European economies, although rapidly recovering from the damages of World War II, were not yet strong enough to produce the necessary counterbalance to Soviet power on their own. Britain, having already opted to terminate its military commitments in India, Palestine, and Burma because of, in part, economic reasons, was fighting a colonial war in Malaya, while maintaining forces in Gibraltar, the Suez Canal zone, the Persian Gulf, Hong Kong, and sub-Saharan Africa.[25] Only large contingents of American forces could counterbalance the Soviet army in continental Europe.

American combat divisions in Europe would also help convince the French to accept German rearmament, already under consideration at the State Department in 1949. Since German rearmament might threaten France's security, the French would only go along with it if assurances were given of an Anglo-American commitment to the continent. The only way to provide such forces would be to engage in a general increase in military spending.

In Acheson's mind, the United States had to avoid following the pattern of the 1930s: trade wars, economic misery, and above all, an unwillingness of the United States to create, and prepare to use, a working military force to act as a deterrent. If the West could build up forces, it would be ready to play what amounted to a new version of the old Anglo-Russian great game of an earlier era. With the United States consuming almost 50 percent of the raw materials produced in the non-Communist world,[26] it could not afford, as Acheson saw it, to allow Soviet expansion anywhere without feeling the impact at home. Acheson did not place much faith in the view held by some Foreign Service officers that local nationalists and the difficulties of administering subjugated nations might make extensions of Soviet influence a means of Soviet overstretch.

Having lived through the most violent and revolutionary three decades in Western history since the mid-seventeenth century, Acheson saw the international order as prone to instability. A military build-up had the potential to psychologically reaffirm the West's ability to control events.

Perhaps the only agreement on security policy between Acheson and Johnson was that the Europeans should increase their defense spending, which, as Johnson saw it, could relieve the United States of the burden of European defense, and, as they both agreed, could help contain Soviet opportunism. The two departments lobbied NATO nations, with marginal success, to increase military budgets.[27]

Acheson and Johnson's mutual enmity took many forms. They disagreed on military policy, with Acheson preferring a massive build-up of forces, while Johnson preferred downsizing. They disagreed on foreign policy, with Johnson committed to an Asia-first strategy, while Acheson saw Western Europe as the "keystone of the world." To some, Acheson seemed disinterested in Asian affairs, and willing to subordinate Asian issues, such as Indochina, to the need to maintain European unity.[28] They differed in taste, with Johnson holding to his blunt West Virginia ways, while Acheson preferred to play the urbane East Coast establishment lawyer. By 1950, Johnson was so eager to oust his rival that he told Averell Harriman, then a special adviser to the president, that he would support any efforts by Harriman to become secretary of state if Harriman helped remove Acheson from power. Acheson, never one to mince words when in disagreement, responded in his memoirs that "evidence accumulated to convince me that Louis Johnson was mentally ill. His conduct became too outrageous to be explained by mere cussedness. It did not surprise me when some years later he underwent a brain operation."[29]

The combination of rebellion from within the Department of Defense and attack from Acheson made Johnson suspicious of plots to circumvent his authority. Johnson insisted that all contacts between the two departments be personally approved by either himself or General James Burns, his liaison officer for State. This action only made Acheson more irate.

If he was to succeed in his efforts to convince the president, Congress, and the public of the need for an arms build-up, Acheson had to build a team at State that could quietly work with the military to circumvent Johnson's authority, draw public attention to the growing Soviet military menace, oppose Truman's budget ceilings at every opportunity, and work to convince the president of the futility of such arbitrary impositions. The first problem Acheson had to solve in this effort was that of building a team at the State Department that could work with him to create the arms build-up. The only major opposition to be overcome was from the director of the State Department's Policy Planning Staff (PPS), George Kennan.

GEORGE KENNAN'S OPPOSITION TO AN ARMS BUILD-UP

George Kennan had risen to the position of founder and director of the Policy Planning Staff through his acknowledged expertise on Soviet government. He had been dedicated to the task of studying the USSR since before American recognition of that country in 1933. Stationed at the American embassy in Moscow throughout much of the 1930s and the war years, he was fluent in Russian and on personal terms with high-ranking Soviet foreign policy officials. His reputation in Washington, and his career prospects, had been consolidated by his long telegram from Moscow to the White House in February 1946. The telegram attempted to explain some of the historical and cultural reasons for Soviet aggrandizement, and coined the term *containment* to describe the appropriate American response to dealing with the USSR. Truman had found the telegram so valuable that he had copies sent to various key officials in his administration. It was also reprinted anonymously in *Foreign Affairs* magazine.[30]

By 1949, Kennan had clarified and refined the concept of containment. At the time of the long telegram, Kennan had not made clear distinctions between military and political efforts to contain Soviet power, and had not clearly stated the geographical and economic limitations, if any, that were to be imposed on efforts to combat Soviet designs.[31] But questions concerning his article from those in government and in the media, particularly from journalist Walter Lippmann, combined with the unfolding of events in Greece, Iran, Czechoslovakia, and Berlin, led Kennan to elaborate on his views.

Kennan's suggested policies were far less reliant on a strong military than were Acheson's. He opposed Truman's pledge, given in a speech before Congress designed to gain acceptance for an aid package for Greece, to support peoples everywhere who were resisting Communism.[32] He believed that Stalin could be contained if the West prevented certain critical economic areas, such as Western Europe, North America, the oil regions of the Middle East, and Japan, from falling into Communist hands, and he did not think it necessary to possess more military force to do so.

The North Atlantic Treaty, Kennan felt, was unnecessary.[33] While intending to give a message of firmness and resolve, the creation of an alliance system could foster contrary impressions. Nations would soon be categorized as falling inside or outside the American defense sphere. It was not necessary to create the alliance in order to signal Moscow of America's intentions, for it was clear to everyone after the two world wars that the United States would intervene militarily to prevent an upset in the continental balance of power. Including a foreign state in an alliance could make things difficult for the United States by tying her down to expensive, rigid commitments to regimes of potentially opposing interests. Rising anti-Americanism, bred by the stationing of U.S. forces on foreign soil, would replace anti-Sovietism as the dominant political force.

Kennan lobbied against American military aid for Europe, feeling that this arrangement would only make the Atlantic alliance so dependent on thinking in terms of the military balance of power that it would be inflexible in its ability to negotiate with the Soviets.[34] He also distrusted a growing tendency domestically to think of the Cold War in military terms, fearing that this would prohibit the U.S. diplomatic corps from operating pragmatically, coolly, and flexibly with the difficult Soviets.

Kennan sought a no-first-use policy for atomic bombs, even in the event of a war initiated by the Soviet Union.[35] Nuclear attacks on the USSR, Kennan said, would "stiffen the courage and will to resist of the Russian people."[36] The mere act of preparing for atomic war would also contribute to a nuclear arms race of great cost and danger to all.

Most critically, for the needs of this book, Kennan did not favor an arms build-up, preferring to rely on economic and political policies, such as the Marshall Plan, to strengthen friendly states against Soviet pressure. Kennan felt that American resources were limited, and he did "not believe in the reality of a Soviet military threat to western Europe."[37] He told his coworkers that "the best evidence available to us indicates that the Russians are not planning to start a war," since they were "too preoccupied with Tito and the Far East."[38] Kennan believed that Soviet military capabilities were greatly exaggerated by American officials, and said that "basic Russian intent still runs to the conquest of western Europe by political means. In this program, military force plays a major role only as a means of intimidation."[39] Two Marine divisions, he said, would be sufficient to support the military needs of containment.[40] Unlike Acheson, he felt that the United States could negotiate with the Soviets (perhaps for a united, neutralized, and demilitarized Germany, combined with Soviet withdrawal of forces from eastern Europe)[41] without first creating a militarized situation of strength.

During a meeting with Department of Defense planners in the summer of 1949, Kennan declared that the military requirements of American foreign policy could be met under the current budget ceiling ($13.5 billion annually), if the money was directed toward small, mobile, well-trained, and highly mechanized task forces.[42] These forces would be designed for the localized conflicts of limited scale that might prove necessary in upholding the policy of containment.[43] Kennan's views ran counter to the Department of Defense policy, made in light of the budget ceilings, of not even planning for small conflicts. The Pentagon was devoting whatever it had toward the possibility of a major war. Kennan told his counterparts at Defense that a total war with the USSR was too remote a possibility to be taken seriously and that such a conflict might not be winnable if it did occur. It was virtually impossible for anyone to occupy the Soviet Union, according to Kennan. He also expressed doubts as to efficacy of Strategic Air Command's plans for nuclear bombardment.[44]

Kennan lobbied against a large military establishment in PPS meetings as well. When speaking in opposition to the strategic bombing faction in one meeting, Kennan mentioned, as an alternative, what he considered to be the French view of European security: having the ability to stop a Soviet advance at either the Elbe or the Rhine, and then tying the Soviet army down in fighting at that front until their weaknesses were exposed and a settlement was reached.[45] He added that "we should not even contemplate trying to occupy all of Russia and Siberia."[46] He seems to have believed that the French version of security could be met without an increase in military spending.

Kennan's mentioning of the French plan may have reflected his belief that war was unlikely as much as it reflected belief in the plan's viability. Kennan seems to have felt that any argument against military spending, conventional or nuclear, was useful, considering the unlikeliness of war. He was convinced that the balance of power was stable.[47] Where Acheson saw a dangerous Soviet threat, Kennan felt that "both sides have somewhat over-extended lines and are attempting to consolidate their positions."[48] The American atomic weapon was a "superfluous deterrent."[49]

Kennan challenged Acheson's premises directly. When, at an October 1949 meeting of the PPS, Acheson suggested that "unless we face up to what we want, decide how to get it, and take the necessary action, the whole structure of the Western World could fall apart in 1952," Kennan struck back, claiming that "the Western World need not necessarily collapse simply because we stopped financing it . . . perhaps the main strain might be felt in this country unless we can decide how we can swallow our own surpluses."[50]

Acheson did not take such criticism lightly. In response to some of Kennan's pleas for a less militaristic policy, Acheson snapped that "if that is your view, you ought to resign from the Foreign Service and preach your Quaker gospel, but don't do it within the department."[51] In response to Kennan's broaching of the French plan, Acheson mocked it with the remark that "if the Red Army got started [the American military] would not be able to stop it, even with the bomb."[52] His distrust of Kennan seems to have continued even after leaving government office. One historian quotes Acheson as referring to Kennan years later as "a footnote of the Truman Presidency."[53] Most significantly, Acheson gradually began to remove Kennan from policymaking circles. From September 1949 onward, the PPS no longer reported directly to the secretary of state, but had to go through the operational division chief.[54]

Despite his confidence in challenging the secretary of state's views, Kennan does not seem to have engaged in any significant effort to construct a consensus on the inadvisability of an arms build-up. His challenges of Acheson were those of a lone dissenter. There is little record of cooperation between Kennan and the other major bureaucratic opponent of the arms build-up, Louis Johnson, and no hint of an effort to smooth over differences over atomic policy with Johnson in order to forge an alliance against the proposed conventional arms build-up. Kennan did not possess the ear of Truman, nor of the JCS. When Kennan criticized an NSC draft report on U.S. security objectives, even Charles Bohlen, his longtime associate at the U.S. embassy in Moscow, disparaged Kennan's overly rosy view on security affairs, claiming that:

We are not now in the military phase of our relations with the Russians. But we must look ahead. Certain things must be done now in terms of a long-range projection ... if in 1953 we should find the Russian war wounds are healed, her industry re-established, her military on a firm footing and in possession of the atom bomb, we might be in a position to say: 'What should we have done in 1949?'[55]

By late 1949, Kennan had lost any control over his own Policy Planning Staff. Minutes of the meetings increasingly show Kennan debating several people at once, including Acheson.[56] He spent increasing amounts of time alone, holed up in an office in the Library of Congress, working on a lengthy paper as part of his futile effort to convince the administration of a no-first-use policy.[57] He was paid less and less attention. Kennan offered to change jobs, and Acheson consented. Effective December 31, 1949, Kennan resigned from his position at PPS, becoming a counselor of the State Department. Theoretically, this was not a demotion, but it took Kennan further away from the day-to-day affairs of the department. His replacement as director of PPS was his underling, former investment banker Paul Nitze, a pessimist regarding Soviet intentions, and a fervent believer in the necessity of an American arms build-up. Although Kennan had originally been responsible for persuading Acheson to allow Nitze to become a PPS member, their policy differences led to personal differences between Kennan and his replacement, whom he would later consider militaristic and simplistic in his numerical approach to Soviet-American comparisons. Nitze, in return, considered Kennan naive in his certainty that the USSR would not initiate military action, and privately accused Kennan of opposing the arms build-up because it might relieve the diplomatic corps of its primary position in dealing with the Soviets.

THE SOVIET ATOMIC BOMB AND THE
AMERICAN HYDROGEN BOMB

The Truman administration and the leadership of the armed forces had assumed since 1945 that the Soviets were trying to build their own atomic weapon. The military had even created the Long Range Detection Program (LRDP), in which specially equipped aircraft would look for evidence of a Soviet atomic explosion.[58]

But the president continually underestimated Soviet capabilities in atomic research and espionage. Soon after the war, Truman had the following conversation with J. Robert Oppenheimer, the chief physicist of the Manhattan Project:

Truman: "When will the Russians be able to build the bomb?"

Oppenheimer: "I don't know."

Truman: "I know."

Oppenheimer: "When?"

Truman: "Never."[59]

Truman willfully ignored the information coming in that suggested that the Soviets could succeed quickly. Physicist Niels Bohr, who had worked on the Manhattan Project and who had been approached by Soviet scientists attempting to recruit him, told the American government in January 1948 that Stalin would have the bomb within sixteen or eighteen months.[60] However, as late as July 1949, Truman chose to rely on General Leslie Groves's prediction that the monopoly would last another decade rather than believe a report produced by experts at the Atomic Energy Commission, the Pentagon, and the CIA predicting that the Soviets would achieve fission by mid-1950.[61]

He was wrong to do so. On September 3, 1949, a U.S. Air Force B-29 flying over the North Pacific near Alaska on LRDP duty detected high levels of radiation in atmospheric samples. Further flights were made. The results were the same, and the air force forwarded its conclusion to Washington: the Soviets had detonated an atomic device similar in composition to the one the Americans had detonated at Alamagordo.[62]

The Soviet atomic program had begun in the 1930s. After languishing for some years, Stalin ordered an all-out development program, under the direction of Laventri Beria, the day after the bombing of Hiroshima. The program had been aided by the use of vast amounts of resources, by Communist sympathizers in the Anglo-American atomic establishment who gave the Soviets classified information, usually for ideological motives, and by the existence of a brilliant core of experts in theoretical physics, led by Yuri Khariton. The men were under such pressure that one of them would later claim they would have been shot for failure.[63] Even Beria found that Stalin was spying on him.[64] By mid-1949, Stalin's physicists told him they were ready to produce either a copy of the American bomb or their own atomic bomb. Stalin ordered that the former be tested. It was detonated on the morning of August 29, 1949, near the town of Semipalatinsk, in Kazakhstan.[65] This location, in the Ust Urt desert, would become one of the Soviets' favorite testing sites.

The Truman administration admitted its findings to the public on September 23. The reality that the nation's rival possessed a weapon of mass destruction slowly sank into a worried public. On November 6, 1949, the thirty-second anniversary of the Bolshevik Revolution, official speeches indicated what American officials understood to be a new Soviet assertiveness in international affairs.[66] A different era in the Cold War had begun.

What, if anything, was the United States to do about the Soviet bomb? Truman himself seems to have been slow to rush into action. As late as March 1952, he would write in his diary, inaccurately, that the Soviet bomb might be a "phony."[67] But he could not be certain of anything, and he was in the midst of a tense cold war. Virtually everyone around him accurately assumed that the Soviet bomb was genuine, and Truman found himself at the center of a debate on whether and how to respond to the Soviet weapon.

The State Department Estimates Group, in the Office of Intelligence Research, suggested that the American government should not radically alter its policies.[68] The American ambassador in Moscow, Alan Kirk, essentially agreed, feeling that the only change in Soviet policy resulting from the bomb would be a new propaganda push.[69] Similarly, Louis Johnson told reporters after the announcement of the Soviet atomic explosion, "I warn you, don't overplay this."[70]

Others saw the new strategic environment as demanding new vision. Kennan, who did not believe in the feasibility of nuclear weapons, wanted a new initiative to internationalize atomic energy under the auspices of the United Nations, and he hoped for negotiations to reduce conventional forces in Europe. Kennan also conducted a series of briefings in October 1949 that investigated the strengths and weaknesses of an American declaration opposing the first use of nuclear weapons in any conflict.[71] Despite the possibility that the Soviets might now bomb European cities in the event of a war, the threat of first use was still the backbone of American defense policy in Europe, and its questioning was a matter of serious discussion. The attendees at an October 1949 meeting of the General Advisory Committee of the AEC, including Generals Bradley, Lauris Norstad, and Harris Hull, among others, were unable to definitely favor a first-use policy in the event of a war in Europe,[72] although they did not favor a public statement against American first use either.[73]

A special committee of the National Security Council recommended that the nation respond to the Soviet bomb with an increase in America's quantitative nuclear edge, proposing an increase in the current rate of production, which was four atomic bombs per week[74] (the total number of atomic bombs was 250 in 1949).[75] The committee, consisting of Johnson, Acheson, and AEC Chairman David Lilienthal, cited the recommendations of the JCS in their report. The Joint Chiefs asserted that improvements in the plutonium separation process, in waste recovery, and in the use of U-235 would make increased production feasible, and that a quick decision would be helpful, given the three- to four-year lead times from conception to realization in the production of atomic weapons.[76] There were military benefits to more A-bombs, the JCS claimed, such as "lower unit costs of weapons, probable shortening of war, increased military effectiveness, decreased logistical and manpower requirements for the prosecution of certain tasks in war, and increased flexibility in the conduct of the war."[77] They also cited political factors, such as "continued international tension, springing from the continuing refusal of the Soviet Union to become a cooperating member of the world community," "the growing United States commitments on a world-wide scale," "the growing realization of the necessity to defend Western Europe in the event of Soviet aggression," and "the military prostration of our Western European allies" as reasons for increases in atomic production.[78] The committee also relied on AEC reports for information on the economic feasibility of an increase in bombs and on State Department conclusions regarding the positive impact of the nuclear deterrent.[79]

Others wanted to increase America's qualitative edge by developing hydrogen weapons. Physicists Ernest Lawrence, Luis Alvarez, and Isador Rabi were particularly forceful in advocating such development.[80]

Acheson and Nitze either did not agree with these views or saw them as missing the critical need, which was a conventional arms build-up. Whereas the Estimates Group had specifically noted that the Americans could draw strength from their quantitative lead in atomic production, Acheson and Nitze prophesized that this edge would be hard to maintain if the Soviets shifted to large-scale atomic production. American estimates in early 1950 assumed that the Soviets would have ten to twenty atomic bombs by mid-year and, quite possibly, one hundred by 1953.[81] Acheson and Nitze felt that the qualitative edge would be even more difficult to keep. Although American scientific research was considered sound, technological progress tends to occur in unplanned jumps, not smooth rises. It was impossible to predict which side would lead in developing new technologies. (The concern over the United States's technological lead was later shown to be warranted. The Soviets would construct a usable hydrogen bomb and test it on August 12, 1953, while by 1955 the United States still had not downsized their own fusion device, first successfully tested on November 1, 1952, into a weapon that could be carried by a bomber.)[82]

Acheson and Nitze partially agreed with Kennan's arguments against the usefulness of atomic weapons in international affairs, but drew different conclusions. The appropriate response to the nullification of America's nuclear deterrent was not negotiation, but conventional rearmament.

At one PPS meeting, Kennan, desiring a unilateral American declaration not to use atomic weapons first, told the other members of the staff that in light of the Soviet nuclear weapon, "it may now be impossible for us to retaliate with the atomic bomb against a Russian attack with orthodox weapons."[83] Nitze responded that the Soviet atomic weapon "might make conventional armaments, and their possession by the Western European nations, as well as by ourselves, all the more important."[84] Nitze worried that the Soviets might use satellite armies to achieve their aims,[85] in what he would later term "piecemeal aggression against others, counting on our unwillingness to engage in atomic war unless we are directly attacked."[86]

Conventional forces were more suitable for such campaigns, since nuclear weapons were difficult to use in measured quantities as a means of intimidation. The situations of strength argument that was the backbone of Acheson's diplomacy was dependent on large conventional forces deployed globally, so that force, or the threat of force, could be used in local conflicts.

Backing up the Acheson-Nitze viewpoint were the reports that had been ordered by Secretary of Defense Forrestal in the wake of the interservice public disputes of 1948. These reports were completed at about the time of the Soviet bomb, and they cast doubt on the effectiveness of air force strategic bombing claims. The Harmon Report, completed July 28, 1949, stated that nuclear strikes would destroy only 30 to 40 percent of Soviet industrial capacity,[87] which "would not force the surrender of the Soviet Union."[88] No matter how atomic weapons were used, whether on rail lines, oil refineries, or other targets, they would fail to

per se, bring about capitulation, destroy the roots of Communism, or critically weaken the power of Soviet leadership to dominate the people . . . for the majority of the Soviet people, atomic bombing would validate Soviet propaganda against foreign powers, stimulate resentment against the United States, unify the people, and increase their will to fight . . . the capability of the Soviet armed forces to advance rapidly into selected areas of Western Europe, the Middle East, and the Far East would not be seriously impaired.[89]

One navy analyst pointed out that the Allies had dropped the equivalent of 500 atomic bombs on Germany during World War II without destroying its war-making capacity.[90] Using different means of comparison, historian David Holloway noted that the Soviet Union suffered more casualties and physical destruction in the first four months after the 1941

Nazi invasion than all 200 nuclear weapons in the 1949 American arsenal could have achieved, and had still managed to win that war.[91] The Hull report, written by the Department of Defense's Weapon Systems Evaluation Group and chaired by Army General John Hull, stated in its January 23, 1950, report that so many American bombers would be destroyed in the initial attack, which would destroy only 35 to 60 percent of the intended targets, that a second strike would not be possible.[92]

The armaments faction, led by Acheson and Nitze, began constructing an informal case for an American conventional arms build-up. They cited the Soviet edge in of conventional military power compared to the United States and the changes in military doctrine brought about by the Soviet bomb. General Bradley, chairman of the Joint Chiefs of Staff, told Congress in October 1949 that Soviet possession of the atomic bomb made any operation similar to the Normandy landings of 1944 impossible,[93] hinting that Europe could be lost unless the Soviet steamroller was stopped as it tried to roll to the Atlantic, which he considered an unlikely outcome. With the Soviets having established their bases of supply well to the east of the Pripet Marshes, he told AEC Chairman Lilienthal, they could mount a deadly and powerful offensive, and the only thing protecting Europe was the small stockpile of atomic bombs.[94]

Although the Soviets did not yet have bombers capable of flying to North America and back, the Truman administration could not be sure of when that capability would exist. The possible destruction of the North American industrial centers would de-emphasize the role of production potential in winning a war, while increasing the need for powerful forces deployed by the start of a conflict.[95] There was also the need for more troops to maintain order in the aftermath of a nuclear strike upon the United States.[96]

But the case for an arms build-up was not successfully argued in 1949. Truman's budgetary concerns and general unwillingness to seriously rethink an already accepted doctrine (one that represented traditional American policy) led him to adhere to his fiscal limits for the armed forces. He may have been strengthened in his belief by the deficiencies in Soviet delivery capacities, and by institutional inertia. The first U.S. defense budget formulated after the discovery of the Soviet bomb does not indicate a high degree of change in military doctrine. War plans were still based on the assumption that the United States would bomb the USSR with nuclear weapons at the start of a war, and, in cooperation with European allies, fight a delaying action against Soviet thrusts westward until reinforcements could be created and sent from North America. Fighting a broken-backed war, one in which a nation fought on even after the introduction of nuclear weapons left one or both sides with wrecked domestic infrastructure, was an assumption incorporated into military doctrine.[97]

There were, however, at least two direct effects of the discovery of the

Soviet atomic bomb. The first was a boom in hydrogen bomb research. The second was a review of America's global strategy in light of recent events.

Research into more destructive types of atomic weapons was already under way. Serious investigation of a boosted fission bomb had been in progress since 1948. Such a bomb would use a thermonuclear fission reaction to enhance the power of the main fission reaction.[98] Even more spectacular, however, was the concept of a fusion bomb that would use a thermonuclear reaction to attempt to fuse hydrogen atoms.

The fusion of hydrogen atoms creates 25 to 1,000 times more energy than the fission of uranium atoms, so that in terms of explosive power, a very large hydrogen bomb may be just as great an exponential leap in killing power over the atomic bomb as the atomic bomb was over mass raids with conventional explosives. To achieve fusion, it was necessary to use fission bombs just to reach the required temperature. Whereas the fission bomb dropped at Hiroshima had destroyed the center of the city but had left the suburbs virtually intact, a hydrogen bomb could create a fireball with a diameter of four miles and a lethal fallout of more than 10 miles.

The idea had been on the drawing boards of some scientists since at least 1932[99] and had even been researched at Los Alamos during World War II. But in 1946, further practical development of the fusion weapon had been discontinued.[100] Work continued, under the supervision of physicist Edward Teller, but on only a theoretical level. Sidney Souers, the executive secretary of the NSC, left an October 1949 meeting with the president under the impression that Truman was completely oblivious to the H-bomb.[101] But there were new calls to develop the weapon in the wake of the Soviet success in developing a fission device.

Opinion on the development of fusion weapons was very much divided. Some leading atomic physicists vocally opposed the H-bomb, as they had been doing since at least 1945. The General Advisory Committee of the AEC, a panel including physicists Enrico Fermi and Oppenheimer, declared on October 30, 1949, that the construction of a hydrogen weapon was morally reprehensible and should not be undertaken.[102] They also warned that a program to develop the fusion bomb would divert men and resources from the fission program, slowing the manufacture of those weapons.[103] Instead of mass destruction bombs, the committee wrote, the United States should work to create small fission devices for use as tactical weapons.[104] The AEC agreed with the findings and passed them on to the administration.[105]

Kennan, in his last days at the PPS, totally opposed, on moral grounds, any further development of weapons which, in all likelihood, would be used for mass destruction of civilians. Lilienthal also felt humanitarian concerns ruled out such a weapon, and he recommended on November 9, 1949, that no attempt be made to develop a hydrogen weapon.

Johnson, already a supporter of atomic weapons on the basis of their relatively low cost compared with the maintenance of conventional forces, favored fusion development. As a member of the NSC subcommittee concerned with the question, Johnson approved a recommendation to build the H-bomb.[106] The only way that he would revise this decision, he claimed, was if, implausibly, the Soviets agreed to the American plan for the international control of atomic energy.[107]

Nitze argued forcefully for the bomb, especially to Acheson. Neither Acheson nor Nitze, however, wanted any atomic weapon, fission or fusion, to be seen as a substitute for large deployed armies.

In November 1949, Truman appointed Acheson, Johnson, and Lilienthal to investigate the desirability of development of the H-bomb.[108] Lilienthal argued against fusion bomb development in meetings with the other two members, in part because he thought that neither the State nor Defense Departments had thought through the implications of nuclear weapons for world politics.[109] He wanted a top-to-bottom review of America's national security policies before making a decision on the bomb.[110] Acheson also wanted a review, if he could use it to illuminate his desire for an arms build-up. He delayed his approval for the hydrogen bomb project until he received permission from Johnson to conduct Lilienthal's suggested review.[111] Not only would Acheson have tremendous control over the review process, but having Johnson's signature would also make it more difficult for Johnson to oppose the review's conclusions when they were revealed.

It is unclear whether Lilienthal or Johnson realized that Acheson would use the review to recommend a massive increase in the size of the military. Either way, Lilienthal, now the minority voice on the H-bomb committee, knew that he could do little to prevent the building of the fusion weapon. He discussed the matter with Acheson and decided to sign a directive to build a fusion weapon, in return for an agreement to hold the review.[112] A letter, written by the State Department, ordering the State and Defense Departments to make an overall assessment of American foreign and defense policy in light of the loss of China, the Soviet mastery of atomic energy, and the prospect of a fission bomb, was appended to the H-bomb directive.[113] The State Department intentionally gave authority to only two departments, hoping, or perhaps already knowing through back-channel contacts, that they could persuade Pentagon officials to cooperate in recommending increases in the military budget. State Department officials did not want to include representatives from other departments, who might not share their pro-arms build-up sympathies.[114]

Meanwhile, pressure was mounting on the administration for a decision. The existence of a private debate in the administration about the hydrogen bomb had become public knowledge during January, with journalists Drew Pearson and Edward R. Murrow mentioning it on their radio shows, the *New York Times* printing a front-page story on the issue, and former presidential adviser Bernard Baruch urging fusion development.[115] Public sentiment was behind the thermonuclear bomb, and, as historian Alonzo Hamby put it, "No elected politician of any significance was prepared to go to the barricades to defend a negative decision [on the hydrogen bomb issue]."[116] Pollsters found that the public favored the development of the hydrogen bomb by a four-to-one margin.[117] Truman was personally the subject of much lobbying, with recommendations from the JCS, Senator McMahon, who was the head of the Joint Committee on Atomic Energy, and others.[118] Truman may have made up his mind sometime in the third or fourth week of January.[119]

On January 31, 1950, the day that the H-bomb directive and attached authorization of a review were submitted, Acheson, Johnson, and Lilienthal went to see Truman. Lilienthal began to explain the committee's findings and to express his personal reservations about fusion weapons. There was little need. Truman, cutting off Lilienthal in mid-argument, asked if the Soviets might be working on such a bomb (which they had been doing since 1948,[120] without American knowledge). Once Truman was informed that American intelligence was not sure and that the Soviets just might be building a hydrogen weapon, he immediately ordered the development of the H-bomb,[121] publicly announcing his decision later in the day.[122]

THE WRITING OF NSC-68

Acheson and Johnson differed in their approach to the top-to-bottom review authorized by the H-bomb agreement. As we have seen, Acheson helped orchestrate the initiation of the review, hoping to use the review-writing exercise to argue the case for increased military spending. Specifically, he wanted to build a broad coalition for military expansion in the bureaucracy and the White House before launching a campaign in Congress and the press to gain the necessary funds.[123] He delegated his role to Nitze, who, with Kennan no longer on the Policy Planning Staff, and unable to interfere, willingly worked to implement the secretary's ideas, meeting with Acheson daily during the drafting of the review to keep him appraised of its status.[124] Johnson seems not to have felt that the exercise would be remembered as one of the most critical points of his tenure, judging by his decision to delegate Defense's role to Major General (retired) James Burns, assistant to the secretary of Defense for foreign military affairs. Johnson did not keep himself apprised of its progress.

Burns consulted the Joint Chiefs, who declined to participate, but they did assign part of their staff, the Joint Strategic Survey Committee (JSSC), to the exercise. With Burns's consent, Major General Truman Landon, the air force member of JSSC, took charge of the Defense portion of the project. Once Burns, who worked directly for Johnson, removed himself from authority, no one was officially speaking on behalf of the secretary of defense. Since it was a long-standing policy of the JCS that no one, not even their staff, formally spoke for them, the Defense team was formally liberated from having to follow official policy and could challenge Johnson's assumptions if it chose.[125] It is quite possible that the JCS, in contact with allies at State, had planned all along to use the review-writing exercise to attack Johnson, and had orchestrated the delegation of the task to a nominally independent body for that reason. The JCS, whose approval would be necessary if the review was to be held in esteem by the civilian leadership of the Truman administration, were kept apprised of the document's nature on a regular basis during its drafting,[126] and probably influenced the decision by Landon and his staff to argue the case for increased funding, unsurprising given that they were personally opposed to Johnson and politically opposed to his budgets.

Once delegated, the members of State and Defense organized what they termed the State-Defense Policy Review Group. Nitze and Landon played critical roles.[127] The group met numerous times and created several drafts before submitting its report in April.[128]

At the group's initial meeting, Landon and Defense Department colleagues submitted a potential draft based on existing appraisals of American military capabilities. These drafts were optimistic in their portrayal of American power, relative to the estimates from the State Department.[129] The assessments might have been instigated by Johnson, who could only cut budgets if he could maintain the perception that the United States was not falling behind the Soviets in military power. However, Landon seemed to State Department officers to have little faith in his own paper.[130] The State Department members of the groups cajoled Landon on the issue. At first Landon would not consider writing any document that recommended an increase of more than $5 billion per year,[131] but upon consideration, and consultation with the JCS, Landon's team consented to the State Department's position, giving them the lead in creating the review.

The result was a 67-page essay preaching the virtues, for the United States, of gaining conventional military superiority over the Soviet Union. The document was officially titled "A Report to the President Pursuant to the President's Directive of January 31, 1950," until Truman authorized its approval by the NSC, when it was renamed National Security Council Paper 68 (NSC-68).

NSC-68 barely mentioned or ignored entirely certain subjects one would expect to be covered in a review of national defense, such as logistics, training, troop morale, and tactics, because these topics were not necessary to the cause. The only relevant information for the team were observations or measurements that showed the Soviet Union to be expansionist, unstable, and better armed than the United States. The intention, Acheson later wrote, was "to so bludgeon the mass mind of top government that not only could the President make a decision but that the decision could be carried out." To do so meant using forceful prose: "The task of a public officer seeking to explain and gain support for a major policy is not that of the writer of a doctoral thesis. Qualification must give way to simplicity of statement, nicety and nuance to bluntness, almost brutality, in carrying home a point."[132] Nitze's instructions to his writing team were to "hit it hard."[133]

NSC-68 was a forceful and thorough argument, marked by anti-Communist vitriol and using the strongest possible language. It was, at times, moralistic (the United States was a "free society founded on the dignity of the individual," whereas the Soviet Union was a "slave" state), occasionally prone to philosophical pretensions ("Soviet ideas and practices run counter to potentially the best and the strongest instincts of men, and deny their most fundamental aspirations"), and alarmist throughout ("the issues that face us are momentous, involving the fulfillment or destruction not only of this Republic but of civilization itself"). Justifiable concerns many American officials had about the existence of an assertive, powerful, and nuclear-armed government in Moscow were exaggerated for effectiveness.[134]

Nitze's team wanted to gain agreements on seemingly common-sense assumptions before postulating their potentially radical conclusion. The basic assumptions involved judgments concerning the ease with which the United States' prominent position in world politics could evaporate, the inherently expansionist intentions of the Soviet leadership, and the existence of a preponderance of Soviet conventional power. The conclusion was that an arms build-up of massive proportions was necessary.

The first of the nine sections, explaining the background of the "present world crisis," was designed to show that American power could not be taken for granted and that the nature of international politics dictated that swift shifts in status could occur abruptly. NSC-68 stated:

Within the past thirty-five years the world has experienced two global wars of tremendous violence. It has witnessed two revolutions—the Russian and the Chinese—of extreme scope and intensity. It has also seen the collapse of five empires—the Ottoman, the Austro-Hungarian, German, Italian and Japanese—and the drastic decline of two major imperial systems, the British and the French. During the span of one generation, the international distribution of power has been fundamentally altered.[135]

American political leaders could not afford to relax.

Sections two through four of the report were designed to show that the two major states to have emerged from the previous war in a position of enhanced strength had antithetical visions of society. The fundamental purpose of the U.S. government was "to assure the integrity and vitality of our free society, which is founded upon the dignity and worth of the individual." On the other hand, the Soviet government sought "the complete subversion or forcible destruction of the machinery of government and structure of society in the countries of the non-Soviet world and their replacement by an apparatus and structure subservient to and controlled from the Kremlin."[136]

The "conflict in the realm of ideas and values" between the two powers would make a settlement of major international issues agreeable to both sides unlikely.

Sections five through eight compared the political intentions and military capabilities of the United States and the USSR. Repeating the theme of Soviet aggressiveness, NSC-68 found the Kremlin's aim in world politics to be "the elimination of resistance to its will and the extension of its influence and control" to those areas currently under non-Communist government. Not wishing to split hairs in ascertaining the precise reasons for this policy, NSC-68 simply ascribed a combination of three possible motivating factors: "[The Kremlin] is inescapably militant because it possesses and is possessed by a world-wide revolutionary movement, because it is the inheritor of Russian imperialism and because it is a totalitarian dictatorship."[137]

The Soviets did not view coexistence with the non-Communist world as possible, believing that "the most mild and inoffensive free society is an affront, a challenge and a subversive influence" that might appeal to citizens suffering under the dictatorship of Soviet Communism.[138]

Conducting its policy in an "utterly amoral and opportunistic" manner, the Kremlin placed no limit on the means to achieve its ends.[139] It typically made use of Communists abroad, a powerful espionage service, and the popular appeal of its anticolonial ideology among the peoples of the non-Western world. The only factors inhibiting Soviet use of military force were expediency and practicality.

The Soviets were enlarging their armed forces, in case a moment should arise in which it would be expedient and practical to use them. The USSR had a commanding lead in conventional firepower, NSC-68 argued, and the termination of the American atomic monopoly removed an essential guarantee against its use. Relying on reports by intelligence organizations in the military and the CIA, especially the JCS report cited in section 2.5 of this book, NSC-68 predicted that, in the event of war, the Soviets would be capable of successfully conquering vast tracts of territory at various points along the frontiers of Soviet power, in, among other places, Scandinavia, central Europe, the Middle East, and the Far East. NSC-68 also attempted to give numerical evidence of the growing Soviet atomic capability.[140]

Although the economic deficiencies of the Soviet economy, the inherent inflexibility of the Marxist-Leninist system, the distrust of the Communist government by citizens of the USSR, and the nationalism present in the satellite states of Europe potentially weakened the power of the leaders in the Kremlin, these factors would not, according to NSC-68, lead to a demise in the power of such leaders unless "an adversary which effectively affirmed the constructive and hopeful instincts of men" was willing to exploit them.[141]

Section nine, offering "possible courses of action," posed the question of whether the United States was willing to be that nation that stood up to the Soviet Union and whether it was willing to arm itself to contain Stalin's ambitions.[142] Time, according to NSC-68, was running out. As Soviet power was waxing, America's ability to counter it was waning.

There were four possible options:

1. continuation of current policies, with current and currently projected programs for carrying out these policies;
2. isolation;
3. war; and
4. a more rapid building up of the political, economic, and military strength of the free world than provided under the first option, with the purpose of reaching, if possible, a tolerable state of order among nations without war and of preparing to defend ourselves in the event that the free world is attacked.[143]

All of these choices, according to NSC-68, were unpalatable, and all but the last were unacceptable.

A continuation of the present funding levels would ensure that the West would fall further behind the USSR militarily, endangering Western security and accepting enormous losses in the event of a war. NSC-68 claimed that:

The relative military capabilities of the free world are declining, with the result that its determination to resist may also decline and that the security of the United States and the free world as a whole will be jeopardized [if current funding policies are carried out].[144]

There was also a psychological danger in allowing the Soviets to gain too much of a lead on the United States in military capabilities:

Should the belief or suspicion spread that the free nations are not now able to prevent the Soviet Union from taking, if it chooses, the military actions outlined in Chapter V, the determination of the free countries to resist probably would lessen.[145]

Isolationism, the second option, was also dangerous:

With the United States in an isolated position, we would have to face the probability that the Soviet Union would quickly dominate most of Eurasia, probably
without meeting armed resistance. It would thus acquire a potential far superior
to our own, and would promptly proceed to develop this potential with the purpose of eliminating our power.[146]

The third option was initiating hostilities with the USSR. This was the
air force's preventive war doctrine, although NSC-68 did not mention that
service by name.[147] NSC-68 concluded that an American preventive attack
would not "force or induce the Kremlin and the Kremlin would still be
able to use the forces under its control to dominate most or all of Eurasia,"
leading to "a long and difficult struggle during which the free institutions
of Western Europe and many freedom loving people would be destroyed
and the regenerative capacity of Western Europe dealt a crippling blow."[148]

Apart from this, however, a surprise attack upon the Soviet Union, despite the
provocativeness of recent Soviet behavior, would be repugnant to many Americans. Although the American people would probably rally in support of the war
effort, the shock of responsibility for a surprise attack would be morally corrosive.
Many would doubt that it was a "just war" and that all reasonable possibilities
for a peaceful settlement had been explored in good faith. Many more, propor-
tionately, would hold such views in other countries, particularly western Europe
and particularly after Soviet occupation, if only because the Soviet Union would
liquidate articulate opponents. It would, therefore, be difficult after such a war to
create a satisfactory international order among nations. Victory in such a war
would have brought us little if at all closer to victory in the fundamental ideological conflict.[149]

The potential of negotiating with the Soviet Union was discussed, but
the authors of NSC-68 intentionally chose not to make negotiations a separate option. They did not want to give Truman the impression that he
faced a choice between negotiations and an arms build-up. They preferred
that he see an arms build-up as necessary for success in negotiations.
    NSC-68 posited that negotiations with the Soviet Union could only be
successful if Soviet leaders were in a position where they had little choice
but to negotiate. The terms that NSC-68 stipulated that the United States
use as its minimum demands in negotiations with the USSR were not ones
the Soviets would agree to unless given little other choice. NSC-68 admitted that agreement "by the Soviet Union [was] impossible without
such a radical change in the Soviet policies as to constitute a change in
the Soviet system." To be precise, the negotiating stance of the United
States, according to NSC-68, should have been to demand the seven con-

cessions that Secretary of State Acheson mentioned in his March 16, 1950, speech: "1. Treaties of peace with Austria, Germany, Japan and relaxation of pressures in the Far East; 2. Withdrawal of Soviet forces and influences from satellite area; 3. Cooperation in the United Nations; 4. [UN] Control of atomic energy and of conventional armaments; 5. Abandonment of indirect aggression; 6. Proper treatment of official representatives of the U.S.; 7. Increased access to the Soviet Union of persons and ideas from other countries."[150]

Without an arms build-up, negotiations would be to the detriment of the West. Moscow had a distinct advantage in bargaining leverage in any peace conference, according to NSC-68, not only because of its military superiority, but also because of the Soviet political structure. The Soviets could "know more about the realities of the free world's position than the free world [could] know about its position" because of the secrecy in the USSR.[151] The Soviets also did not have to worry about public opinion or the wishes of allies. Negotiating would mean tacitly accepting Soviet transgressions of the Yalta arrangements, thereby psychologically weakening the populace at a time when it needed to be warned of the Soviet threat, and giving Moscow the impression of a lack of resolve. Besides, there was virtually nothing the West could offer the Soviets that would not contribute to their ability to defeat Western society. Any loss of territory would be not only an economic, but also, far more importantly, a psychological blow to anti-Communists around the world.

What was needed was an arms build-up, so that the United States would have "the military power to deter, if possible, Soviet expansion, and to defeat, if necessary, aggressive Soviet or Soviet-directed actions of a limited or total character."[152] The United States could then use the threat of force to contain Soviet ambitions along the entire perimeter of the Soviet-dominated world, compelling the leadership in Moscow to discontinue its violent opportunism, and, with any luck, stifling Soviet ambitions until the current Kremlin leadership was replaced by moderates.[153] If the Soviets were prevented from destroying non-Communist societies, the grip the Communist Party had on power would eventually erode, as the Kremlin struggled with limited means to keep its citizens from trying to recreate the Western world within the Soviet sphere. "The existence and persistence of the idea of freedom is a permanent and continuous threat to the foundation of the slave society"[154] and, if free societies were protected, liberty would prevail in due time.

"Superiority" for the United States and its allies over the Soviet bloc was a high priority, "both initially and throughout a war." The United States did not possess this advantage, and could not achieve it without a mobilization of enormous proportions.

As Nitze would later say, forcing the Soviets to modify their international policies would require "more power than to win military victory
in the event of war."[155] Because Acheson did not want to scare Truman
away from NSC-68's conclusions before the president had digested the
themes of the document, no proposed budgets were offered.[156] In private,
Nitze told Oppenheimer and other attendees at a policy group meeting
that supplying Western Europe alone with a reasonable amount of conventional armaments might require $40 billion, almost three times the U.S.
annual military budget.[157] His estimate may have been influenced by his
participation, in August of the previous year, in a British-American planning team that had, according to Nitze's later recollection, "estimated that
the cost of the military equipment for a force strong enough to hold the
Rhine was $45 billion."[158]

Although NSC-68 did not specifically call for the stationing of American
troops in particular areas, the description of a militarized containment
made it implicitly clear that the build-up of American forces could make
possible a strategy of forward defense. American leaders would have the
option of defending against Soviet encroachment on what were rapidly
becoming the front lines of the Cold War, those places where the USSR
and its allies bordered American allies, in central Europe, the Middle East,
or East Asia.

To relax Truman's knee-jerk fiscal authority, the authors lobbied the
president by mentioning the three methods by which the government
could find the funds: "increased taxes," "reduction of federal expenditures
for purposes other than defense and foreign assistance," or borrowed
funds. Using Keynesian terminology, the authors wrote that the government could drive the economy to full capacity with loans and maintain it
there without inflation through the use of price controls, as had been attempted in World War II. "One of the most significant lessons of our World
War 2 experience," NSC-68 stated, "was that the American economy, when
it operates at a level approaching full efficiency, can provide enormous
resources for purposes other than civilian consumption while simultaneously providing a higher standard of living."[159] Nitze himself probably
did not believe this statement, since he had claimed in an October 11,
1949, NSC meeting that "it might be necessary . . . to lower rather than to
raise civilian standards of living in order to produce arms as against consumer goods,"[160] but the authors realized the usefulness of economic doc-
trines that had been previously used by the left to justify public works
and relief programs in the 1930s. The use of controls was still well regarded in the Truman era, with a 1948 poll finding that 47 percent of the
general public favoring price controls.

NSC-68 made little effort to explain how the U.S. economy was to grow
while paying for an arms build-up, perhaps because of the expectation

that, one way or another, the Cold War would soon end, and because the authors probably felt that talk of long-term growth would hurt their cause.

It is difficult to assess the originality of NSC-68. In using vigorous anti-Communist proclamations, the report differed only in degree from previous Truman administration statements of policy.[161] In assuming that the Soviets were opportunistic and amoral, and in accepting the existence of Soviet conventional military superiority, it merely restated the accepted wisdom in the corridors of power in Washington.[162] In positing that the political confrontations between West and East would continue "until a change occurs in the nature of the Soviet system,"[163] NSC-68 followed in the footsteps of Kennan, whose long telegram had stated that containment would exist until it helped bring about structural change in the USSR. However, unlike the long telegram and subsequent efforts by Kennan to elaborate on that document, unlike either the majority or the semi-isolationist Old Guard opposition in Congress, unlike the secretary of defense, and unlike the president, NSC-68 claimed that in order to carry out the policy of containment, it was necessary to embark on an arms build-up of sufficiently radical size to gain superiority over the Soviets in conventional military forces, and to be willing to use these arms to prevent any expansion of Soviet influence. Such ideas differed from Kennan's suggestions that economic and diplomatic policies alone were sufficient, that only certain key regions were absolutely vital, that the balance of power was stable, and that American resources were too limited to increase the nation's military power. The report also differed from the congressional majority's reliance on nuclear weapons, from the Old Guard's emphasis on an Asia-first policy, and from Johnson and Truman's faith that they could win the Cold War while winning the annual budget battles. The document that began circulating amidst the echelons of power in Washington had the potential to alter the thrust of American foreign policy.

THE TRUMAN ADMINISTRATION'S REACTION TO NSC-68

Nitze and his staffers knew that the more signatures of approval they could collect on the document from leading officials, the more inclined Truman would be to pay attention to it, and the more difficult it would be for him to reject it. So they invited all of the civilian service secretaries, the JCS, and various luminaries from the atomic and foreign policy establishment to briefings. The JCS, having known of and approved of the direction of the document, required little persuasion. The report preached to the converted. With the partial exception of Bradley, the Joint Chiefs had been advocating greater military spending already, and they readily signed the document. Getting the other signatures required more work.

The State-Defense Policy Group met one or two individuals at a time, realizing that to bring in more would increase the possibility of discord and hamper their ability to explain the document in a manner most appropriate for the audience. Sometimes after giving vague assurances that the document would be amended to take into account any misgivings of the individual concerned, Nitze and his men got the desired signatures.[164]

One of the most critical signatures would, of course, be the secretary of defense. On March 22, 1950, Johnson and the Joint Chiefs were invited to a meeting to discuss a preliminary draft of NSC-68. To avoid press attention, they entered through the basement and went to Nitze's office. Accounts of what happened in that room vary, but it is possible to attempt some reconstruction.[165] By most accounts, Nitze and Acheson began explaining the document, which they had intentionally avoided showing to Johnson, with the exception of a vague two-page summary. Johnson asked if Acheson had read it, to which the reply was affirmative. Knowing that his bureaucratic rival had been a part of the project must have alerted Johnson that the report could be designed to work against his interests. Johnson told Acheson that he preferred not to be called into conferences without having had the opportunity to read the material at hand. Always leery of directives from the State Department, Johnson had even more reason to be angered when he realized that Nitze and Acheson were trying to use the fact that so many in his own Pentagon had already signed the report that he would look foolish if he rejected it. Johnson became livid, stood up, banged his fists on the table, shouted that he had not known of the document's formulation, and argued, perhaps with some accuracy, that the document had been an attempt by members of his own department and his enemies at State to circumvent his authority. He then stormed out of the room. The meeting had lasted only approximately 14 minutes.

Once back at the Pentagon, however, Johnson realized that by siding against his service chiefs, who had endorsed the document, he would make himself seem unable to control his own department. The report was going to be completed no matter what Johnson did. The State Department team had told the president of Johnson's boorish behavior at the meeting, and had received Truman's approval to complete the report. As Acheson would later snigger, "Johnson was not left in a strong position."[166] Nitze used the last week in March, while Johnson was in The Hague attending a conference of NAT defense ministers, to drum up even more support at the Pentagon for the document.[167] In addition, Johnson was coming under increasing public scrutiny for his cost-cutting measures. Joseph and Stewart Alsop, well-connected sibling journalists whose editorials were nationally syndicated, undertook a campaign from January to March 1950 to vilify Johnson, claiming that his cuts were leaving America unprepared for a potential war with the Soviet Union. Perhaps receiving information from Johnson's many enemies in the armed forces and the State Department, they cited significant decreases in available warships, submarines, light bomber groups, troop transport groups, and other critical measures.[168]

Probably realizing that there were no precise budget recommendations or specific recommendations for deployments in NSC-68 that could come back to haunt him if he signed it, Johnson relented.[169] On April 11, he added his signature.

During the creation of the document, Nitze, using caution and the rigorous application of rules regarding security clearances, had done his best to ensure that those who might oppose an arms build-up were denied access to the document.[170] Such officials included those in the Department of the Treasury and the Bureau of the Budget whose bureaucratic role was to place the needs of the economy first, and those State Department officials who opposed an arms build-up. After Kennan, in his new role as counselor, advised against the proposed build-up in February, claiming that "drastic measures to reduce the exorbitant cost of defense" were needed, Acheson had sent him away on a fact-finding trip to Latin America to get him out of the country when the important discussions took place.[171] Bohlen, who had some doubts about Nitze's perceptions of the Soviet Union, was not recalled from Paris to discuss the document, as had been considered, and did not read the final document until 1951.[172]

However, once the document was submitted to the White House, Truman, following procedure for any wide-ranging proposal, had drafts distributed to critical high-ranking officials throughout the executive branch. Many comments were submitted to Truman on the matter. NSC-68 was neither uniformly heralded as a panacea nor was it wholly discarded. It did not "bludgeon the minds of top government" into advocating radical changes in military spending, as Acheson had hoped. Within State, there was much criticism. The head of European affairs, George Perkins, felt that the existing American measures in Europe, economic and political, were sufficient, as did his assistant, Llewellyn Thompson.[173] Budgeting advisers also expressed reservations. The deputy chief of the Division of Estimates in Bureau of the Budget, William Schaub, wrote a critique of NSC-68 a month after it was submitted. He was concerned by the unwillingness of Nitze's team to delineate the nation's commitments, the lack of attention to nonmilitary solutions, the attempt to link individual freedom to the all-too-flexible concept of self-determination, and the failure to explain how the United States could pay for the version of containment the report proposed. But

the gravest error of NSC-68 is that it vastly underplays the role of economic and social change as a factor . . . we cannot win the Cold War by a predominant reliance on military force even if combined with large scale dollar assistance. Nor is it

sufficient to add preachments of the concepts of democracy in terms too sophisticated for understanding or too remote from the particular issues foremost in the
minds of peoples. Only as we develop methods for capitalizing on the emerging
social pressures can we beat the Russians at their most dangerous game and safely
take advantage of a rising tide of nationalism.[174]

George Elsey, of the White House staff, feared that NSC-68 would "in-
vite extravagant and well nigh uncontrollable demands by the military
services."

The Bureau of the Budget was even more critical, going so far as to
deny Soviet military superiority and to insist on maintaining the current
ceilings.[175]

All of these critiques would have mattered little to the authors of
NSC-68 if only the president had listened to the document's recommendations. He did not. Harry Truman signed the document on April 11,
which theoretically made it policy, but signing such a general outline of
beliefs, with little in the way of formal proposals, did not entail the assumption of any firm commitments. Truman was still firmly in the middle,
convinced that the United States needed to act as a defender of the democratic bloc, as Acheson insisted, but insistent that this could be done
while trimming military budgets, as Johnson was doing. Truman did not
ask for an arms build-up. On the contrary, even after approving NSC-68,
he pushed for a $13.5 billion defense budget for fiscal year 1951, the lowest
in the post-World War II era. As part of his efforts to get the budget package down to that sum, he exhorted Johnson in an April 20, 1950, memo
that "I am sure as I sit in the President's chair that we have material on
hand, probably rusting in some instances, that will mount up to half a
billion dollars."[176] Truman announced in a May 4, 1950, press conference
that "the defense budget next year will be smaller than it is this year, and
we are continually cutting it by economies. And we are not alarmed in
any sense of the word."[177] When told 19 days later by Frederick Lawton,
the director of the Bureau of the Budget, that the bureau had a number of
serious questions concerning NSC-68, Truman, according to Lawton's record, "indicated that we were to continue to raise any questions that we
had on this program and that it definitely was not as large in scope as
some of the people seemed to think," and also told Lawton to use his own
judgment in deciding whether to press the JCS to complete the fiscal year
1951 ceilings in time.[178] At a news conference on May 20, Truman responded to a query on the defense budget by stating that a "ceiling has
been placed upon it."[179] In June, Truman told *New York Times* correspondent Arthur Krock that he still wanted to keep the lid on defense expenditures.[180] He also reemphasized his optimism, declaring that the outlook
for world peace was greater than at any time since V-J Day.[181] On June 7,
Nitze, frustrated in his efforts to increase military funding, left Washington

for a vacation.[182] Later, on June 22, Truman was asked at a press conference how he felt about the 70-group air force some in Congress were proposing. Truman responded, "I am opposed to an air force group for which we can't pay." The reporter then inquired whether the country could pay for a 70-group air force. "No, we cannot," the president responded.[183] The U.S. military continued to shrink, reaching post-World War II lows in manpower and readiness. As of June 30, 1950, there were 593,167 army personnel on duty,[184] an extremely small increase on the army personnel levels of fiscal year 1948. Also as of June 30, air force manpower was 411,277,[185] and combined navy manpower was 450,780.[186] This figure was the lowest navy manpower level in the post-World War II era.[187]

The lack of forces was so glaring that Navy Chief of Staff Admiral Forest Sherman had informed Acheson, Johnson, and the other members of the Joint Chiefs of Staff in April that the United States should consider abandoning American military commitments in Japan and Okinawa, and withdrawing to a defensive perimeter based on Guam and the Philippines.[188] In the weeks before the Korean War began, the navy was mothballing ships and planning to reduce the number of operating aircraft.[189] Admiral Sherman announced that financial limitations would prevent the navy from constructing any aircraft carriers in fiscal year 1951, even though the increasing size of warplanes made a larger carrier necessary.[190] In the first few days of the Korean War, the navy would find that it did not have as many shells as the Chinese had junks (wooden sailing vessels common to China at the time), and that, in the event of a predicted Chinese invasion of Taiwan, the Chinese would succeed.[191]

Truman sent a letter to the NSC on April 12, requesting that the council consider NSC-68, and that it "provide me with further information on the implications of the Conclusions contained therein. I am particularly anxious that the Council give me a clearer indication of the programs which are envisaged in [NSC-68], including estimates of the probable cost of such programs."[192] The NSC decided to organize an ad hoc committee to meet the president's request at its April 20 meeting.[193] Initial cost estimates were to be finished by July 1 and final estimates by November 1. There is scant evidence that Truman was planning on heeding these cost estimates even when they were produced. Perhaps the single characteristic most commented upon by Truman's associates was his decisiveness.[194] When he wanted something done, he did it. The expected cost estimate completion times suggest that Truman did not want higher defense expenditures.

Truman also seems to have been unaffected by the pressure from the arms build-up faction after he chose to reject their proposals for budget increases. On May 15 and May 22, 1950, columns by Ernest Lindley in *Newsweek* contained predictions that 1952–54 would be a period of maximum danger from the Soviet threat, a prediction also contained in

NSC-68.[195] It is unclear whether Lindley came to this conclusion himself (it was not very different from the conclusions reached in the public report by the President's Commission on Air Policy in 1948) or if the information was leaked to him.[196] Possibly, some of the men advocating the arms build-up, not content with the president's reaction, created the leaks to coerce Truman. If so, they probably meant the leak as a shot across Truman's bow. Although NSC-68 was not yet named in public print, it would be apparent to Truman what could come next: an account in the newspapers about how the president was dangerously cutting military expenditure against the advice of many of the senior advisers and military chiefs.[197] Whatever the source of the Lindley article, Truman pushed ahead, oblivious to attacks on his defense policy.

Despite Truman's reluctance to agree with its budgetary implications, NSC-68 has come to be seen by many historians as significant,[198] and correctly so. NSC-68 was significant enough that its delivery to top officials must be included among the series of critical events both foreign (the Berlin blockade, the discovery of the Soviet A-bomb, the fall of the Guomindang in China, and the signing of the Sino-Soviet treaty) and domestic (the start of the McCarthy witch hunts, and the Old Guard's assault on Truman's softness) that, when combined with the ideological, bureaucratic, political, and personal dispositions of the American leadership, helped foster an environment in which American-Soviet relations were considered in militaristic terms.

This is not to say that NSC-68 caused the arms build-up. It was merely one more factor fostering an environment in which an arms build-up could be contemplated, although the arms build-up did not result from its conclusions. Had it not been for the events in Korea, it is unlikely that serious increases in military budgets would have occurred. It seems doubtful that Truman would even have agreed to the mild $3 billion per year increase in appropriations that the estimates committee was considering before June 25,[199] and unthinkable that he would have implemented the more than $30 billion per year increase that took place during the Korean War.[200] It is also improbable that the United States would have supported a militarization of the North Atlantic Treaty. Johnson informed the Senate in the weeks before the Korean invasion that no integrated command or treaty organization was contemplated.[201] As Acheson would later write, "it is doubtful whether anything like what happened in the next few years [after the drafting of NSC-68] could have been done had not the Russians been stupid enough to have instigated the attack on South Korea."[202] The NSC "adopted the conclusions of NSC-68 as a statement of policy" in September 1950,[203] which makes it appear that they did not consider it to be a statement of policy before the Korean conflict.

NSC-68 was written without a single congressional representative or aide on the staff, and there seems to have been no concurrent activity in Congress that would have led to the same conclusions without the Korean War. Many in Congress shared Truman's background in state or local government, tended not to think in terms of tens of billions of dollars, and understood, perhaps more than those who wrote NSC-68, the potential reelection difficulties that accompanied tax increases. After he was allowed a peek at the finished document, Senator Walter George was unconvinced.[204] In the time immediately before the Korean War, Senator Millard Tydings, a Democrat from Maryland, was proposing a world disarmament conference, and Senator McMahon was advocating the abolition of nuclear weapons through a "moral crusade for peace" combined with a $50 billion "global Marshall Plan."[205] In the weeks after NSC-68's completion, the Senate watered down Truman's request to extend the expiring draft from a three-year extension to a two-year one.[206] Despite Acheson's tour of the nation, during which he made a case for the arms build-up by trying to shock his audience with evidence of Soviet military power, the truth, as Charles Bohlen later explained, was that without the Korean War

there was absolutely no chance that [NSC-68's] recommendations for huge increases in defense spending would [have been] adopted. It would have involved additional tens of billions in appropriations, increased taxes, and all the disadvantages which accompany a large increase in armaments. In a democracy such as ours, with diverse groups competing for government funds, it was hardly likely that in time of peace any Congress would seriously consider such an increase in the military budget.[207]

Was NSC-68 "one of the most important documents in the nation's history," as Dean Acheson termed it?[208] It depends on the extent that one feels NSC-68 was responsible for the arms build-up of 1950–51, which was indeed a critical event in the history of American foreign policy. The more inclined one is to believe this, the more inclined one might be to consider NSC-68 to have been the equivalent of the Monroe Doctrine, or of the Fourteen Points, and certainly the equivalent of the Truman Doctrine, or the New Look, which posited changes in basic strategic doctrine that were no more radical than the arms build-up envisaged by Nitze's team.

NSC-68's prescience is easier to judge. In light of subsequent events in Korea, and the evidence from Soviet archives of Moscow's efforts to help start that war, NSC-68 was fairly accurate in its portrayal of a totalitarian state willing to use military means for political ends. In light of the U.S. Army's difficulties in the early stages of the Korean War, it was very accurate in its estimation that the United States was not militarily prepared to achieve containment.

WORK ON THE FISCAL YEAR 1951 AND FISCAL YEAR 1952 DEFENSE BUDGETS BEFORE THE KOREAN WAR

Defense budgets are the result of many factors: political, economic, strategic, technological, intelligence-related, and others. They are the sum of these various factors made concrete, actual statements of a nation's beliefs on the importance and nature of its national security apparatus. As such, they demonstrate, perhaps better than policy memorandum do, the true beliefs of a nation. The work on the fiscal year 1951 and fiscal year 1952 defense budgets in the months before the Korean War demonstrate concretely that the creators of the American defense budgets were not yet committed to an arms build-up.

These budgets were similar to those immediately preceding them. Although there was considerable public debate over the status of American military power relative to the Soviet Union, there was no consensus by the majority in favor of a budgeting increase. The budget process operated in the usual manner, under Truman's designated ceilings, and without a visible impact by those, such as the working group that created NSC-68, who were working for a momentous change in military funding.

Following orders, General Eisenhower and the Joint Chiefs of Staff submitted details of a proposed fiscal year 1951 budget to the Department of Defense in August 1949.[209] On September 15, 1949, the Department of Defense announced its proposed budget, based substantially on the Eisenhower recommendations. The budget was for approximately $13.04 billion,[210] just above the $13 billion ceiling stipulated for fiscal year 1951 in NSC-52/1.[211] During the next few months, the department made adjustments that increased the proposed amount to $13.394 billion.[212] Following the usual procedure, Truman had the Bureau of the Budget investigate the proposal. The bureau trimmed the budget down to approximately $13.078 billion.[213] The actual amount to be requested from Congress would be $873 million less, with the money the president had refused to spend the previous year used to cut the budget.[214]

This proposed budget was to be divided as follows: $4.018 billion for the army, $3.881 billion for the navy, $4.433 for the air force, and $746 million for other purposes, such as the contingency fund, retirement pay, and the Office of the Secretary of Defense.[215] Under the budget, the plan was to have an army of 630,000 personnel with 10 understrength divisions, 12 separate regiments, and 48 antiaircraft battalions; a 239-warship navy; two Marine divisions at 36 percent strength; a combined navy-marine personnel of 461,000; and a 48-wing air force with 416,000 personnel.[216] All these personnel levels were well below the ceilings allowed under the Selective Service Act.[217] The 48-wing plan, which was for 20 strategic bomber groups, 16 tactical air support groups, and 12 air defense groups, was forced on the air force by Johnson, despite the opposition of both secretaries of the air force, W. Stuart Symington and Thomas Finletter (who took over in April 1950), each of whom supported the air force's contention that 70 wings was the minimum requirement.[218] As it was, many of the 48 groups operated below full strength.[219]

From January to March 1950, the House and Senate Appropriations Committees heard testimony on the budget and considered administration proposals.[220] Johnson continued to push for economy, claiming that by removing waste and duplication, his office was actually providing the combat force with greater funding. The House Appropriations Committee seems to have been reasonably satisfied with this line of argument, and they brushed aside Eisenhower's modest proposal, made before the Senate on March 29, to spend an additional $500 million for the defense of Alaskan air bases, some modernization of army equipment, reinforcement of antisubmarine warfare efforts, and improvements in mobilization programs.[221] The House Appropriations Committee chairman, Clarence Cannon, a Democrat from Missouri, believed that any further increase in the defense budget would undermine the nation's fiscal health and play into the hands of the Soviets, who wanted the United States to spend itself into bankruptcy.[222] He was confident that defense needs were being met by the Atomic Energy Commission, the Marshall Plan, military assistance, and other programs.[223] The only budget increase of significance that passed was Johnson's April 1950 request for an additional $300 million for air force and navy aircraft procurement and $50 million for destroyers and special antisubmarine warfare ships,[224] and even this constituted a proposed increase of less than three percent.

Only in the Senate did some cracks begin to appear in the economy program, as indicated by the Senate Appropriations Subcommittee's recommendation, on June 20, to raise the total of new obligational authority to nearly $15.6 billion.[225] The basic purpose of the increase, however, was for greater spending on strategic air capabilities, not on conventional forces, and the decision was not a great victory for the authors of NSC-68.

Work on the fiscal year 1952 budget followed similar patterns. In February 1950, Johnson laid down planning guidelines. Manpower, projected at 1,500,000, was to be the same as it was then thought it would be at the end of fiscal year 1951.[226] The funds would also be similar to what was then planned for fiscal year 1951: a May 10 estimate was for a $13.7 billion budget.[227]

The guidelines were obviously contrary to the massive increase proposed in NSC-68 the month before.[228] As we have seen, Johnson signed that document reluctantly and seems never to have agreed with its conclusions. He specifically informed his staff on May 25 that they could proceed without letting NSC-68 interfere.[229]

OPPOSITION FROM THE RIGHT: THE RETURN OF THE OLD GUARD

In 1950, the bipartisan agreement on foreign policy collapsed. Republican congressional leaders who had pursued a cooperative bipartisan foreign policy since 1942, adhering to the expression that "politics stops at the water's edge" to explain the preference to minimize public debate on international affairs to avoid casting doubt on U.S. policy abroad,[230] were replaced. An older faction of Republicans, which had been relatively dormant for almost a decade, returned to positions of influence. They were known as the Old Guard.

Senator Arthur Vandenberg of Michigan, who had been the most prominent of the bipartisan Republicans, became ill in late 1949, and his influence declined as a result. Another bipartisan Republican, Senator John Foster Dulles of New York, lost his seat in a special election held in the fall of 1949.[231] Old Guard members sensed an opportunity for power. In late December 1949, Senator Kenneth Wherry, a Republican from Nebraska, proclaimed that he wanted no more commitments "made by bipartisan bigwigs."[232] Senator Robert Taft of Ohio, generally acknowledged as the leader of the Old Guard, chimed in on January 8, 1950, saying that "There isn't any bipartisan foreign policy and there has not been any for the past year."[233]

The Old Guard believed in limited federal spending and limited foreign intervention. They did so for both ideological motives, in that they remained faithful to a traditional view of America's political economy and international position in the post-New Deal and post-atomic bomb world, and for political motives, in that they had a domestic constituency who would pay for a large share of Truman's social and foreign programs in taxes. They opposed the new breed of foreign policy activists and relatively liberal-spending Republicans typified by Thomas Dewey. Old Guard members had been a potent force in the era before Pearl Harbor, helping to pass neutrality legislation. Many of them were bitter about the way, as they saw it, that Roosevelt had maneuvered the nation into war in 1941, and many members had spent the period immediately before the war fighting Roosevelt's efforts to aid Britain and actively contain Japan (several books published after the war claimed that the Roosevelt administration had received intelligence on a coming Japanese attack and did little to stop it). Old Guard members also disagreed with Roosevelt's decision to focus on Europe once the war began instead of Asia, which some felt involved the nation in an unnecessary dispute in order to save Britain, of which Roosevelt was considered overly fond. The unique American version of democracy, Old Guard members felt, could best be defended by maintaining the economic and political health of the United States. Efforts to export this ideology might ruin the democratic concept of limited government at home, and might be counterproductive to the cause of democracy in general. The Old Guard was particularly opposed to the European multilateralism that Acheson favored, since they felt that it put Europeans in a position to order or restrict American actions while the United States paid the large share. Enemies of the Old Guard, and even some friends, referred to them as nationalists. Certainly they interpreted national security in a more literal sense than the Truman administration, which saw maintaining a certain type of international order, in terms of trade, structure of government, international institutions, and much else, as part of the purview of such policy. Taft had voted against the ratification of the North Atlantic Treaty, believing that it was "more likely to lead to war than to peace," and was convinced that "there is no threat" to Western Europe "at this time."[234] The most virulent of the Old Guard made little distinction between Western European social democracies and Eastern European totalitarian states. The Old Guard's views on foreign aid might have best been summed up by Senator William Jenner, a Republican from Indiana, who felt that aid represented "the squandering of American resources and manpower down the ratholes of Europe and Asia."[235]

Not only were the Old Guard senators convinced that an alliance and aid relationship with Europe was bad foreign policy, but they also feared that any alliance or military commitment would necessarily lead to a defeat of their domestic economic policies of free markets unfettered by excessive regulation, taxation, or debt. As evidence, they cited World War II, which had increased the federal government's portion of the gross national product, created vast debt, and led to the regulation of all major industries and the introduction of wage and price controls. Senator Taft declared that unless cuts were made in the budget, the nation would be "driven down the road, by taxes and constantly increasing debt, to bankruptcy and dictatorial government."[236]

The Old Guard members were not opposed to a powerful non-Communist Western Europe, nor to bringing Western Europe into closer trade ties with the United States and Britain, nor to European economic recovery, as their opponents sometimes claimed. However, they saw American attempts to buy the type of Western Europe that all agreed would be in America's best interest as overly damaging to the U.S. economy, and prone to tie the United States to positions beyond its control. They agreed with Truman's premise that the nation's economic vitality demanded limits on defense spending, but they did not necessarily share Truman's confidence that the United States could commit itself to European security within those limits. The Old Guard thought it better to encourage the Europeans to defend themselves.

The Old Guard's senior members tried to fashion a broad anti-Truman coalition on foreign policy. They found a good deal of support in the

"China Lobby," an informal network of activists, business leaders, and politicians, mostly affiliated with the Republican party, who wished to see a more anti-Communist stance in America's China policy, for reasons political, commercial, and ideological.[237] The evacuation of the Guomindang forces to Taiwan in 1949, the signing of the Sino-Soviet Treaty of Friendship of February 14, 1950, and the Communists' successful invasion of Hainan in April 1950 did little to lessen the support for the nationalist regime, and may have increased the vocality of its proponents.

Differences between China Lobby members, genuine isolationists, and those Old Guard members who were simply antimilitarist or skeptical toward Europe were smoothed over. Even old progressives, liberal pacifists from the early years of the century, were active in working against Truman.[238]

This coalition at times sought to profit from the political damage done to Truman by the concurrent hearings on Communist activity in the United States. The hearings began following the unmasking of several atomic scientists and federal government officials who had worked for the Soviet Union for ideological motives. Alger Hiss, a State Department official who had been a friend of Acheson and of the Roosevelt family, was convicted on January 20, 1950, for perjuring himself regarding his activities with the Communist Party of the United States. Dr. Klaus Fuchs, a German atomic scientist who held British citizenship, was arrested on February 3, 1950, in England for giving atomic secrets to the Soviets. Soon afterward, Fuchs admitted his guilt.[239] Further investigations that spring would reveal a number of American accomplices to Fuchs, including Harry Gold and Alfred Slack, who had also worked on the Manhattan Project to develop the atomic bomb during World War II.[240] In the minds of much of the public, the Soviet development of a weapon of mass destruction became increasingly linked with the revelation of the atomic spies.

Seeing a political advantage to be gained, Senator Joseph McCarthy, a Republican from Wisconsin, began accusing the State Department of harboring Communists on February 9. His charges helped lead to the creation of a Senate investigatory committee, chaired by Senator Tydings .[241] McCarthy used the Tydings Committee forum to attack government personnel, especially those involved with the formulation of foreign policy, who, he hoped, could be linked to Communism. He forced the State Department leadership to defend itself at the time the anti-Truman coalition was trying to block the aid funds for Western Europe that were necessary to persuade European governments to organize their defenses in accordance with American war plans.

Truman took the challenges of the Old Guard and the McCarthy charges seriously. In a March 1950 letter to a cousin he claimed, "I am in the midst of the most terrible struggle any President ever had. A pathological liar from Wisconsin [McCarthy] and a blockheaded undertaker from Nebraska [Wherry] are trying to ruin the bipartisan foreign policy. Stalin never had two better allies in this country."[242]

Truman attempted to counter the Old Guard's influence by hiring Dulles as a State Department consultant in April.[243] He dispatched the former senator to Japan to help negotiate a peace treaty, hoping that his participation would lead to future Senate ratification.[244] The president also lent his efforts to support a plan by Senator Thomas Connally to create eight foreign affairs subcommittees, one for each section of the State Department, so as to allow greater liaison between Congress and State.[245] In a move evocative of his famous whistle stop reelection campaign of 1948, Truman traveled by rail across the nation for 10 days, delivering 57 speeches, mostly on foreign policy, in 12 states. He publicly defended his record on the Greek-Turkish aid program, the Marshall Plan, and the North Atlantic Treaty, and warned against isolationism.[246]

The Old Guard responded vigorously. They renewed their efforts to grant aid to Taiwan by blocking, as a protest measure, the passage of an aid bill for Korea. Former President Herbert Hoover, an icon for Old Guard supporters, even recommended that the United Nations be reorganized to exclude Communist states.[247]

This renewal of the Old Guard's strength posed a challenge to the authors of NSC-68 and their plans to increase defense spending. However, there was one place outside the Western Hemisphere that the many members of the coalition led by the Old Guard felt strongly enough about to reverse their general antipathy towards foreign intervention: East Asia. A war there could gain across-the-board support for an arms build-up.

CHAPTER 4

Transformation

THE TRUMAN ADMINISTRATION'S DECISION TO ENTER THE KOREAN WAR

On June 25, 1950, the North Korean (DPRK) Peoples' Army launched a surprise invasion of South Korea. Using armored penetrations and amphibious landings[1] and supported by air strikes, the Soviet-equipped North Korean forces rapidly pushed deep into South Korea (ROK).

Without antiaircraft guns or long-range artillery, and suffering from a tank shortage (all equipment the United States had denied the ROK to prevent it from attacking the North), the South Koreans were driven back during harsh fighting.[2] Although some American officials had warned of a North Korean strike, and although there had been ominous cross-border raids and skirmishes for more than a year, the invasion caught the Truman administration by surprise, as did the ability of the North Korean forces to dominate the field of battle.

The Soviet press hailed the North Koreans as liberators and joyously claimed that the advancing DPRK forces were greeted by the local populace with "shouts of welcome, bouquets of flowers, and flags of the Korean People's Democratic Republic."[3] However, Moscow's joy was soon to be qualified as the Soviets discovered something they quite likely had not expected: the United States was about to intervene in the war, and initiate a worldwide arms build-up.

There were few reasons for the Soviets to expect the Americans to intervene in Korea. In February 1948, the National Security Council had stated that "Korea is of minor strategic importance," and that the maintenance of U.S. forces in Korea would "require a military and financial long-term cost and risk far out of keeping with the strategic benefit."[4] After the withdrawal of the U.S. Seventh Infantry Division in 1949, the only American military presence in Korea was an advisory group, which, according to Pentagon contingency plans, was to be withdrawn in the event of war.[5] During the debate on policy regarding the Chinese Civil War, the administration had decided that mainland Asia was not the place to fight. The United States had neither the political will to become militarily involved in the turmoil of postwar mainland Asian politics, nor the forces to carry out such a policy.

But, within days of the North Korean invasion, Harry Truman impulsively decided to send American forces to repulse the onslaught. This American intervention was not only made with little regard for existing policies, but also contradicted those policies. As General Vernon Walters would later claim, "If a Soviet KGB spy had broken into the Pentagon or the State Department on June 25, 1950, and gained access to our most secret files, he would have found the U.S. had no interest in Korea. But the one place he couldn't break into was the mind of Harry Truman."[6]

Truman, worn down by foreign policy setbacks, such as the Soviet development of atomic weapons, the Communist victory in China, and the signing of the Sino-Soviet Friendship Treaty, and annoyed and harassed by his political opponents on the issue of internal spying, was tired of events pushing him around. Truman was concerned about the United States's reputation among its allies,[7] and seems to have seized on the Korean War as a means to wrest control of affairs and end the contradiction in policy indicated by his signing of NSC-68 but neglect of its goals. Truman was not in the mood to allow the Korean campaign to develop on its own, even if that was the planned course of events. Hearing of the invasion while taking care of family business at his home in Independence, Missouri, Truman, in the decisive and energetic fashion for which he was famous, set in motion a policy of action. He told Acheson by telephone the morning after the North Korean attack that he wanted to "stop the sons of bitches no matter what." He flew back to Washington promptly, spending his time on board thinking about the failure to stop aggressions in the 1930s in Manchuria, Ethiopia, and Austria, according to his later recollection.[8] During the limousine ride from Andrews Air Force Base to the White House, he told Acheson and Under Secretary of State James Webb, "By God, I'm going to let them have it."[9] Over the next few days, in a series of meetings with his military and political subordinates, he committed America to war.[10] First he ordered the shipment of aid to the ROK government. Second, he commanded U.S. air and naval units to intervene in South Korean airspace and territorial waters. Third, he approved the use of warplanes on missions north of the 38th Parallel. Fourth, he agreed to send U.S. troops to hold vital ROK airfields and port facilities. Fifth, and most dramatically, he issued the order, on June 30, for American troops to fight the North Koreans. Truman also strengthened American forces in the Philippines, sped up delivery of material to the French in Indochina, and sent the Seventh Fleet to patrol the Straits of Taiwan, in a bid to prevent the Beijing regime from carrying out its planned invasion of Taiwan.[11] A motion to build an international fighting force was introduced in the UN General Assembly by the United States. It passed.

Truman was not restrained by his advisers. With the partial exceptions of Johnson, Nitze, Bradley, and Secretary of the Army Frank Pace,[12] most administration personnel made little effort to challenge the president's view. It is interesting but not fulfilling to speculate on what their attitudes would have been had Truman not come back from Missouri proclaiming his desire to punish the North Koreans for their invasion. As it was, they might have been overwhelmed by the wave of public desire for action in light of the bold gambit by a Soviet-backed power. Or their desire to escape Truman's legendary temper might have led them to hide any misgivings they might have had about the intervention. With advance warning of how the president had reacted to the invasion, his staff backed him on his rigorous stance.[13] Pentagon generals, realizing how weak the U.S. military was, were reluctant to be drawn into the war,[14] but dutifully obeyed the orders of the commander in chief.

It is by no means clear that Truman's decision was predictable, seeing how some of his choices were at odds with what other leading figures seem to have either expected or desired, and it was only through rapidity of action that he accomplished the desired result. Truman only cursorily consulted congressional leaders about his decisions. He acted so fast that Senator Taft complained that Congress was presented with the use of American ground forces as an accomplished fact.[15] In the two days after the North Korean invasion, most members of Congress were unsure about future action, and many hoped that the United Nations could resolve the crisis. Few had any firm plans, and many made general statements of support for South Korea.[16] The Senate Republican Policy Committee was divided in its recommendations, with Eugene Millikin, a Republican from Colorado, claiming that "the incident should not be used as a provocation for war," while other senators, such as Margaret Chase Smith, a Republican from Maine, supported American action in Korea.[17] Newspaper editorials were similarly divided, with some newspapers, including the *Denver Post* and *Cleveland Plain Dealer*, advocating American military participation as part of a UN force. Others, such as the isolationist *Chicago Tribune*, warned that the United States should not participate in the war; however, most newspapers generally advised that the United States somehow try to contain the new North Korean plunge.[18] One newspaper article, produced by the *United Press*, a national press organization with extensive

Washington connections, inaccurately but confidently predicted on the first day of the war that "the United States will not put its armed forces into any direct action in the Korean conflict."[19] The Joint Chiefs were startled by the president's tough talk the day after the invasion,[20] and even the first American soldiers sent into Korea were surprised by Truman's decision.[21] But Truman's decisiveness helped consolidate a sense of purpose in the public, which, with the exception of some of the most bitter Truman haters, seized on Truman's moves with ardent fervor. As the *New Republic* explained, "when Truman's executive order [to intervene in Korea] hit the wires, Washington took a new look at the President. It found that he had fooled them even more than he did on Election Day 1948."[22] Polls taken by the State Department indicated that in the wake of the North Korean attack, 75 percent of the American public approved sending troops to Korea.[23] Faced with a president elevated to new heights of popularity, and perhaps seduced by the mood of assertiveness themselves, congressional leaders, including even the Old Guard, decided not to oppose U.S. involvement. Had a debate on a declaration of war taken place, it is possible that the Old Guard would have tried to embarrass the administration, but unlikely that they would have contested Truman's key decisions.

THE TRUMAN ADMINISTRATION'S DECISION TO BEGIN AN ARMS BUILD-UP

The Korean War was viewed by almost all American political leaders in a Cold War context. It was thought that the Soviet Union bore responsibility for initiating the conflict, and that in doing so the Kremlin was raising the stakes in the poker game of world politics, replacing a cautious policy of fifth-column activities and coups with one of piecemeal warfare. The Soviets had acted in a less restrained manner than many American analysts had considered likely. There was no guarantee that they would abstain from making moves elsewhere.

The day after the North Korean attack, the president told senior political advisor George Elsey that he was "more worried about other parts of the world" than Korea, especially the Middle East.[24] He asked Pace on June 28 to pay special attention to Soviet activities in the vicinity of Yugoslavia and in northern Europe.[25] The same day, he directed the National Security Council to reexamine "all policies affecting the entire perimeter of the USSR."[26]

A cause of concern for all administration officials was the perceived parallel between the North Korean armed forces, prepared and equipped by the Soviets to attempt national unification, and the East German armed forces, which seemed similarly trained.[27] The NSC felt that a renewed blockade of Berlin, or a blockade of Vienna, could not be ruled out,[28] and they were told by the National Security Resources Board that the demands of the Korean campaign would make another airlift impossible.[29] Several Eastern European nations were enlarging their military forces under the auspices of former Soviet military personnel who served as defense ministers,[30] and the possibility of the Soviets using these satellite armies to restore Soviet dominance over breakaway Yugoslavia had to be considered. Rear Admiral Roscoe Hillenkoetter, the director of the CIA, told the National Security Council Consultants' Meeting on June 29 that he considered a Bulgarian attack on Yugoslavia to be the most likely contingency.[31] Kennan added that Soviet forces might join in.[32] Bulgarian troop movements near the border had already become public knowledge,[33] and the Soviet press had begun comparing Josip Tito to Hermann Goering.[34]

General MacArthur informed Johnson that he thought a move on Iran would be next.[35] In a July 1 meeting, the NSC also fretted over the possible seizure of power by the Tudeh Party of Iran, which was sympathetic to the USSR, and the possibilities of Chinese Communist actions in Korea, the straits of Taiwan, Hong Kong, Macao, Tibet, Indochina, or Burma.[36] Since the Chinese regime was considered strongly influenced by the Kremlin, it was assumed that the Soviets might persuade the Chinese to probe the anti-Communist world anywhere along the vast Chinese borders.

There were large differences of opinion among U.S. analysts over the likelihood of direct Soviet involvement in any of these possible military actions, but virtually no one ruled Soviet participation out entirely. To quote the NSC: "[Our] analysis has been predicated on the assumption that the Kremlin does not intend to engage in a general war in the near future for the reasons stated in NSC-68. That assumption may be wrong."[37]

In the event that it was to be shown wrong, the lack of American forces would be glaring. On July 14, Acheson told the Cabinet that the United States lacked the means to meet the Soviet threat. The initial setbacks in the Korean War showed this.

It is becoming apparent to the world that we do not have the capabilities to face the threat, and the feeling in Europe is changing from one of elation that the United States has come into the Korean crisis to petrified fright. People are questioning whether NAT really means anything, since it means only what we are able to do. Our intentions are not doubted, but our capabilities are doubted.[38]

Acheson continued:

In this situation the question is what the United States can do to affect these trends. Obviously it must do all possible to deal with the Korean situation and other present dangers, but it must do more now. Prompt action is worth more than perfect action. In the very early days of next week some action must be announced.[39]

The actions that Acheson wanted the president to announce consisted of asking for more money for the armed forces, and "if it is a question of asking for too little or too much, he should ask for too much."[40] Acheson had stated these pleas in a very dramatic fashion because of his concern that other parts of the executive branch did not seem to realize the scale of the radical changes in policy that would be necessary to reorient the American economy towards military production. The mid-year report by the Council of Economic Advisors, which was predicated on the assumption that the fighting in Korea would remain localized, and that the president need not be granted any emergency powers, particularly incensed Acheson.[41] He wanted the fighting in Korea to remain localized, but was not content with any assumption that it would do so. Nothing less than the deployment of a large conventional force to central Europe, for an indefinite duration, would satisfy Acheson.

The Joint Chiefs of Staff, seriously considering the possibility that an all-out war would shortly arise,[42] were similarly inclined. Although they still felt that American atomic superiority and manufacturing capacities would enable the United States to achieve victory in such a war, they feared that the Soviets were rapidly increasing both the production of nuclear weapons and the means to deliver them on American forward bases and U.S. industrial centers, in an effort to nullify the U.S. atomic deterrent or bomb out of existence the American economic advantage.[43] If the Soviets could negate the American atomic advantage and seize Western Europe, they would attempt to assimilate the trained workforce and industrial infrastructure into a Moscow-centered sphere of influence. "If Soviet Russia ever controls the Eurasian land mass," Bradley warned, "then the Soviet-satellite imperialism may have the broad base upon which to build the military power to rule the world."[44] The need for an arms build-up seemed obvious.

Apparently shaken by the North Korean attack, Truman became more involved in foreign and military policy formulation. He attended more NSC meetings and scheduled regular meetings with Bradley.[45] His views grew increasingly hawkish because of the events in Korea, perhaps combined with months of steady efforts by Acheson and his allies to wear him down on the issue of defense spending. His conversion became evident in his personnel decisions. He chose Gordon Dean, known for his aggressive attitudes about the use of atomic weapons, to fill the vacancy as director of the AEC; named Lieutenant General Walter Bedell Smith, known for his toughness, to replace Hillenkoetter, who had gained a reputation for unassertiveness, as director of the CIA; and began using Stuart Symington, long an advocate of military spending, to coordinate the movement of the supplemental defense budgets (see section 4.5) through Congress.[46] Foreign policy meetings took on more of a military character.

Most executive branch leaders who had opposed increasing arms budgets before the war either lost power or shifted their opinions in the summer of 1950. Louis Johnson, despite initially opposing the use of American troops in Korea, grudgingly accepted the need for an arms build-up after Truman ordered it. As we will see, even this would not be enough to save his job. James Webb, who had been a proponent of limited military spending when he was director of the Bureau of the Budget, had, after becoming under secretary of state and working in the heart of the pro-armament camp, become a crusader for the ideas of NSC-68.[47] Bohlen, who had been relatively dovish on the subject of an arms build-up when discussing NSC-68 a few months before was, by July, recommending the mobilization of the National Guard under federal control, a program of controls to allocate raw materials to war industries, new weapons development programs, increases in military aid to Europe, and the creation of new production capacity for military equipment.[48] On July 13, Bohlen summarized the new administration thinking:

The character of the new Soviet inspired aggression has revealed various interpretations as to Soviet intentions. However, despite these differences in estimate, *all* studies on this subject which have been conducted in State and Defense agree on the following conclusions:

1. The Soviet Union has the military capacity at the present time of taking, or inspiring through satellites, military action ranging from local aggression on one or more points along the periphery of the Soviet world to all-out general war.

2. While estimates of probabilities of Soviet action vary it is completely agreed that there is not sufficient evidence to justify a firm opinion that the Soviet Union will *not* take any one or all of the actions which lie within its military capabilities . . . It is therefore obvious that it is urgently necessary for the U.S. to initiate measures necessary to bring about a rapid build-up of the United States military position both in manpower and in production.[49]

Incoming reports from the Korean battlefields were a factor that led Truman to radically increase military spending. Fewer than 24 hours after the North Korean attack, he asked Bradley about the availability of extra recoilless rifles to send to the Far East and was informed that there was a shortage of both the rifles and the ammunition.[50] The lack of rifles would be just one of the problems facing the U.S. Army. Despite the administration's public pronouncements to the contrary,[51] the condition of the first

American ground units to arrive in Korea indicated the woeful state of American conventional forces. They were occupation troops from Japan, used to a relatively soft life of mild duties (as cheap civilian labor was used to perform base functions), and a generally pleasurable lifestyle more akin to that of a colonial occupation army than a modern combat force. For their basic weapons, the troops had to use such pre-1945 equipment as the M-1 rifle, the Browning Automatic Rifle, .30 and .50 caliber machine guns, 75mm recoilless rifles, 2.36 inch bazookas, 105mm howitzers, and Pershing and, more often, Sherman tanks.[52]

The North Koreans attacked with Soviet T-34 tanks, off the sides of which American 75mm shells exploded harmlessly. Given their age, the shells sometimes did not explode at all. There was insufficient ammunition for the 105mm guns to destroy the tanks that the 75mm guns could not destroy. Antitank mines were unavailable. Communications broke down as scarce telephone wire was lost during successive retreats, and World War II-era radios kept going dead because they were too dilapidated for the task.[53] When the Americans committed light tanks to battle, they lost 10 almost immediately.[54]

There were so few American troops available that General MacArthur, commander of the UN forces, ordered the integration of Koreans directly into the ranks of the U.S. Army.[55] The military, lacking sufficient aircraft to transport the troops it did have to Korea, had to sign contracts with commercial airliners.[56] Tactical bombing was poor, aerial reconnaissance abilities were far below World War II standards, and maps were difficult to find.[57] According to General Matthew Ridgway, "Every division was short 1500 rifles and all its 90mm. tank guns, missing three infantry battalions out of nine, lacking one firing battalion out of three in the divisional artillery, and all regimental tank companies."[58]

The mountainous terrain, poor roads, and a swift-moving enemy who often maneuvered at night and hid during the day forced the Americans into a fluid infantry-based type of warfare utterly different from what American defense planners had envisioned. Before the war, the Pentagon had decided not to plan for the possibility of a localized conventional war, deciding that budgetary limitations dictated a focus on a possible total conflict in which nuclear weapons would be used early and often[59] and large motorized forces would be assembled over time in America and then shipped abroad. But it would take months to build new armored divisions, and there were few roads in Korea to support them anyway. Truman, who was resolute on the issue of presidential approval for any atomic action, never approved the use of atomic weapons in the Korean War, and would not allow bombing of the Communists' bases of manufacture and supply in the USSR and China. The bombing of North Korean cities that did occur, on a vast scale,[60] was of little immediate aid to the

American ground troops first arriving in Korea. The UN forces, composed primarily of Koreans and Americans (soon to be joined by ground forces from 13 other nations and assorted naval and medical support from several others), were hurled backward by the oncoming North Korean forces.[61] The U.S. Army's Twenty-fourth Infantry Division, which entered Korea with 16,000 soldiers on July 1, had only 8,660 troops left by July 22.[62] In one 17-day period of almost constant fighting, the division was forced to retreat 70 miles.[63] Major General William Dean, its commander, became detached from his forces during the July 20 battle for Taejon, and, in an embarrassment to the army, became the highest-ranking American officer ever captured by a foreign army.[64]

The decision to engage in a large arms build-up was made during this crucial period between the North Korean invasion and Operation CHROMITE, the UN's amphibious landing at Inchon on September 15. The North Korean attack weakened the Truman administration's faith that the Soviets would not initiate war. Just as importantly, the U.S. losses at this stage of the war, to an army of a relatively small and poor nation, made clear just how unprepared the American military would have been in the event of a war with the Soviets, and helped convince Washington of the necessity of an arms build-up on a vast scale.

The timing of the attack, coming less than a year after the discovery of the Soviet atomic bomb, seemed to suggest a link between Soviet military capabilities and a willingness of Communist nations to engage in hostilities. Although in retrospect reports of a possible general war seem unduly alarmist, it is easy to see how key officials, anxious over exaggerated criticisms of subversion at home and genuine reports from a war abroad, and haunted by inadequate military power, could be convinced of the need for an arms build-up.

In the first few days of July, Truman cancelled the $13 billion ceiling on the defense budget and ordered the Pentagon to draft a new appropriations bill.[65] On July 11, Johnson told the JCS to defer work on fiscal year 1952 in order to handle the reassessment of fiscal year 1951 needs.[66] The army wanted three new divisions to replace forces assigned to the Korean operation, the navy wanted to take four aircraft carriers out of mothballs, and the air force wanted to have funds to make use of the combat planes it had in storage.[67] The requests were accommodated, and Truman turned to Congress to gain support for an even larger build-up. On July 19, 1950, he asked the legislatures for a $10 billion supplemental military budget, almost as much as that year's entire planned fiscal defense budget. As we will see in the section on fiscal year 1951, the request passed easily. The same day, Truman also ordered a strengthening of the NSC to better coordinate policy, and suggested Congress consider a program to allocate materials and restrict consumer credit.[68]

To flesh out these forces, manpower was increased dramatically. Truman ordered a new draft, and by July 17, 20,000 men had been called on to serve.[69] On July 6, the Joint Chiefs of Staff and Johnson recommended, and Truman approved, the raising of authorized army strength from 630,000 to 680,000.[70] On July 14, he approved another recommendation to increase authorized strength to 740,500, and on July 19 he approved an increase to 834,000.[71] This new army was to have 11 divisions, 12 separate regiments, and 72 antiaircraft battalions.[72] Truman also approved a proposal to call four National Guard divisions into active federal service on July 31.[73] In the second half of 1950, the size of the American armed forces swelled from 1,460,000 personnel to 2,360,000.[74]

On September 9, Truman announced that a combat-ready American army would be deployed to Europe.[75] This was only the third time the United States had sent such an army to Europe, and this was the first time that it was done while Europe was at peace.

On August 1, 1950, little more than a month after the start of the Korean War, and during the period of tremendous effort by the administration to augment military capabilities, the Joint Chiefs of Staff advised Johnson that goals for the manufacture of atomic weapons should be sharply increased.[76] Johnson forwarded this request to the president. His proposal was seconded by Senator McMahon of the Atomic Energy Committee on August 3.[77]

Truman agreed to look into the recommendations, and assigned a joint Department of Defense-Atomic Energy Commission team to investigate.[78] The team used JCS suggestions on military needs and AEC recommendations on feasible costs and availability of fissionable materials. The final report, finished in September, concluded that the nation should expand nuclear production to meet higher targets by 1956.[79] The report was given to Truman and the rest of the NSC, and on October 9 Truman approved the recommended expansion, for $2.5 billion over six years.[80] He would later approve further increases: $1.06 billion in the second supplemental bill for fiscal year 1951 defense, and $59 million in the fourth supplemental bill for fiscal year 1951 defense.[81] The AEC surpassed the World War II Manhattan Project in size and scope.[82]

U.S. national security expenditures jumped from 4.6 percent of gross national product in fiscal year 1950 to 6.9 percent in fiscal year 1951 to 12.7 percent in fiscal year 1952. The majority of this build-up would not end when the Korean War did. Military expenditure remained at least 9 percent of the gross national product per year (nearly double the fiscal year 1950 total) through 1962,[83] and at least 5 percent of the gross national product per year until the mid-1990s. Over the first two decades of the Cold War, the U.S. defense budget was, on average, approximately half the size of the entire British economy.[84] After armistice negotiations had begun in Korea, and the level of world tension had eased slightly, Truman would claim that in planning defense spending, his administration had not caved in to extremists who, in the initial stages of the Korean War, had advocated an even larger build-up.[85] However, as officials of his own administration would later point out, the most important reasons that the arms build-up in fiscal year 1951 had not been even greater were fears of bottlenecks in production, the need to lay a firm base of capital expenditure before production could rise, and a general desire to make the build-up as efficient as possible. Truman himself admitted that, when inflation was discounted, the increase in military spending in the first year of the arms build-up (fiscal year 1951) was almost half of the increase in the first year of World War II, an outstanding testimony to just how huge the later arms build-up was.[86]

By 1952, according to Secretary of the Air Force Thomas Finletter, the value of American plant facilities and equipment used for military production was greater than "the 1950 total combined assets of General Motors, Standard Oil of New Jersey, United States Steel, and American Telephone and Telegraph combined."[87] That same year, *US News & World Report* magazine described the military's economic holdings as a $200 billion investment, "more than four times the present book value of all the plants and equipment of all U.S. manufacturing corporations."[88] In the days before the Korean War, General Marshall had warned Congress that if it failed to pass a $1.2225 billion assistance program, Western Europe might be overrun, forcing the United States to become an armed camp, spending as much as $30 billion per year on the military.[89] Within months, the administration was requesting more than $40 billion for an annual defense budget.

The situations of strength group had won the debate on armaments policy. The perception that the start of the Korean War indicated a new aggressiveness by the Soviets, and the difficulties encountered by the American troops sent to Korea, were the levers that enabled the necessary legislation. It would be difficult to imagine a more perfect conflict for their purposes. The North Korean invasion was perceived as an act of naked aggression by an ally of Moscow, which served to provoke both public and presidential opinion. Even more, it was on mainland Asia, which was perhaps the only region outside the Western Hemisphere where some of the congressional Republicans would consent to the use of American force. It would have been difficult for any Congress to turn down military appropriations proposals at the start of a war of unknown duration and at a time when quite a few believed that Korea would be a mere precursor to a larger conflict. General Bradley must have understood this mood when he testified in the House of Representatives on July 25, 1950, pressuring Congress for funds by claiming that "the cost [of the arms build-up] will be heavy, but not as heavy as the war which, we are now convinced, would follow our failure to rearm."[90]

It is difficult to overestimate the impact of this arms build-up. It was a new phase of containment. Without the Korean War, or an incident similar to it, it is doubtful that America would have adopted such a militarized stance on worldwide security issues. Bohlen's comment, quoted in the first sentence of this book, is on target. Although Truman would later claim, in an official address to Congress asking for military funds, that the decision to ask for an increased military budget "should have—and, though no doubt in smaller measure, would have—been taken" even in the absence of the Korean War, the evidence suggests otherwise.[91] It is worth repeating Truman's claims, mentioned in the introduction and made during a January 1953 discussion with a journalist, in which he talked about Stalin's decision to allow North Korea to invade South Korea: "It's the greatest error he made in his whole career. If he hadn't made that mistake, we'd have done what we did after World War I: completely disarmed. And it would have been a cinch for him to take over the European nations, one by one." Instead of this, Truman said the beginning of the Korean War had these far reaching results: "It caused the rearmament of ourselves and our Allies. It brought about the North Atlantic Treaty [sic]. It brought about the various Pacific alliances. It hurried up the signing of the Japanese Peace Treaty. It caused Greece and Turkey to be brought quickly into the North Atlantic Alliance."[92]

Truman specifically stated, when sending wartime requests for armaments to Congress, that the funds would be used for a general build-up and overseas deployments to Europe, and not just war costs. Even in the days immediately preceding the Inchon landing, in a time when American forces were backed into a corner of South Korea and seemingly almost driven into the sea, Truman felt he had to balance General MacArthur's requests for troops in Korea with the needs of Europe. The overriding basis on which to judge policy was the strategic comparison with the Soviets worldwide, not the situation in Korea. NSC-68/1 stated that "the programs which have been initiated pursuant to the President's message to the Congress of 19 July 1950, constitute an initial implementation of the long term United States build up as well as of specific measures to meet the situation in Korea. The invasion of Korea imparts a new urgency to the appraisal of the nature, timing, and scope of programs designed to attain the objectives outlined in NSC-68. The ending of the Korean operation, however, will not appreciably affect these [budget] estimates."[93]

In particular, the balance of power in Europe disturbed the Truman administration. In August 1950, American civilian and military officials in Germany informed Washington that in the event of conflict in Germany, "forces in order of 3 Allied divisions with necessary support troops would be required to defeat the 55,000 present DDR [East Germany] paramilitary troops; and in the event the latter increase to a maximum strength of 150,000, forces in order of 5 Allied divisions with necessary support troops would be required,"[94] all of this not including the possibility of fighting Soviet forces. The primary goal of the arms build-up was to create a conventional defensive force capable of fighting the Communists at the border between the two German states. While it would be an overstatement to claim that Truman followed a Europe-first policy as Roosevelt did in World War II, it is true that certain new items, such as the B-50 medium bomber and the C-124 transport, were deployed against the potential Soviet menace in Europe, rather than sent to Korea.[95] As early as July 7, 1950, a request by MacArthur for additional forces was rejected, in part because of the need to build up the armies in Europe.[96] The rejection of this request prompted MacArthur to later complain that "the Far East was again at the bottom of the list . . . I could obtain only a trickle of soldiers from Washington, under the plea that they were needed in Germany."[97] Germany was given greatest priority, mostly because of its critical economic importance, but also perhaps because of perceptions of Soviet intentions. It was believed that the Soviet army was positioned with its strongest force in East Germany, with little or no Soviet troop strength in Bulgaria and Hungary. A successful tap on the communications line from the Soviet embassy in Vienna, created by the British in 1949 and made more effective by the CIA's success at building an electronic deciphering machine in 1951, confirmed this information.[98]

During fiscal years 1951–53 (a period from July 1, 1950, to June 30, 1953), the United States spent $116.9 billion on national security expenditures. The Korean War, almost all of which was fought during this period, is estimated to have directly absorbed only about $40 to 50 billion.[99]

THE PRIMACY OF THE ARMS BUILD-UP IN AMERICAN STRATEGY, 1950–51

The Korean War was a seesaw affair, with each side taking turns in winning. There were five phases. The first phase, one of almost total victory for the North Koreans, lasted from June 25 to September 15, 1950, during which time the North Koreans pursued the South Koreans and UN forces into a small beachhead at the southern tip of the Korean peninsula. The second phase, which began with the UN landing at Inchon, a port near Seoul, was a period of success for MacArthur's forces, with the UN forces driving north of the 38th Parallel. The third phase began with the massive Chinese attack of late November 1950, which pushed the UN forces below the 38th Parallel. The fourth phase of the war saw this Chinese attack blunted, and somewhat reversed, by a series of UN victories in the spring of 1951 that stabilized the front near the original line. The fifth phase, lasting more than two years, was a time of protracted but discontinuous trench warfare with little movement in what the UN termed the Main Line of Resistance, fought during the armistice negotiations. While American war aims regarding Korea were subject to change as the front lines shifted and as concerns about a possible general war with China grew, American aims globally changed little during the war.

The primary American foreign policy aim during the Korean War was to reverse the perceived disadvantage in the conventional balance of power among, on the one hand, the USSR and its allies and, on the other, those states willing to join the growing anti-Stalinist crusade known as containment. The Soviet Union was considered the main basis of comparison, and central Europe was considered the most important area.

While the decisions in the theater of operations were based on concern about China, it is worth repeating that the American military build-up had much more to do with the perception of Soviet power. The Chinese intervention increased American losses in the war and terminated American hopes to unify the Korean peninsula under the ROK regime, but it did not have as decisive an impact on American global strategy as the June 25 invasion of South Korea by North Korea. As Acheson's remark that "we are fighting the second team, whereas the real enemy is the Soviet Union"[100] would indicate, the administration's primary goal was to build up the necessary force to deter the Soviets, or, failing that, win a future war against them.

Most plans for an arms build-up had been approved before the Chinese intervention, and the worldwide arms build-up was to continue at full pace, even after armistice negotiations began in Korea. In late September 1950, when it seemed likely that the Korean War would soon be over, the Truman administration approved NSC-68/1, which contained plans to spend more than $40 billion per year in fiscal years 1952, 1953, and 1954. It claimed that these "estimates of forces are based on the assumption that hostilities in Korea will terminate in fiscal year 1951," strong evidence that the build-up was already meant to be global in nature and indefinite in duration.[101] The NSC approved NSC-68/2, a more fleshed-out version of the plan, on September 30, 1950.[102] The Truman administration had become convinced of the need to prepare for a Soviet military threat by the attack on South Korea and by the weakness of the first American forces sent to Korea, and maintained this conviction even after feared Soviet thrusts into Yugoslavia and Iran failed to materialize.

The battles in Korea constituted only one of three elements that absorbed the bulk of military spending, the other two being the American military deployment to Europe and investment for long-term development of military technology. This last category included basic and applied research, as well as the creation of production capacities. As late as June 1951, a full year after the beginning of American involvement in Korea, and a few weeks before the beginning of armistice talks there, the Office of Defense Mobilization would claim that "Military production is still mainly in the 'tooling up' stage—the period during which orders are placed, blueprints drawn, subcontracts worked out, and production lines organized."[103] That this was the situation was not primarily a result of sloppy planning. Rather, the build-up—its goals, its funding, its organization—was based on preparation for a potential war several years in the future. More weapons could have been produced during 1950–51 if the administration had been determined, at any cost, to circumvent the bottlenecks of limited machine tools and too few engineers and draftsmen. However, the demand was not so immediate, and it was more cost-efficient to create a smoothly rising curve in military preparedness, investing in research and design, rather than to produce larger quantities of existing weapons.

The Korean War was so useful to the arms build-up faction that there has been speculation that the armistice negotiations were intentionally prolonged in order to complete the deployment of U.S. forces to Europe.[104]

EXPANSION OF THE FISCAL YEAR 1951 AMERICAN DEFENSE BUDGET AFTER THE START OF THE KOREAN WAR

As we have seen, the pre-Korean War proposals for a fiscal year 1951 budget suggested that fiscal year 1951 would have little quantitative or qualitative difference from the previous two budgets. Before the budget had passed, however, the North Korean military attack had begun.

Congress immediately granted the Department of Defense permission to spend funds from the fiscal year 1951 budget. After Johnson lost his policy battle against the use of ground forces in Korea, he seemed to decide that he could no longer afford to be a budget-cutter. He delegated to the services the right to spend fiscal year 1951 money on July 14,[105] while Congress continued to work on the budget. By the time it passed, on September 6, 1950, the $14.680 billion budget[106] was vastly insufficient, since more than that had already been spent during ten weeks of war.[107] Truman told Frederick Lawton, director of the Bureau of the Budget, that he was dissatisfied with the budget but had to sign it, given the war needs.[108]

As we have seen, support was very high on Capitol Hill for the war and a general arms build-up, and the Truman administration had little trouble finding funds. The only proposal to blunt the thrust of the arms build-up, made by the skeptical Senator Taft in spite of the mood of pro-military hysteria that followed the start of the war, was that the tax increases to pay for the funds should be proposed before the November elections. Truman, always devoted to balanced budgets, happily obliged.[109]

The president perceived the events in Korea to mean that the Soviet Union was openly challenging the West militarily. He wanted more arms and armies everywhere. On July 19, he publicly announced that he would soon ask Congress for $10 billion in military appropriations supplemental to the budget.[110] As we will later see, he also used this date to launch his bid for price and wage controls. The new willingness of both the executive and the legislative branch to dole out money for an arms build-up led Acheson to proclaim on July 21 that "I do not recall any period of four weeks in the history of the United States when so much has been accomplished."[111]

However, it seems that although Truman changed his views on the necessity of large standing armies overseas, he would never relinquish his distrust of the professional officer corps. He would back huge new defense appropriations spending, but would dole out the money in individual packages for specific plans. The president told Lawton on July 22 not to put "any more money than necessary at this time in the hands of the Military."[112] Truman considered it possible that the military would use the war as an excuse to fund every conceivable unnecessary project, such as those his World War II Committee on Procurement had uncovered. Fraud, duplication, and waste had to be avoided.

The money would have to come from specific supplemental appropriations bills. There would be four of these in fiscal year 1951.

The Pentagon, in response to Truman's request, revealed the first proposal, for $10.6 billion. This proposal developed into the first supplemental bill. Truman trimmed it to approximately $10.487 billion and submitted it to Congress on July 24. The proposal provided $4.535 billion for the air force, $3.064 billion for the army, $2.648 billion for the navy, and an additional $240 million contingency fund.[113]

Then the Department of Defense, because of the urgency of the war, submitted requests for more funds to the president on July 29. These were for $950 million for naval aircraft, $85 million for army construction projects, $90 million for similar navy projects, and $35 million more for the contingency fund, for a total of $1.16 billion.[114] On the recommendation of the Bureau of the Budget, Truman trimmed $4 million from the navy projects and submitted the $1.156 billion request to Congress on August 4.[115]

Rather than pass the new requests separately from the first proposed package, Congress combined the two. The House of Representatives passed the two, intact, as one bill, for approximately $11.643 billion.[116] The Senate then added $93.188 million in extra appropriations, to cover new requests for wool clothing, ship construction facilities, naval medical care, and other items.[117] A conference settled the final amount at approximately $11.729 billion.[118] This supplemental defense appropriations request was combined with a number of other funding requests. These included a request for more than $4 billion in supplemental foreign aid, plus new money for a variety of domestic, nondefense needs. The new

bill totaled approximately $17 billion.[119] Among other things, the bill pro-
vided funds for an expansion of the air force to 58 groups.[120] It passed on
September 27.[121]

The preparation of the second supplemental appropriations bill began
before the first one had even passed. On August 24, Secretary of the Army
Pace informed Johnson that the army wanted a bigger force. He claimed
that the first supplemental appropriations bill had been based on the use
of four divisions in Korea, but that the United States would soon be using
eight. Also, the army was spending money on equipping South Korea, for
which there had been no mention in either the fiscal year defense budget
or the supplemental appropriations act. Pace declared that the army
would run short of funds in five major areas between the end of September
and the middle of December.[122] Johnson and Pace brought up this matter
with the president, but Truman decided that he should not introduce another appropriations bill until at least the middle of November. Some
military assistance funds were diverted to the army in the meantime.

The Joint Chiefs got to work on producing an appropriations package
that could be ready by mid-November. The first stage, establishing target
needs, was accomplished on September 22. It based needs on the assumptions that the Korean War would be over by June 30, 1951, and that
priority would go to Korea (this would seem to be obvious in wartime,
but of course the administration was more interested in building up
American capacities generally, and particularly in Europe). The army was
to have 17 divisions and 1,263,000 personnel by the end of fiscal year 1951,
with all overseas units and half of all domestically based units at 100
percent strength and the rest at 85 percent. The navy was to have 322
major warships, 12 carrier groups (with naval combat units at 85 percent
strength), and 689,000 sailors. The air force was to have 70 wings and
688,000 personnel, and the Marine Corps was to have 166,000 personnel.[123]
Funding such a program, if passed, would cost approximately $20 billion.

Having signed defense bills for more than $25 billion in September
alone, Truman was concerned about costs. Fearing restrictions from the
president (this was especially likely given the army's success in the immediate stages after the September 15 Inchon amphibious landing), the
JCS scaled back the plan on November 13 by removing one army division
and two air force wings, and eliminating the planned rehabilitation of
certain reserve factories.[124] The 68-wing air force was to have 25 strategic
bomber groups, 28 tactical air support groups, and 15 air defense
groups.[125]

But the JCS cuts were not enough trimming for the president. He had
the Bureau of the Budget cut the JCS plan by almost 50 percent, reducing
it to $10.9 billion. However, war in Korea intervened again. The Chinese
attack, which began November 25 before the bill had been introduced in
Congress, created a new hunger for funds. The supplemental bill was

rewritten, this time for a budget of slightly more than $16.845 billion,[126] and introduced in Congress on December 1.[127] The bill was part of a package that included appropriation bills for the Atomic Energy Commission, the Selective Service System, the Tennessee Valley Authority, the Coast Guard, the Bureau of Public Roads, the Subversive Activities Control Board, and others, all forming a package of more than $18.081 billion in spending.[128] The supplemental defense budget bill was to have the following costs: $1.687 billion for military personnel, $3.935 billion for operation and maintenance, $1.888 billion for aircraft procurement, $381 million for ship procurement, $6.325 billion for other procurement, as well as other expenses.[129] When related costs were added to the aircraft procurement budget, the total was approximately $2.144 billion.[130] This estimate was to be added to previous procurement funds that the air force had saved, giving the air force an estimated $9 billion in cash and contract authority for the purchase of aircraft.[131] Considering that these funds were to buy planes in addition to the more than 1,400 military aircraft previously purchased and paid for but not yet delivered, it is clear that the increase in air power was on a radical scale.[132] It was expected that the rate of aircraft construction would increase 500 percent in one year.[133]

Even more staggering, however, were the army's costs. The army was to receive a total of more than $9.211 billion, compared with the navy's $2.979 billion, and the air force's $4.603 billion.[134] A comparison of these figures shows the trend after the beginning of the Korean War to reconstruct the ground forces, which had lost most budget battles with the air force in the pre-Korea era when relying on atomic bombing capacities was the prime military policy.

Coming as it did during what was certainly the most critical point of the war, and at what, with the possible exception of the Cuban Missile Crisis, was perhaps the most dangerous point of the Cold War, the debate on the bill involved heated discussions on the direction of American foreign policy. For three weeks, Congress grilled senior administration officials about the future. Why did the United States need the money? Why not more money, on the scale of World War II? Why not, the China Lobby asked, expand the war in Asia? Marshall, Deputy Secretary of Defense Robert Lovett, and Bradley testified on behalf of the administration, that the budget was just right, since it signaled a commitment to establishing the facilities for a long-term build-up that might or might not prove necessary, rather than an unnecessary expansion of funds that would be squandered.[135]

The Eighty-first Congress delayed the bill until January 2, 1951, its last day of existence, but passed the bill intact, along with two other defense bills.[136] One was a $3.1 billion civil defense bill, with the money to be spent by federal, state, and local agencies.[137] The other authorized the president to modify defense contracts so as to start construction, using some of the funds just appropriated.[138]

There was a third supplemental defense appropriations bill that did not include any funds for the military.[139] The bill was for approximately $365 million, to be doled out to 18 agencies for civil defense, for the Voice of America radio network that transmitted American propaganda, and for other Cold War matters.[140] One of the bill's provisions was the Kem amendment. This amendment declared that until the war in Korea was over, the United States would not provide aid to any nation that traded items considered useful in the manufacture of military equipment with Soviet bloc states.[141] The Kem amendment was a source of friction within NATO, since some European governments considered the eastern European nations and the USSR to be valuable trading partners, and feared that a strict interpretation of the amendment might make the importation of such basic items as coarse grains and timber from the USSR difficult.[142] The amendment seemed, to its critics, to confirm Soviet claims that American aid was a means to reorient European trade across the Atlantic. Truman, who vocally opposed the amendment, managed to delay its implementation while trying to create alternative legislation.[143]

The fourth supplemental defense appropriations bill of fiscal year 1951 was for $6.642 billion, $6.379 billion of which went to the Department of Defense, and $59 million of which went to the Atomic Energy Commission.[144] The bill was signed into law on May 31, 1951.[145] Its passage brought total fiscal year military spending to $48.2 billion.[146] This figure roughly equaled the total Department of Defense appropriations for the four previous fiscal years (1947–50).[147]

During the fiscal year, there had also been a $4 billion bill for new military assistance, passed on August 1.

Johnson, with his typical aggressiveness, sought to control the arms build-up from his office in the Pentagon. He told the service secretaries and the Joint Chiefs on July 3 that they were not to seek individual appropriations bills from Congress, nor to make any public speeches. Everything would have to go through the Office of the Secretary of Defense. Johnson also tried to interfere in the president's directives on Far East policy, preferring to give MacArthur, who had a history of making statements without checking them with Washington, a much looser rein when making public pronouncements on foreign policy.

Johnson's efforts at consolidating power convinced Truman that Johnson needed to be removed if the administration was to have the unity necessary to complete the arms build-up. Johnson had served his purpose in banging heads together at the Pentagon during the harsh interservice bickering in the late 1940s, and he had helped consolidate the power of the Office of Secretary of Defense, which under Forrestal had been weak. But the press blamed Johnson for the poor showing of the army in the first few weeks of the Korean campaign, since he had been so publicity-hungry as a budget-cutter in the time preceding the war. The British naval attaché in Washington referred to Johnson as "one of the most unpopular men in the United States."[148]

Truman decided that George Marshall, former army chief of staff and secretary of state, should replace Johnson. He asked Johnson to resign in September (and later claimed he had made up his mind to fire him in late June). The president had to bring Johnson back a second time and order him to resign, since Johnson, ever assertive, was trying to find a way to avoid resigning. On hearing the news of Johnson's departure, Acheson and Nitze had a champagne toast.[149]

THE FISCAL YEAR 1952 AMERICAN DEFENSE BUDGET

The fiscal year 1952 American arms budget was transformed by the Korean War. As we have seen, the proposals for fiscal year 1952 under consideration in early 1950 were for a budget similar to fiscal year 1950, but the war changed that, more than tripling its eventual size.

In the first hectic months of the war, work on the fiscal year 1952 budget was slow. On August 10, Johnson informed his staff that work on fiscal year 1952 would have to be delayed until fiscal year 1951 could be reconsidered and the costs of NSC-68 calculated.[150] These calculations, which took the form of NSC-68/1, NSC-68/2, and so forth, became the basis for budgeting fiscal years 1952–55. These documents set targets, but it was recognized that these were likely to be modified, and had value primarily as a starting point for all discussions.

As we have seen, the new fiscal year 1951 budget was passed on September 6, 1950. As one of Johnson's last tasks as secretary of defense, he ordered the resumption of fiscal year 1952 preparations on September 13, 1950.[151] By this time, NSC-68 was nearly fleshed out. On September 21, NSC-68/1 was finished.

The Joint Chiefs of Staff, armed with knowledge of planned funding, produced troop level estimates. On September 22, 1950, they estimated fiscal year 1952 manpower at 1,350,000 for the army, 863,000 for the air force, 712,000 for the navy, and 170,000 for the Marines.[152]

The development of the fiscal year 1952 budget was similar to the development of the supplemental 1951 budgets in that plans and estimates changed as the situation in Korea changed. It seemed in early fall that the war would soon be won, so Deputy Secretary of Defense Lovett instructed the Joint Chiefs to lower their estimated needs.[153] They did so on November 13, decreasing their troop estimates from 3.1 million to 2.8 million.[154] Nevertheless, such a level was still estimated to cost almost $40 billion in fiscal year 1952, a massive increase that was accounted for by the global build-up, not costs in Korea.

Once the People's Republic of China intervened on a large scale in November, all of the estimates had to be revised upward. Officials decided to hasten the build-up. NSC-68/4, completed in December 1950 to replace NSC-68/2, called for the completion of the build-up by the end of fiscal year 1952 (June 30, 1952) rather than the end of fiscal year 1954 (June 30, 1954).[155] The Joint Chiefs were informed of this at a December 6 meeting,[156] and sent detailed estimates of fiscal year 1952 force goals to the NSC on December 14.[157] These estimates called for an 18-division army, 397 major combat vessels for the navy, and 95 wings for the air force.[158] Considering that before Korea the JCS had been pleading for a fiscal year 1952 force of 10 divisions, 281 major combat vessels, and 58 wings, the scope of the changes in late 1950 is clear.[159] This period, immediately after the Chinese counterattack, may have marked the point at which budgetary estimates reached their maximum in the entire 1945–60 era. Lovett informed the Bureau of the Budget on December 20 that the planned budget for fiscal year 1952 might be $60 billion, which would have been a nearly five-fold increase in two years.[160]

The Bureau of the Budget and the president felt these new figures were too high. Worried that too much spending would have an adverse inflationary impact, Truman ordered the Bureau of the Budget to discuss lowering the planned fiscal year 1952 budget with the Department of Defense.

These talks, in early 1951, took place at a time when the Department of Defense was preoccupied with completing the supplemental bills to flesh out the fiscal year 1951 budget, and it was a long time before fiscal year 1952 could be finished. It was not until April that a compromise was worked out: the Truman administration decided to introduce a budget to Capitol Hill, on April 30, 1951, for $56.2 billion, not including a separate $4.5 billion bill for military construction.[161] Although the Korean War was in one of its bloodiest stages, the administration confidently expected that its attrition campaign would soon force the Chinese to negotiate, and so the budget was based on the accurate prediction that any fighting in Korea during fiscal year 1952 would be on a smaller scale than at present. Therefore, war supplies, such as ammunition, were not favored as much as long-term investments in technology. The military was to spend less on armament in depth and more on armament in breadth.

The armistice negotiations in Korea, which were to last until July 1953, began in July of 1951, and the level of fighting subsided. Although American forces faced a significantly lower level of conflict than before (there were sporadic battles over hills, fought mostly to win bargaining leverage), Truman still pushed for the continuation of the arms build-up. As Truman informed Congress days after armistice negotiations had begun:

We have no reason to believe that the events in Korea have fundamentally changed the basic Soviet intentions . . . we must press on to build our defenses.[162]

Congress seemed to agree. The House passed a version of the Truman budget for approximately $56 billion, and the Senate passed a budget for approximately $59.5 billion in September.[163] When a joint House-Senate committee finally produced the fiscal year 1952 military budget in October 1951, more than three months after the start of the fiscal year, it was for approximately $56.94 billion.[164] In addition, the public works bill was slashed to $3.9 billion before it passed.

The air force created its 95-wing program (surpassing the 70 wings it already had), and won theoretical approval to eventually expand to 143 wings.[165]

The fiscal year 1952 budget represented a stage of military preparedness that would, in a broad sense, be representative of American doctrine for the next two decades. While the actual production of many weapons was not completed until well into fiscal year 1953, 1954, or even 1955, it was fiscal year 1952 that saw the fleshing out of deployed divisions, and the increased commitment to atomic research and other components of the arms build-up.

CHAPTER 5

Globalization

AMERICAN DEPLOYMENT TO EUROPE AND THE PROMISE OF GERMAN REARMAMENT

Western European governments generally supported the American decision to intervene in Korea because it showed American willingness to prevent Soviet expansion.[1] The British, as a Foreign Office memorandum put it, sent a sizable contingent of troops to Korea "in order to safeguard the future of the United Nations Organization, and to deter the Soviet Union from attempting aggression elsewhere (e.g., in Persia)."[2] However, the critical result of the war, for Britain and for the rest of Europe, did not lie in Korea, nor in the UN, nor in Persia, but in Germany. The question of whether and how to address the Soviet preponderance of military power along the dividing line between the two German states vexed Western Europe from 1950 to 1955.

The important result of the war for Europe was the development of a new NATO combat-ready army in areas of the Federal Republic of Germany close to the German Democratic Republic, with six divisions of U.S. troops deployed there.[3] These American forces, and the U.S. military aid funds, shifted the balance of power on the continent. As Churchill said toward the end of the war, "Korea does not really matter now. I'd never heard of the place until I was seventy-four. Its importance lies in the fact that it has led to the re-arming of America."[4]

The inclination, present before the Korean conflict, to lobby Washington to at least maintain, and perhaps increase, American military commitments in Europe became a primary foreign policy objective of most

European NATO governments after June 1950. The American occupation forces in Germany, and the three bomber groups in England, did not constitute a powerful fighting force, and the North Korean outburst suggested that the world situation might soon become more violent.

Europeans were well aware of the weaknesses of existing armies in western Europe and had never been comfortable with the reliance on the atomic deterrent, even before the Soviets achieved atomic fission. The Europeans considered it probable that in a nuclear conflict, atomic bombs would be dropped on Europe, maybe by the Americans as a means of destroying Soviet forces as they advanced across Europe, and maybe by the Soviets, either as a military tactic or in retaliation for U.S. strikes on the Soviet Union. It was not beyond reason to imagine that the Americans would bomb European industrial areas rather than allow them to fall into Soviet hands. Wanting American economic and military capacities to balance their power with the Soviet bloc, but not wanting this power to be manifested through the use of nuclear weapons, the Europeans actively sought greater American commitments of conventional forces in central Europe.

The potential parallel between what had happened in divided Korea, and what the East German Army could try in divided Germany, was not lost. Walter Ulbricht, the Communist Party leader in East Germany, even hinted at this when he claimed that "if the Americans in their imperialist arrogance believe that the Germans have less national consciousness than the Koreans, then they have fundamentally deceived themselves."[5] The Soviet army's maneuvers in East Germany at the time of the North Korean invasion seem to have heightened fears.[6]

There were opponents of the American deployment within Europe, mostly the same people who had opposed the creation of NATO: the hard left, a number of nationalists on the right, and members of Communist parties sympathetic to the USSR. There was also a sizable minority of the public that feared that by intervening against the Communists in Korea and by sending troops to Europe, the Americans might provoke the Soviets into war.

The majority, however, sided with the thrust of Truman's policy. The Norwegian ambassador, Wilhelm Morgenstierne, told Acheson that the Norwegians felt that the benefits of the American policies far outweighed the risks.[7] The Berlin newspaper *Der Abend* claimed that a defeat of the West in Korea would mean "that the Kremlin would be tempted more strongly to continue the series of unpunished attacks with new actions of surprise."[8] The *Economist*, of London, describing Truman's speech regarding the use of force to prevent Soviet-sponsored aggression, wrote, "That is the voice of Palmerston . . . the warning has gone out—to the east German *Bereitschaften*, to the Cominform conspiring against Tito, to the would-be 'liberators' of south-east Asia. The policy of encouraging situations of strength is serious."[9] In 1953, the French newspaper *L'Aurore* would opine: "What would have happened if Truman had given a free hand to the Communists in Korea? It seems clear enough to us. After Korea it would have been Indochina. After Indochina it would have been the whole of Southeast Asia. And what would have then prevented the Communists, faced with disarmed nations, from attacking Europe?"[10] As Bohlen would later write, "after Korea, where the Communist section of a divided country launched a military assault on the non-Communist section, a mere pledge on paper was no longer enough. Europe overreacted to Korea as much as, or more than, the United States."[11] Western European political leaders hoped that American troops might placate public worries, and perhaps send Moscow a much-needed message of firmness.

Consequently, the Truman administration's desire, following the start of the Korean War, to create a preponderance of NATO conventional power in Europe coincided precisely with European goals. The result would be a large American combat force in Germany for decades.

The second major issue in the build-up of NATO forces was the rearmament of Germany, which proved more controversial. Before the Korean War, the British and the Dutch had already been discussing German rearmament, with the Dutch States General even publicly debating it,[12] but neither side had come out directly in favor of it. The Dutch prime minister, Dirk Stikker, declared on May 13, 1950, that German rearmament was "premature" and that "it is essential that the defence of Western Europe be strengthened first."[13] In the United States, German rearmament had been privately considered by the State Department in late 1949,[14] and General Bradley had commented publicly that, from a strictly military point of view, German rearmament was desirable.[15] Even John McCloy, the American high commissioner in Germany, had hinted, in March 1950, that if there was a build-up of Western Europe in general, German rearmament could be considered.[16] However, Truman had termed a proposal for rearming Germany "as wrong as can be" as late as June 16, 1950.[17]

He rapidly changed his mind on the issue after the start of the Korean conflict nine days later. The possible detrimental effects of a rearmed Germany (opponents of German rearmament cited a potential renaissance of German militarism or a West German effort to reunite Germany) still existed, but Truman now considered the need for German armies too great to resist. There was also strong pressure from both the military and Congress to encourage German rearmament. Congressional approval for appropriations allowing a deployment of U.S. forces in Europe or increased U.S. military aid to Europe would be difficult to obtain if the impression existed that the United States would be paying a disproportionate share of the expenses for the defense of Europe. With the outbreak of the war, the British and the Dutch also rapidly came to favor German rearmament.

The Truman administration became so favorably disposed towards German rearmament in the months after June 25 that the administration even rejected proposals for partial German rearmament. Suggestions for enlisting Germans into the U.S. Army, increasing the monetary contribution of the West German state to NATO, or building a paramilitary force similar to the East German *Volkspolizei*, of which the British were in favor, were rejected as insufficient or not agreeable to the Germans.[18] Another proposal, sent to the White House by McCloy, calling for German rearmament within a pan-European army, was dismissed as too difficult and time-consuming to implement.[19]

Tapping into the German economy was critical to win Congressional approval of the deployment of American combat-ready forces to Europe, but Conrad Adenauer's government was not keen on releasing German funds for military purposes unless they were for German forces. Adenauer sensed what American polls of the German populace revealed: the German people wanted rearmament, despite fears that rearming might aggravate tensions.[20]

The Adenauer government had been concerned, even before the Korean War, that the occupying powers did not inform it of war plans,[21] and was sufficiently shocked by American defeats in the first few weeks of the Korean War that it asked for explanations of how the United States intended to succeed in the event of a war with the Soviets in Europe.[22]

Adenauer's demand, in September, that "13 armored divisions [be] transferred to the Eastern borders of the Federal Republic" as rapidly as possible, or "the Soviets will take advantage of our defenselessness in order to begin a preventive intervention in Germany,"[23] showed a genuine concern over possible Soviet aggrandizement and a desire to strengthen the hand of Germany in getting approval for rearmament on its terms. The more convinced the Americans were of the need for vast forces in central Europe, the more they would help Adenauer lay the foundation for a German army. Indeed, toward the end of 1950, the strong desire among most NATO countries for German forces allowed the Adenauer government to use such an outcome as a negotiating ploy, insisting that Germany gain a voice in NATO planning, and proposing a direct link between the formation of German military units and the removal of controls by the International Ruhr Authority.[24] Adenauer was so assertive that he virtually dictated many of the terms for German rearmament. In one meeting McCloy made 122 concessions to obtain Adenauer's cooperation, leading some to joke that "Adenauer is the real McCloy."[25]

The French, who had one eye on the Western balance of power with the Soviets and the other on the French balance of power with Germany, proved to be the biggest obstacle to German rearmament. They tried to prevent the inclusion of Germany in the North Atlantic Treaty as well as a revival of the German army. The French government announced that "it is quite impossible to even discuss the question of a restoration of Germany's military forces."[26] To ally with Germany against the Soviets would be to contravene France's experiences of the first half of the century, when it was usually the Russian Empire/Soviet Union that guaranteed French security against German ambitions. The French saw German rearmament as a slippery slope. They had been persuaded to allow German production of material for NATO units, and had even consented to allowing the West German state to have a police force.[27] If they also consented on German rearmament as a NATO nation, would they eventually be asked to agree to ever larger increases in German military power, and then see Germany leaving NATO to become an independent and dominant force in Europe? The issue was not merely political for the French; there was an emotional distrust of the Germans. It had been fewer than six years since German occupation had ended. Jules Moch, the French minister of defense, had lost two sons in a German concentration camp, which he used to explain his antagonism towards the German military in talks with Frank Pace, the American secretary of the army.[28]

In early September 1950, at the New York meeting of the North Atlantic Council, Johnson proposed a package offer by which the Europeans would have to accept German rearmament and increase their own military spending to induce the United States to send four divisions to Europe. This proposal was not that different from what would eventually occur, but it would not occur by Johnson's design. As we have seen, Johnson's tenure was soon ended for other reasons. Marshall, in agreement with Acheson, felt that although a U.S. offer of troops and German rearmament were both desirable, it did not make sound diplomatic sense to link the two issues, since doing so would make the United States appear overly forceful. So he decoupled them.[29] On September 12, 1950, at the NATO Council Meeting in Washington, Acheson, without prior consultation with the French or the British,[30] formally proposed German rearmament without directly mentioning American deployment. Marshall and his British counterpart, Manny Shinwell, spent the conference lobbying the French, especially Moch, to agree to defense at the Rhine and to a German military. They succeeded on the first count, but Moch was a tough sell on German rearmament, at first denying that the Federal Republic of Germany should be allowed to have even a paramilitary force.[31] Only after Marshall bluntly told the French that American aid to France would be decreased if they did not cooperate on the German rearmament issue did Moch agree to a German force, and even then he insisted that it consist of less than one brigade, making it the smallest force in NATO except for Iceland's.[32] The tripartite communiqué announcing the decisions showed the lack of complete agreement on the rearmament issue, promising to study "the participation of the German Federal Republic in the common defense of Europe," but referring to German units as "mobile police forces" designed to maintain "internal security."[33]

After the conference, the French, realizing that they were in the minority on the German rearmament issue (the Belgians and Luxembourgers provided what Foreign Secretary Ernest Bevin termed "half-hearted support" for the French), sought to create a compromise plan to avoid the possibility that full German rearmament would be thrust upon them by the British and the Americans.[34] On October 24, 1950, they announced a new proposal, the Pleven Plan, named after French Prime Minister Rene Pleven. Under the terms of the Pleven Plan, a single commander would lead the various national forces of European NATO countries, plus a pan-European force of 100,000 troops, including Germans.[35] There would be no German general staff. The plan was designed to help resolve the perceived need for a conventional deterrent against the Soviets while restricting German control over a German force. The French hoped that the plan would help satisfy the American demands for German participation, but that the actual pan-European force would be small and slow to develop.[36] The British Foreign Office was prepared to explain the Pleven Plan to the Germans, but did not feel that it was mandatory for the Germans to participate.[37] The Americans barely accepted it in theory, but wanted more German military help than the French had anticipated.

The Soviets reacted to the talks on German rearmament with virulent public attacks. The Kremlin hoped to split the Western alliance by appealing to western Europeans opposed to a renewal of German arms.[38] Given the strong anti-Soviet sentiments in the wake of the fighting in Korea, these appeals came to naught.

The Americans and the British placed new pressure on the French after the November 25 Chinese counteroffensive in Korea, when concern over the spread of the fighting in Korea intensified.[39] Adenauer, taking advantage of the Anglo-American insistence on German rearmament, told a journalist on December 11, 1950, that

we must insist on full equality with regard to arms and command. This is necessary in order to counter the impression that our soldiers are to be used merely as cannon-fodder. Without heavy equipment German troops would have no chance of defending themselves and without their own commanders they would consider themselves second-class soldiers.[40]

If a plan for a partial German rearmament, under which German units would not be equal to their NATO counterparts, was put forth, Adenauer declared that "we would find ourselves in the unfortunate position of having to reject it."[41]

The French government persisted in its desire to contain German power. On December 12, 1950, the French foreign minister, Robert Schuman, declared that German military units would at no time "be at the disposition of a German government."[42] The French still insisted, either in spite of or because of Adenauer's declaration, that all German forces be within the pan-European army, adding that German units were not to have more than 1,000 men,[43] and demanding a stronger American presence to balance the German forces. The next day, December 13, in London, under the shadows of the major UN setbacks against the Chinese in Korea, NATO negotiators pushed the French into a compromise arrangement: German divisions would be created, under an integrated NATO command structure, with a strong American presence in Europe.[44] The conferees decided to postpone the Pleven Plan until a January conference in Paris,[45] but British and American doubts about the plan had already been leaked to the press.[46] The French appeared to have been dragged into the London agreement by the British and the Americans; the very next day the French proposed postponing the implementation of the new agreement until a conference of the four occupying powers of Germany had been convened and the issue of German rearmament had, once again, been considered.[47] In private talks with the British and the Americans, the French had tried to justify the proposal for a four-power conference by claiming that if the Communists were willing to intervene with Chinese troops in Korea, they might be willing to intervene with Soviet troops in Germany to prevent German rearmament.[48] At approximately the same time, Moscow declared its desire for a four-power conference to discuss the demilitarization of Germany, in accordance with the Potsdam Accord.[49] Hoping to pressure the West, Stalin also published ominous warnings on the inadvisability of German rearmament.[50] The Truman administration feared that the Soviets would try to use a conference to side with the French to prevent German rearmament. Given that the Soviet and French proposals for conferences came almost simultaneously, it seemed that there was an understanding between the two, either tacit or explicit, to work together against German rearmament. This tactic could undermine the fragile agreement with France to trade U.S. deployments to Germany for French approval of German rearmament, introduce chaos into the administration's European policies, and upset relations with Adenauer's government in Germany.

The administration followed NSC-68's proposals and declined the Soviet invitation, hoping that after the build-up of forces in western Europe, the Atlantic nations could then negotiate with the USSR from a situation of strength. The administration felt that it needed the ability to effectively dominate each step of a military escalation crisis with the Soviets if it was to be able to bargain effectively.

The French continued their attempts to implement the Pleven Plan. Although the Americans and the British would have preferred the immediate creation of German units, they accepted the delays and complications inherent in creating a pan-European army, desiring continued French cooperation in NATO and sure that German rearmament was inevitable. The attempted implementation of the Pleven Plan, under the name European Defense Community, would be delayed and, ironically, destroyed before birth by the French National Assembly in 1954. German rearmament did not occur until May 5, 1955.

NATO chose Eisenhower, then a civilian president of Columbia University in New York City, to become the first NATO Supreme Allied Commander in Europe (SACEUR). The SACEUR title was intentionally chosen because it recalled the victorious Anglo-American Supreme Allied Command of World War II. Truman officially notified Eisenhower of the offer on December 19, 1950.[51] Eisenhower would soon rejoin the army. The SACEUR post was the highest position except for the NATO Military Committee, which was (and still is) composed of one member of each nation, usually the chief of staff of the armed forces.[52] It would become a NATO policy to give the SACEUR post to an American general.

Eisenhower was sent on a fact-finding mission through the western European and Canadian capitals in January. Upon returning to the United States, he told Truman that he wanted 10 to 12 American divisions, to be part of a 50– to 60–division NATO force.[53]

On February 1, he informed Congress that no limit should be placed on the number of American troops sent to Europe and that a 40-division allied force, composed mostly of French troops, was a good goal for 1953. The issue of how many divisions were to be sent to Europe became an issue of close congressional scrutiny. It would not be resolved until April, as we shall see.

Meanwhile, the French continued their efforts to lessen the extent of German rearmament. During a visit to the United States on January 29 and 30, 1951, Pleven succeeded in getting the Americans to agree to a five-to-one ratio of non-Germans to Germans in NATO forces.[54] Pleven expressed his concern to American officials that German rearmament might lead to war, either because the Soviets would see the move as a threat and launch a preemptive strike, or because the Germans, once rearmed, might leave NATO and attempt to unify Germany.[55] In a March 1951 visit, French President Vincent Auriol repeated these points.[56]

Truman responded that the United States still possessed enough of an atomic edge to deter the Soviets from attacking in the immediate future. The administration did not seriously consider the possibility of Adenauer launching a war to reunite Germany. The prime thrust of Truman's policy was to rearm rapidly to a position of strength, so that when the time of perceived maximum danger was reached in a couple of years, the West would be in a solid position.[57]

The Americans realized that the French were not prepared to sabotage the sovereignty of Germany, or to sabotage NATO, or even to withdraw from NATO, and therefore had little leverage to enforce their views on German rearmament. Had the French pulled out of NATO over the issue of German rearmament, their actions may quite possibly have had the opposite impact on intentions, making the allies more likely to rely on German military power.

Attempting to prevent German rearmament would also have cost France one of its highest priorities: a pan-European economic organiza-tion. On May 9, 1950, Schuman announced the plan for the integration of French and German coal and steel industries that he had privately broached with the German government. During the 1950–51 talks on Ger-man rearmament, the Germans attempted to link the completion of the coal and steel plan with rearmament. The French decision to accede to a German armed force helped pave the way for the signing of the European Coal and Steel Community agreement in April.

On May 19, 1951, following congressional approval, part of the U.S. Fourth Division, the first of four army divisions to be sent to Europe as part of NATO under the command of General Eisenhower, departed from New York City.[58] By 1952, the American presence in western Europe had increased to six divisions, 503 aircraft, and 82 warships, involving ap-proximately 260,800 personnel, more than 20,000 more than were used in the Korean conflict at that time.[59]

There was an arms build-up throughout NATO in the Korean War era. Between 1949 and 1951, military spending as a percentage of gross na-tional product rose from 2.7 percent to 4.3 percent in Belgium; from 3.9 percent to 5.7 percent in Italy; from 5.9 percent to 8.7 percent in the United Kingdom; and from 5.7 percent to 9.7 percent in France.[60] The total man-power of NATO increased by three million in three years.[61]

The number of NATO divisions increased from 15 to 35 during 1951, and operational aircraft from 1,000 to 3,000.[62] The number of NATO air-craft was 5,200 by 1953.[63]

PUBLIC CONCERN OVER NATIONAL SECURITY AND DOMESTIC ATTACKS ON TRUMAN'S POLICY

In the winter of 1950–51, public attitudes in the United States toward the state of world affairs were characterized by anger, gloom, fear, and frustration. There was a bloody war of attrition in Korea that seemed to have little hope of U.S. victory, except in the unlikely event that the war spread, in which case victory might entail involving the nation in nuclear warfare. Not since the latter stages of the War of 1812 had America been in the position of fighting a war that seemed likely to end without victory. Most Americans perceived the Soviets as the real enemy, and many felt that a war with the USSR was likely.

Stuart Symington, chairman of the National Security Resources Board, asked President Truman in a January 1951 memo, "Who doubts any longer that the Soviets will attack when ready? . . . As things are now going, by

1953 if not 1952, the Soviet aggressors will assume complete command of the world situation."[64] The *Wall Street Journal*, in the first week of 1951, warned that "1951 is the first full year of the great arms race to avert or fight World War III."[65]

In the fall of 1950, local authorities began to designate certain buildings as air-raid shelters.[66] David Lilienthal, recently resigned from the directorship of the AEC, was asked by friends to recommend places to move to that would be safe from atomic bombing.[67] The administration tried to allay public fear by announcing that it was protecting the skies over New York City with the latest jet fighters. *Look* magazine ran a cover story entitled "Could The Reds Seize Detroit?"[68]

Not understanding Truman's decision to wage a war of limited means for limited ends, many Americans took their frustrations out on the administration. The White House was deluged with telegrams calling for an all-out war on Communist countries, the dismissal of Acheson, and even the resignation of Truman.[69] Calls for widening the war were popular. Senator Lyndon Johnson said that he foresaw "a time when we will decide that we have had enough of indecisive fighting—of battles without victories."[70] Several senators hinted that the atomic bomb should at least be considered. Senator Owen Brewster, a Republican from Maine, in a debate over his suggestion that General MacArthur be given discretion over the use of the bomb, suggested that his opponents didn't respect the position of the "100,000 American boys now in the hills of Korea . . . denied the use of the one weapon which might save the lives of thousands."[71] Two local draft supervisors in Montana were replaced after they publicly declared that they would not draft any more men until the United States used the atomic bomb in Korea, which they saw as preferable to sending more young Americans there.[72]

Others took their frustrations out by engaging in a natural attitude of people at war: denigrating the enemy. Anti-Communism reached a fever pitch. There were anti-Communist movies, such as *I Was a Communist for the FBI* (1951); anti-Communist books, such as the Mickey Spillane series, which sold 13 million copies by 1951 by celebrating the killing of "Red sons-of-bitches"; anti-Communist comic books[73]; and even a "Fight the Red Menace" childrens' card series.[74] The Cincinnati Reds baseball team changed its name temporarily, since the word *red* had become so pejorative.[75] Senator Joseph McCarthy's virulent attacks on suspected Communists rivaled the Palmer raids of the 1919 Red Scare.

The language of government became increasingly strident. Few argued with Truman's choice of words in referring to the "Soviet imperialists."[76] Nor was anyone surprised when the secretary of defense stated that "the Soviet government threatens the peace of the world,"[77] or when a congressional representative claimed that the American people faced a choice between "slavery to a heartless and pitiless dictator like Stalin, or great sacrifices to preserve the liberties of mankind."[78] Five people who wrote "PEACE" on a wall in Brooklyn, New York, were sent to jail because the judge suspected they were Communists.[79] The Soviets were powerful, Stalin was dictatorial, the eastern European states had been violently brought under Moscow's control, the United States was at war with a Soviet ally, and the popular perception was that Moscow was not to be given the benefit of the doubt in international affairs.

The anti-Communist hysteria was bolstered by some long-standing ethnic prejudices. Retired Lieutenant General Clarence Huebner, serving in the CIA's Office of National Estimates, informed his co-workers that since the Russians were animals who had little regard for human life, they would crash their fighter aircraft into American bombers in the event of an American strategic raid on the Soviet Union.[80] Huebner's ideas were disregarded by the other office members. Eisenhower, trying to explain his calmness in the midst of crisis, wrote in a private letter, "It is just not sensible to think that 190 million backward Eurasians can conquer the entire western civilization with its great history and its great economic, political and material resources."[81]

The Republican opposition, taking advantage of much of the public frustration, sharply criticized the administration in the Senate. The gains in the November 1950 elections, in which the Democratic majority had been reduced from 12 (54 to 42) to 2 (49 to 47), bolstered the confidence of the Republican leadership.[82] Republican senators castigated Acheson for the speech he made on January 12, 1950, at the National Press Club, declaring that the American defense perimeter in Asia was to the east of Korea. They also ridiculed the Truman administration for its indecisiveness: first the administration decided to cross the 38th Parallel and then, when met by force, elected to pursue a limited war. This decision opened the administration to charges of confusion, appeasement, and even charges of treachery from the most hostile opposition. On December 15, 1950, the Republican leadership publicly asked for the resignation of Acheson.[83] The attacks on Acheson, coming as they did during a crucial week that saw the Western nations agree to rearm Germany and send American combat forces to Europe, made it clear that Truman's enemies in Congress wanted a showdown on America's new commitments abroad.

THE GREAT DEBATE

Many of the Truman administration's actions from June 1950 to the spring of 1951, including sending troops to Korea, pushing for higher defense spending, increasing military aid to Europe, supporting the rearmament of Germany, deploying combat-ready armies to that nation, and extending the alliance system, represented a turning point in American foreign affairs. Some of the goals, many of the priorities, and a dramatic part of the means of American policy were altered. Although Truman tried to appear consistent for public relations purposes, these policies amounted to a great divergence from those of his first administration.

It would have been surprising had such changes not run into opposition. Given the American constitutional system and the relatively transparent nature of the nation's political processes, long-held tenets of American policy, such as small peacetime military budgets or limited peacetime involvement in European power politics, could not be abandoned without a public rethinking of American international practices.

This rethinking happened behind closed doors through most of 1950, within the corridors of power at the White House, the State Department, and the Pentagon, and during the debates over the hydrogen bomb, NSC-68, the Korean campaign, and the militarization of NATO. In the winter of 1950–51, against the wishes of Truman, this great rethinking of American foreign policy priorities spilled into the legislative chambers.

The initial decision to send U.S. troops to Europe had been made in the desperate days before the Inchon landing in September 1950, at a time when much of Congress was united strongly behind any anti-Soviet act by the president.[84] However, the Chinese intervention in Korea and subsequent embarrassing revision of war aims by the United States, made the Truman administration seem vacillating and unsure of geopolitical strategy to much of the public, and political opponents sought to take advantage of the opportunity.

On December 20, 1950, the day after Truman formally announced that a U.S. contingent would participate in a North Atlantic alliance force under Eisenhower's command and that an additional 70,000 troops were to be sent to Europe, former President Herbert Hoover attacked the new forward defense strategy. He claimed that American ground forces would not be capable of stopping a Soviet attack if one took place and that Europe would become "the graveyard of millions of American boys and would end in the exhaustion of this Gibraltar of western civilization." Hoover added that the deployment of troops would waste precious American resources even in the event of peace. He preferred to see the Europeans prepare their armies, with the United States focusing on using air and sea forces to protect the Western Hemisphere, and he wanted to withhold military aid from Europe until there was more evidence that Europe was willing and able to defend itself.[85] Journalists characterized this speech as the beginning of the Great Debate on foreign policy.

Hoover's speech was applauded enthusiastically by disparate elements that were angry or confused about the Truman administration's handling of international affairs. Many Americans were frustrated by the lack of success in Korea, and quite a few saw the decision to wage a limited war there as senseless. They could not tolerate the Truman administration's focus on limited wars and foreign deployments, either because they were policies for the passive and the patient, and therefore lacking the appeal of military action, or, conversely, because the policies were foolhardy, recklessly expending American money and blood in Europe and Korea with no guarantee of success.

Any formulation of foreign policy requires an evaluation of a nation's ideas, interests, and ideology. For many who valued the origins of the United States as a revolutionary state, detached from the European traditions of alliance politics, the administration's decisions to revise the tenets of Washington's farewell address were unforgivable. In this sense, the Great Debate had some similarities with the one concerning ratification of the Versailles treaty in 1919–20. In both situations, Democratic presidents tried to couch their efforts in advancing such American political values as free trade and representative democracy abroad, but were countered by traditionalists at home who felt that involvement in an international political order dominated by national interest politics was bound to end with the United States futilely spending its blood and capital for peoples who would never be converted to alien American political notions. Such policies would only serve, in the long term, to weaken America and American principles.

While it is difficult to define popular beliefs in any numerical fashion, it seems that Truman's belief in a limited Korean War for limited ends and a strengthening of American forces in Europe was supported by either a plurality, or at best, a small majority of the citizenry. The anti-Truman sentiment was particularly popular in traditional isolationist segments of the population, where suspicions persisted that American participation in either or both of the World Wars had represented an American sacrifice for a continent that had already begun to destroy itself. Arnold Lunn, a British writer who traveled across the United States in the fall of 1950, observed that:

If isolationism is reborn it will owe its rebirth to the growing conviction, particularly in the Middle West, that American Capitalism is financing European Socialism without getting any adequate recognition or thanks, and that American G.I.s are expected to fight for a Europe which the Europeans are too apathetic to defend.[86]

Much of the Great Debate took the form of conservatives casting Truman and, particularly, Acheson, as men who unpatriotically placed the interests of Europe above the interests of America. The feeling among such conservatives was that the administration was willing to send American boys to die in Korea just to get enough anti-Communist hysteria whipped up to help the Europeans.

Leading the attack, the Old Guard launched a desperate battle to forestall this new, expanded form of containment. It was not wholly clear what containment was to be replaced with, since the Old Guard allied itself with groups of various interests: China Lobby supporters, isolationists, semi-isolationists, and those who preferred an all-out war on China or a strike against the Soviet Union. This disparate group, most popular in the Midwest and West but backed by such Washington notables as journalists Walter Lippman and Arthur Krock, was united only by the vehemence with which they viewed the Truman-Acheson containment strategy.[87]

Buoyed by the 100-to-1 ratio of pro-Hoover to anti-Hoover letters his office received after the former president's speech, Senator Taft attacked Truman's plans in a 10,000-word speech delivered in the Senate on January 5, 1951. Taft was willing to send a small force to Europe, feeling that it was necessary as a symbol of American determination, but he was adamant about maintaining a ceiling on the size of the force that was much smaller than Truman wanted. He asserted that the Europeans seemed less fearful of a war with the Soviets than with the Americans, and that Americans "have no business going over there trying to prod them into a great military program which, in my opinion, is almost certain to produce war."[88] He was particularly incensed by the manner in which the administration was ignoring the Senate. The U.S. troops were supposed to serve under a North Atlantic Treaty command, and the administration was citing Article Three of the treaty as indicative of the power to form such a command. Taft argued that Article Three established no such right, and that the administration should seek Senate approval of the package deal with the European allies before embarking on its policies. Truman's unilateral decision to send troops to Korea in June; unilateral declaration of a state of national emergency on December 15, which gave him wide powers over setting economic controls and imposing a draft; and unilateral decision to send troops to Europe led Taft to declare that the United States was drifting away from its constitutional principles, and remaking itself into a garrison state with overly strong central authority.[89] In the hope of countering the president's strategy with one of his own, Taft proposed a ceiling of 20 percent on the share of American forces that could be sent overseas. It was preferable, Taft claimed, to strengthen American air power, as Congress had suggested when it was overruled by the Truman administration on the issue of a 48-group air force, bolster U.S. sea power, and allow the Chinese Nationalists and the Europeans to provide the land power.[90] Taft questioned the desirability of the arms build-up:

The key to all the problems before this Congress lies in the size of our military budget. That determines the taxes to be levied. It determines the number of boys to be drafted. It is likely to determine whether we can maintain a reasonably free system and the value of our dollar, or whether we are to be weakened or choked by Government controls which inevitably tend to become more arbitrary and unreasonable.[91]

Following Taft's lead, Senator Wherry, a Republican from Nebraska, introduced a resolution in the Senate on January 8, 1951, proposing that troops not be deployed to Europe until Congress voted to do so, contradicting Truman's stance that the constitution gave the president proper authority to make such a decision. According to Wherry, Truman was backing away from the assurances he had given the Senate, during the ratification process for the North Atlantic Treaty, that U.S. troops would not be sent to Europe.[92] The same day, Truman jumped into the fray with a not-very-well disguised attack on the Hoover faction in his annual State of the Union address to Congress.[93] On January 11, Representative Frederic Coudert, a Republican from New York, introduced a proposal almost identical to Senator Wherry's in the House.[94]

Although the Old Guard was overwhelmingly Republican, the Great Debate was by no means a strictly partisan affair. Some Republicans, such as William Knowland, Earl Warren, Thomas Dewey, Harold Stassen, Henry Cabot Lodge Jr., and John Foster Dulles, sided with the administration on NATO policy. Some Democrats, such as Senators Walter George (Georgia) and Paul Douglas (Illinois), sided with the Old Guard in demanding congressional approval for troops to be sent abroad.[95] The debates on military aid to Europe in 1949 had shown that some Southern Democratic senators, such as John McClellan (Arkansas), Russell Long (Louisiana), Olin Johnston (South Carolina), and Harry Byrd (Virginia), could be sympathetic to the Republican Old Guard.[96] This pattern now threatened to repeat itself.

The Great Debate was centered in the Senate, where Wherry's resolution was debated in committee from January 23, and where the Old Guard called Acheson for testimony and continuously grilled him, looking to put the administration's policies in disrepute. Acheson thought condescendingly of a number of the senators, which kept the pitch of the debate at the highest possible level of distrust and discord.[97]

The Old Guard focused on three questions. The first was whether the United States could afford to wage a militarized containment campaign on two fronts, Europe and Korea. The second was the strategic value of such a strategy when compared with other options. The third was the constitutionality of Truman's decision. The administration helped remove the thrust of much of the Old Guard's attack on the first issue by having Secretary Marshall announce, on February 15, 1951, that only four more divisions would be sent to Europe, one armored and three infantry, bringing the total U.S. Army force under NATO command to six divisions,[98] all part of the Seventh Army.[99] On the second issue, the administration had to counter charges made by Taft that any major war with the Soviets would be decided primarily by the exchange of nuclear weapons, and that sending any troops to Europe would be sentencing them to death for little or no strategic benefit. To make the case, Acheson, using language similar to that of NSC-68 and stressing key points the administration had come to adopt in the immediate aftermath of the North Korean attack, warned the Senate of the threat of proxy warfare, in which the Soviets could gamble on the success of a satellite attack in Europe, knowing that "the free nations could respond only with weapons of all-out general war, or not at all."[100] Acheson's appearances were buttressed by an administration publicity blitz that included numerous appearances by the popular and supportive Eisenhower in the Senate. The third question was never fully resolved, perhaps because Truman could not afford to wage unnecessary battles. The Senate decided to vote on the issue of troops to Europe, and added a clause that declared that the president would have to gain their approval before any extra forces could be sent overseas. This clause was termed the McClelland amendment, after its author. It was never clear how binding the amendment would have been, since Truman never forced a showdown on his constitutional authority. It is not even clear whether the Senate's vote on sending the troops to Europe issue was necessary, and Truman, not admitting that his actions were in any way unconstitutional, did not make a large issue out of the matter. The McClelland amendment passed by 49 to 43, and the resolution in favor of deployment passed on April 4, 1951 (coincidentally the second anniversary of the signing of the North Atlantic Treaty) by a vote of 69 to 21, with 6 abstentions, thus ending the Great Debate.

The course of the Great Debate had, in no small way, been governed by events in Korea. In the first few weeks of winter, as the Chinese counteroffensive continued to gain ground in Korea, the popularity of proposals for extreme change in American policy had been high. Calls for a withdrawal from Korea and western Europe, perhaps in addition to a buildup of forces domestically, were common. Another popular option was for a general war with China, not limited geographically or in war aims to the Korean peninsula. This was publicly considered by senators such as Wherry and Styles Bridges, a Republican from New Hampshire.[101] Many people were prone to swing from one view to the other, indicating how intensely frustrated the American body politic was with existing policy, which required patience, firmness, and endurance, all with little hope of immediate payoff. But the course of the Great Debate changed as the situation on the battlefield developed. The Chinese armies were slowed in January and thrown back in April. The Truman administration's popularity, which had been at rock bottom in December, was slowly on the upswing. The seeming inability of the United States to control events or contain the Communist armies was slowly replaced by a new faith that containment was working, deflating the Old Guard's hopes of leading a popular uprising against the administration.

THE EXPANSION OF AMERICAN GLOBAL POWER

The summer of 1950, when the Truman administration began its arms build-up, was a definitive moment in the growth of America's worldwide influence. Although the U.S. had been a wide-ranging actor on many parts of the world stage for generations, it was only at the time of the Korean War that the American government embarked on an effort to systematically employ American power on a large scale worldwide for an indefinite period.

The expansion of American influence can be seen in four respects. One was the expansion of U.S. military commitments through deployments of troops and forces. The second was the proliferation of treaty commitments obligating American forces in the event of war. The third measure was the change in American spending on aid programs, and the fourth was the growth of noncombat U.S. operations in foreign nations.

As for army deployments, besides the obvious and huge American deployment to central Europe, which outlasted the Cold War, there was a deployment to South Korea, where American troops are still stationed, to guard against a possible strike from the north. The air force saw an even more widespread deployment, with SAC acquiring the use of bases in the Azores, Iceland, Libya, Morocco, Newfoundland, Saudi Arabia, and Turkey, among other places.[102] For the navy, the decision to station the Seventh Fleet in the Straits of Taiwan would prove difficult to undo. The United States risked war over Taiwan in the crises over Quemoy and Matsu Islands in the 1950s, and, as late as the 1970s, found it necessary for credibility purposes to insist that Beijing recognize American interests on both sides of the Straits of Taiwan as a prerequisite for American recognition of the Beijing government.

As for security agreements that the United States signed, the Korean War set off a boom in alliances. In August and September 1951, at the San Francisco Conference, the United States and Japan signed security arrangements that would last longer than the Cold War. At the same conference, Australia, New Zealand, and the United States created a new tripartite alliance (ANZUS),[103] and the United States and the Philippines signed a bilateral defense pact.[104] The Republic of China, located on Taiwan, also signed a mutual security arrangement with the United States.[105] The fear of Communist encroachment in southeast Asia led to negotiations for a security agreement, which was accomplished in 1954 with the creation of the South East Asian Treaty Organization (SEATO), which allied the ANZUS states with Thailand, the Philippines, Pakistan, Britain, and France.[106] These commitments had been sought by some of the governments involved, such as Australia and the Philippines, before the Korean War, but the United States was unwilling to pursue them until the North Korean invasion radically altered American security planning.[107]

Aid increased both in scale and geographic scope. Nations that had previously been considered unsuitable for aid, such as Yugoslavia, were reconsidered.[108] The United States was drawn deeper into an aid race with the Soviet Union in what would come to be known in the 1960s as the Third World. By early 1951, the two superpowers were competing to provide famine relief to India.[109] These efforts helped lead to the Colombo plan for civilian aid to the nations of South Asia. The Truman administration also increased funding for the Point Four program, so named because it was the fourth point that Truman mentioned in his January 1949 inaugural address. The intensified sense of competition with the Soviet Union led to the September 1950 passage of a $26.9 million aid bill.[110] Eventually, Point Four would give much larger sums of technical assistance for agricultural projects in Latin America and elsewhere.

Even more important was military aid, which was given to fund the arms build-up among NATO powers, to bolster the ROK forces, and to help allies fighting Communist insurgencies, such as the Philippines, which was then fighting the Huk guerrillas.[111] The aid not only fleshed out the containment policy throughout the world, but it also helped fashion the anti-Soviet nations into a more united bloc, by building NATO and other allied armies around standard American types of equipment and weapons. Perhaps most importantly, military aid was a carrot dangled to help convince the allies to work toward a more rigorous defense posture, convincing them that it was possible to create a realistic deterrent to Soviet military action. Truman convinced Congress of the necessity of the aid programs by telling them that "the cost of supplying equipment through our aid programs is only a fraction of the cost of raising a comparable force ourselves."[112] Military aid had been given on a fairly large scale even before the United States decided to embark on its own arms build-up, but such programs became massive afterward. Within days of the North Korean invasion, Congress passed a $1.222 billion military aid bill, and the administration began shipping more weapons to the Philippines, Thailand, Burma, Indonesia, and the French authorities in Indochina.[113] The total amount of American equipment supplied to allies, from March 1950 to the end of June 1951, was 1.5 million tons, not including aircraft and naval vessels.[114] According to the Office of Defense Mobilization,

The bulk of this equipment, 930,000 tons, has been shipped to the countries of western Europe; 400,000 tons have gone to the Middle East, and 170,000 tons to the Far East. The major items of equipment already transferred include: 4,000 tanks and combat vehicles, 2,500 major artillery pieces, 16,500 general purpose vehicles, 850 aircraft, 150 naval vessels and small craft, small arms, mortars, recoilless rifles, bazookas, electronic equipment, [and] millions of rounds of ammunition.[115]

A training program was created to teach more than thirteen thousand foreigners how to use the equipment,[116] and American military missions were created where before there had been none, such as in Saudi Arabia. All of this occurred before the creation of the Mutual Security Program, which received $8.299 billion in fiscal year 1952, the first year of its operation.[117]

Between June 25, 1950, the start of the Korean War, and January 1, 1953, the United States government appropriated $15.9 billion for foreign military assistance.[118] This figure should be compared with the approximately $12 billion that the United States spent on the entire Marshall Plan during its three years of existence.

As for noncombat operations, it was the Korean War era that saw the spectacular growth in espionage on the Soviet Union, and in noncombat operations designed to weaken it. The U.S. Air Force established new listening posts, with technologically advanced radio interception equipment, along Soviet borders.[119] More boldly, it extended its covert overflights of the USSR, which continued throughout the 1950s, despite the casualties of those airmen whose planes were shot down.[120]

An even larger expansion took place at the CIA's Office of Policy Coordination (OPC), which was in charge of various overseas operations and was a forerunner of the Directorate of Operations. The OPC's budget grew from $4.7 million to $82 million between 1949 and 1952,[121] and OPC personnel in the same period increased from 302 to 2,812,[122] in addition to 3,142 overseas contract employees.[123] The CIA supported groups in Sovietized Europe that opposed Moscow's control and had more than forty covert operations ongoing in central Europe by 1952.[124] Once the Korean War began and MacArthur was forced to recant his order prohibiting CIA activity in his jurisdiction in the Pacific,[125] the agency began playing a major role in that region, in operations such as supporting organizations in mainland China that were fighting the consolidation of power by the Communists.[126] By that year, the OPC was operating out of 47 foreign stations, training guerrillas, engaging in covert actions, and laying the groundwork for the rest of the Cold War.

THE USSR INITIATES AN ARMS BUILD-UP, 1950–51

Although Stalin was advising the Chinese during the Korean War that "Americans are not capable of waging a large-scale war," and "Americans don't know how to fight,"[127] it seems such statements were made to keep the Chinese fighting in Korea, and to deflect Chinese requests for more Soviet military aid on better terms. The increase in Soviet military personnel at the time reveals more concretely the Soviet concern over American military expansion. There had been 2.8 million personnel in uniform in 1948. By the spring of 1953, there were nearly 6 million.[128]

The Americans had made little effort to disguise their build-up. On the contrary, the open nature of American society and the desire to use the arms build-up as a warning to the Soviets dictated that it would not be done in secret. The approximate size and deployments of American troop formations were mentioned in American newspapers of the day.

Anglo-American communications and memorandum of conference talks, particularly the Attlee-Truman meeting in Washington in early December 1950, were probably divulged to the Soviet leadership by Donald Maclean, the head of the British Foreign Office's American desk from November 1, 1950, and a spy for Moscow.[129] The senior intelligence officer for the Joint Chiefs of Staff would later estimate that "It would appear that very nearly all U.S.-U.K. high level planning information prior to 25 May 1951 [the date that Maclean, fearing that his cover was about to be blown, fled to the Soviet Union] must be considered compromised."[130] The Soviets also made use of the work of Kim Philby, the MI6 liaison officer in Washington.

Filtering the information from Maclean, Philby, and others through the ideological, cultural, and personal lenses through which the Kremlin leadership observed the United States, the Soviets seem to have concluded that the arms build-up was an event of great importance, one that threatened the security of the Soviet Union. Soviet concern can be seen by the Presidium of the Supreme Soviet's 1950 order to strengthen border defenses and create air defense lines along Soviet borders for early warning of air attack.[131] The stationing of twenty to twenty-five thousand troops in Siberia along the North Korean border in 1951, and the army maneuvers in East Germany in August 1952, seem to have sprung from a similar desire to prepare for all contingencies.[132] Soviet press coverage of the American arms build-up was voluminous, indicating that the Soviet government sought to warn its citizens that there would be shortages ahead as the Soviets attempted to match Western force increases.[133]

In addition to swelling in size, the Soviet army continued to make rapid strides in modernization. In 1950, the R-2 ballistic missile was completed; the Soviet rocket brigade, specializing in tactical surface to surface missiles, was upgraded to a division;[134] work started on the SS-3 surface to surface missile;[135] and development of the Mya-4 bomber, named "Bison" by the Americans, began.[136] In 1951, the Soviets developed their first computer,[137] and in the spring of 1952, Stalin ordered the production of 100 new tactical bombers.[138]

The Soviets also enhanced their networks of undercover operatives, most of them recruited from Communist parties. According to the memoir of Pavel Sudoplatov, one of the KGB officers in charge of organizing such activities, Stalin requested more effort to create an anti-American network in 1952, believing that many of the ethnic minorities of the United States would willingly work against America for nationalist reasons.[139]

Allied armies were not neglected. Stalin insisted, at a conference of European Communist leaders in Moscow in January 1951, that Communist nations increase military preparedness.[140] At the very least, Stalin may have wanted to break the Western alliance by provoking Western Europeans to make implausible demands on Washington for weapons and troops, and to distract the Americans from Korea, which otherwise could have become a wider war. The Czechoslovakian army alone almost doubled in 1950–51, from 140,000 troops to 250,000.[141] By the end of the Korean War, in July 1953, the total manpower of the armed forces of the Soviet satellite states in Europe had increased to approximately 1,500,000.[142] The cost was enormous, and it is possible that the anti-Soviet demonstrations in East Germany in June 1953 were partly a result of the heavy economic burden of this build-up. Stalin did not neglect Asia, telling Zhou En Lai in September 1952 that "China should turn into a [military] warehouse for Asia."[143]

The Soviets expanded their peace publicity offensives, using offers of negotiations and Soviet press attacks to blame the West for initiating the arms race,[144] and using diplomatic means, such as the offer of a new four-power conference, to try to interfere with the package agreement on sending U.S. troops to Europe and German rearmament.[145]

The Soviets knew, from Maclean's work, that the Americans were not willing to widen the war in Korea, either geographically through the bombing of China or tactically through the use of nuclear weapons. Although the Kremlin had to be careful to avoid any abrupt changes that would alter American plans the way the outbreak of the Korean War had, the Soviets could reasonably operate with the knowledge of the West's limits. They were therefore free to support China and North Korea's efforts to continue the war if doing so was judged to be in the Kremlin's best interests.

The Soviets seem to have felt that the end of the Korean War would allow a more rapid concentration of U.S. forces in central Europe, and until Stalin's death in March 1953, the Kremlin strongly encouraged the Chinese to continue fighting the Americans in Korea.[146]

CHAPTER 6

Actualization

FINANCING THE AMERICAN ARMS BUILD-UP

Two issues were paramount in the Truman administration's decisions on financing the arms build-up. The first involved the appropriate mix of debt, taxation, and domestic spending cuts. The second involved the use of government controls.

The first issue revealed a split between the law-making branches. The president's preference was obvious, given his dislike of debt, his attempts to raise taxes before the Korean War, and his interest in maintaining many of the post-New Deal programs that gave funds to farmers, the elderly, and other groups considered at risk of poverty.[1] Truman termed his attitude toward funding the arms build-up a pay-as-you-go stance. A majority in Congress preferred debt funding, as had been used during World War II. The result was a compromise: some taxes, some debt, and virtually no new major domestic spending programs.

Congress passed three small tax bills during the war but refused to pass Truman's large one in 1952.[2] During the course of the war, the federal government went from having small annual surpluses to running small annual deficits. Certain Fair Deal programs that Truman wanted were stillborn.

One reason the Fair Deal did not expand was a lack of attention, as can be seen in Truman's 1951 State of the Union address, which was devoted almost entirely to the war in Korea. Truman told a press conference that "first things come first, and our defense programs must have top priority."[3] The Fair Deal may have been politically dead in any case, given the nature of the Eighty-second Congress, elected in November 1950. The

Democratic majority was smaller, with a higher proportion of conservative southern Democrats. In the first week of the session, in January 1951,
92 Democrats and 152 Republicans in the new Congress demonstrated
their attitude by strengthening the power of the House Rules Committee
to prevent new legislation from reaching the floor.[4] The Rules Committee
was dominated by senior southern Democrats who rivaled the northern
Republicans in their opposition to reform. Certain key Truman proposals,
such as government health insurance for the elderly, were unlikely to pass,
and in pursuit of them, Truman might waste political capital, at a time
during the Great Debate when it was unclear if the arms build-up and
deployments to Europe would survive.

Thus, Truman had to choose between an almost certainly doomed attempt to build a Fair Deal coalition in Congress and an effort, for which
the odds were better, to salvage the internationalist coalition.[5] The arms
build-up, and in particular the arms build-up in central Europe, became
the crucial battle for Truman, and his legislative skills and political capital
were devoted toward that end.

On the second major issue, government controls, the Truman administration sought to dampen demand, so prices would not rise when the
supply of nonmilitary goods decreased. Increased taxation could have
achieved this goal to a large extent, but government controls had more
support in Congress.

Truman had already been an advocate of government controls on prices,
rents, interest rates, and wages. He had appealed for them even in peacetime, including an effort to regulate consumer credit in 1948.[6] The use of
controls was one of the key proposals of Truman's January 1949 State of
the Union address.[7] Truman's support for the controls seems to have been
based, at least partially, on his lifelong distrust of big business. He sometimes blamed inflation on "profiteering."[8]

Truman also feared that hoarding by a public afraid of future rationing
or inflation would create shortages and inflation. In his July 19, 1950, radio
address, timed to coincide with the submission of his Defense Production
Bill to Congress, Truman stated:

We have to fear only those shortages which we ourselves artificially create . . . If
prices should rise unduly because of excessive buying or speculation . . . I will not
hesitate to recommend rationing and price control . . . we need laws which will
insure prompt and adequate supplies for military and essential civilian use. I have
therefore recommended that the Congress give the government power to guide
the flow of materials into essential uses, to restrict their use for non-essential purposes, and to prevent the accumulation of unnecessary inventories.[9]

Although he was still hesitant about initiating controls on consumer
goods at this time, Truman was asking for, and would receive, the power

to enact such controls if, at a later date, he felt that the situation demanded it. The Truman administration created the Economic Stabilization Agency (ESA) to implement controls.

On January 26, 1951, the ESA announced a wage and price freeze to take effect on all but a handful of goods and services. The limits were based on average prices and wages for the period of December 19, 1950, to January 25, 1951. A few days later, the ESA clarified its position by allowing that set wage increases according to contract could occur as planned, despite the wage freeze. Price controls were placed on nearly all consumer products, with agricultural goods singled out for particular stringency. Controls on wages covered almost every occupation.

Controls were not unopposed. Republican opponents claimed that controls were a substitution of less efficient bureaucracy for more efficient capital markets, and that industrial planning agencies would cost more than they ever were able to save. Opponents also claimed that the real cause of inflation was excess printing of money, and that controls violated the rights of individuals to conclude contracts independent of government. They also feared that the controls would become permanent. However, the anti-controls group was as doomed as its counterpart anti-NATO group. The popularity of the war in its initial stages enabled Congress to grant the president significant discretionary authority at the outset of the war.

It was not just the war that led to controls. Many liberals had been demanding, even in peacetime, strict controls to prevent inflation and profiteering, management of industry to prevent duplication or shortages, and higher taxes on businesses to slow demand and prevent harmful new taxes on the working poor. Connecticut Governor Chester Bowles, Hubert Humphrey (Democratic Senator from Minnesota), and most of the liberal press (including the *New Republic, New York Post, Nation,* and *Progressive*) advocated the use of controls in 1950.[10]

On December 15, 1950, Truman created an umbrella agency, the Office of Defense Mobilization (ODM), to oversee regulatory agencies, boards, and offices. Charles E. Wilson, the chief executive of General Electric and former chairman of Truman's advisory committee on civil rights, was picked as its head.[11] In addition, Wilson headed the National Advisory Board on Mobilization Policy, a group that, beginning on April 9, 1951, met once a month in the presence of Truman.[12] The board discussed manpower problems, wages, trade with Communist nations, legislation dealing with controls, and procurement issues.

Another voice on mobilization policy was the National Security Resources Board (NSRB). The NSRB had been created in the 1947 National Security Act, the same measure that had created the National Security Council. Like the NSC, the NSRB had a multidepartment composition.

Also like the NSC, the NSRB was designed to be a forum where various bureaucracies created working papers.[13]

Early in the war, Congress elevated the status of the NSRB to give it power to modify production in various ways. Truman had appointed W. Stuart Symington to chair the NSRB. Symington, a former secretary of the air force and senator from Missouri, was regarded as liberal on domestic policies. He would become an intense hawk in the administration during the Korean War.

Spin-offs from these organizations led to a new bureaucracy rivaling the alphabet agencies of the New Deal. Truman formed the Health Resources Advisory Committee (HRAC) to advise the NSRB,[14] the Wage Stabilization Board (WSB) and the Office of Price Stabilization (OPS) to act in concert with the ESA, and a number of ODM committees, such as the ODM Committee on Manpower Policy. These organizations were separate from the various Department of Defense boards that dealt with procurement.

As time passed, the controls implemented by these agencies became as unpopular as those of World War II. Despite the controls, inflation increased dramatically in some sectors of the economy: a report by the Office of the Secretary of Defense to Congress in December 1950 claimed that inflation had already cut the value of the sums appropriated for the military since the beginning of the Korean War by approximately $3 billion.[15] A Senate report found that "eleven basic raw materials used by the military show an average increase in price from April 1950 to December 1950 of 72.3 percent."[16]

As early as April 1951, Congress, against the president's wishes, amended the Defense Production Act to require higher price ceilings[17] as an incentive to producers to make more consumer goods available. Truman opposed the changes, feeling that the threat of inflation was still severe and that price increases at a time when wages were still set low would be unfairly cruel to the poor.[18] But his opposition might have contributed to his increasing unpopularity in polls taken towards the end of his presidency.

THE ARMS BUILD-UP AND THE AMERICAN ECONOMY

The immediate impact of the increase in government spending was to drive up production, employment, and inflation. In constant prices, gross national product grew by more than 5 percent from the second half of 1950 to the first half of 1951. Industrial production increased 10 percent in the same period, unemployment fell to the lowest level since World War II, hours worked per week increased from 40.5 hours to 40.8 hours, living costs increased 9 percent, and wholesale prices increased 16 percent.[19] Increased hiring from the war boom more than offset the negative effects on job growth that may have been caused by tax increases and falling consumer products sales.

The increase in production was, at least partially, a continuation of a peacetime upturn that began in late 1949 and carried through early 1950. Military orders were added to this small boom in the second half of 1950. Much of the financing for the new orders stemmed from increases in the federal debt, postponing the potential negative economic impact of taxation. The result, as shown by an April 1951 survey by the Federal Trade Commission and the Securities and Exchange Commission, was a record business year in 1950 (the previous record was 1948). The 17 percent gain in corporate sales easily surpassed the 13 percent increase in costs, leading to a 61 percent gain in pretax income and a 42 percent gain in posttax income. Annual corporate income jumped from $14.4 billion to $23.2 billion.[20]

Perhaps because of the nature of weapons procurement, in which competitive bidding did not exist on certain technical goods and prices could be based on a cost-plus-profit basis, rather than on a market price, those corporations manufacturing military goods, and the workers they hired, could benefit immensely. The aviation industry, steel producers, communications and radar manufacturers, and certain other firms broke profit records. Lockheed, Bell Aircraft, General Electric, Boeing, and United Aircraft were particularly successful in winning contracts.[21] Lockheed saw its backlog of orders double in the first six weeks of the Korean conflict.[22] The value of aircraft production in the United States increased from less than $2 billion in 1949 to approximately $8.5 billion in 1953, and employment in the industry rose from 281,000 to 779,100.[23] It was a similarly rosy time for producers of certain strategic materials, of which the military's consumption rose from $1 billion during the 1946–50 period to $7 billion in the 1950–53 period.[24] In the last six months of 1950, the Army Ordnance Tank and Automotive Center in Detroit placed more than $3 billion in orders for vehicles and spare parts, more than the total amount for the entire first year of World War II.[25]

Economic spillover from defense spending was distributed disproportionately. Because of many factors, including the existence of right-to-work laws, and pressure from the federal government, which sought to minimize the risk of foreign attack through the dispersal of facilities, manufacturers had, during and after World War II, located many new plants in the South and West, away from the old manufacturing heartland of the Northeast and the Midwest.[26] McDonnell-Douglas, North American Aircraft, and Hughes Aircraft all had plants in California, and Lockheed manufactured in California and Georgia. Boeing was in Washington, and Temco, Chance-Vought, Convair, and Bell Helicopters had plants in Texas.[27] The arms build-up hastened the trend toward enhancing the eco-

nomic power of the South and West. Southern states also benefited from
the increased use of domestic military facilities, a disproportionate number of which were in that region. Southern congressional representatives,
being elected in a region that was only legally bipartisan, could count on
long terms of service. This situation gave them committee and subcommittee chairmanships, strengthening their pork-barreling abilities. It was
natural, given the Southern military tradition, that their priorities should
include the creation of military bases. The military found that the weather
allowed easy year-round personnel training. In 1950, 13 out of the 14
permanent bases of the Tactical Air Command were in states that had
been in the Confederacy, and one was in California. Among the Strategic
Air Command bases east of the Mississippi River, none were farther north
than Savannah, Georgia.[28]

The impact on firms not producing goods or services for the military
was less salutary. Such firms still had to pay the excess profits tax. Although they might benefit from having their labor costs held down by the
controls, there were many uncontrolled rising costs, such as the costs of
capital and imports, even though it was often illegal to raise prices. As
was the case with other examples of price controls, manufacturers often
found that it was possible, in a market of excess demand, to decrease the
quality of items and still sell them. This lowering of the quality of goods
happened at all stages of the production process, hurting manufacturers
who relied on other firms for parts as much as it hurt the consumer.

For automobile manufacturers, the growth of military contracts was
more than offset by the difficulties of competing in a civilian market in
which car prices were controlled, steel scarce, and disposable income
nearly stable. In January 1951, Chrysler, Studebaker, and Packard announced production cuts of approximately 20 percent.[29] The same month,
Chevrolet and Lincoln cut production.[30] In June, General Motors and Studebaker announced temporary shutdowns of plants, affecting more than
164,000 employees. On July 9, Chrysler announced an indefinite layoff of
20,000 workers.[31]

When adjusted for inflation, the nondefense economy was smaller after
the build-up began than before. Inflation, as always, was particularly cruel
to people whose wages or pensions were not indexed to price increases.
Even Truman admitted that "more than half the families of the nation had
no income gains between early 1950 and early 1951, and almost one-fifth
suffered actual declines."[32]

The increased taxes and inflation ate much of the extra income the
American public may have earned. Disposable real income in the fourth
quarter of 1952 was hardly higher than it had been in the first quarter of
1950, even though the economy had swelled during the time leading up
to the war, and had continued to grow once the war began.[33] As Director
of Defense Mobilization Wilson explained in January 1953,

Average income, after adjustment for changes in the buying power of the dollar, has risen by 3 percent before taxes [since the beginning of the war]. After deducting the increased taxes necessary to help pay for the defense program, the average disposable income has increased slightly, from an annual rate of $1,297 in the last quarter before Korea to an estimated $1,337 in the quarter just ended.[34]

A 3 percent rise in almost three years was significantly less than mean increases for most of the twentieth century.

Before the Korean War and the arms build-up, the United States was a net exporter. During the war, it became a net importer. The period witnessed increases in raw material imports to build war goods, but no corresponding increases in production of consumer goods for export. The increase in arms shipments, accounting for only approximately 6 percent of total exports in October 1950, was not enough to make up for the slack in other goods.[35]

During the mobilization period, raw materials accounted for approximately two-thirds of American imports.[36] The vast majority of these goods were earmarked for military use. The allocation of steel, copper, and aluminum for the consumer sector was decreased by as much as 60 percent during the war.[37]

American imports of lead grew almost 25 percent from 1949 to 1950.[38] American rubber imports went from $41 million in September 1950 to $60 million the next month,[39] and American copper imports nearly doubled in the same period.[40] Much of these dollar increases in purchases resulted from the inflation that hit these commodities particularly hard because of the arms build-ups throughout the world.

The inflation in other goods, although comparatively small, was another cause of the trade deficit, at least with nations that had lower inflation. As the British Foreign Office concluded, "the domestic inflation [in the U.S.] may well make it easier for United Kingdom exporters to find markets for their goods in the United States."[41] Between 1949 and 1951, the United States shifted from a net exporter of steel to Europe to a net importer.[42]

Another factor contributing to the trade deficit was the administration's use of controls to decrease exports of materials considered vital to defense. These included cotton and certain metals.[43]

Much capital and brain power was invested in building war plants, crowding out nondefense industries that might have had more profitable export capabilities than defense goods ever had. Defense industries had great needs for importing certain raw materials, but political limitations prevented unlimited sale of military equipment abroad.

Another effect of the U.S. trade deficit was the expansion of dollar supplies outside the United States, which were either invested in American banks or in the growing international dollar markets. This expansion was made more possible by the Bretton Woods arrangements of the World War II era, which had made the dollar the key currency in the world exchange system.

The arms build-up also led to a labor shortage. The war spending drove unemployment down, and the controls on wages made it difficult for firms to hire workers away from existing jobs by offering increased pay. One means of addressing the problem was by importing labor from Latin America. Negotiations were made between the State Department and various Central and South American governments in San Francisco in December 1950, which led to agreements on the subject.[44]

Leaders of organized labor objected to many wage freezes, complaining that the combination of accelerated government purchases of defense products and fixed low wages were allowing big industry to engage in ruthless profiteering at the expense of the worker. Labor leaders' objections led to them refusing to participate in government planning boards and to strikes, which Truman met with force.

When choosing planning board members, Truman split the seats along what he considered politically pragmatic lines: one-third of members from union leadership, one-third from business leadership, and one-third from government. Union leaders, suspecting the other two sides were lined up against them, staged a walkout in the spring of 1951, after the majority sided against them on several important wage disputes. But the unions may have underestimated the impact that the mobilization campaign had on the president. Phillip Murray, a president of the Congress of Industrial Organizations, had once claimed that Truman was the "best friend labor ever had in the White House."[45] Union leaders probably assumed that Truman had to be somewhat sympathetic to union needs because organized labor contributed so many votes for Democrats, but when unions in industries considered important to the arms build-up struck rather than accept the proposals of the Wage Stabilization Board, Truman acted against the strikers.

The first time he did so was over the August 1951 walkout in the copper mining and smelting industry, when 58,000 workers struck, cutting the production of copper, a key war good, by 3,000 tons a day.[46] One of the key unions was suspected by some of having Communist sympathizers in its leadership, which heightened concerns about national security.[47] The Truman administration forced the strikers to obey a federal injunction to return to work while their contract was negotiated under the terms of the Taft-Hartley Act, a piece of legislation much resented by unions.[48]

The biggest strike was in 1952 in the steel industry. Approximately 600,000 workers stopped going to the plants on April 7.[49] This strike occurred at a critical juncture of the arms build-up, since fiscal year 1952 was the second half of a two-year build-up that had initially been designed to take four years. Perhaps influenced by the British nationalization of steel, Truman attempted to place the steel industry under the federal government the day after the strike began, ordering the workers to show up to work. The army occupied the major steel mills and flew the American flag from the buildings.

Before his decision, Truman had asked the chief justice of the Supreme Court, Fred Vinson, whether it was legal. Vinson told him it was, but later found himself in a minority on his own court (supposedly a sympathetic court composed of FDR and Truman appointees), which ruled 6 to 3 against the president's authority in the matter. Truman chose not to provoke a constitutional crisis and backed down. The strike lasted until July 25.[50] The department of defense mobilization estimated that "20 million ingot tons of steel" were not produced because of the stoppage, and reported that "As a result of the loss of production, steel output in 1952 is expected to reach only 90 million tons, 14 percent less than in 1951."[51] A previous report by the same department had estimated Soviet steel production at 39 million tons a year.[52] Although "the impact of the loss of [American steel] production has been partially absorbed by the consumption of inventories, which at the beginning of the stoppage were at an abnormally high level," the strike meant "that 20 to 30 percent of the deliveries of hard goods" and "35 percent of the larger caliber ammunition" would not be completed.[53]

THE REARMED U.S. FORCES

The extent of the American arms build-up can be seen using figures provided by the director of Defense Mobilization[54]:

Table 6.1
U.S. Military Expansion

	Before June 25, 1950	January 1, 1953
Army Divisions	10	21
Marine Divisions	2	3
Air Force Wings	48	Approximately 100
Navy Warships	Slightly More Than 200	Slightly More Than 400
Carrier Groups	7	16

But these numbers only reflect half of the arms build-up. They represent the quantitative differences, rather than the qualitative development of new military equipment. While much of the ground fighting in Korea was done with World War II leftovers (this was true for both sides), the United States was slowly preparing a new fighting force, both in conventional and nuclear forces.

In the United States, the period from June 25, 1950 to January 1, 1953 saw 7 new models of combat aircraft, 8 new models of guns, 8 new models of ammunition, 10 new models of combat vehicles, and 15 new models of radar equipment come into production.[55]

The first step was the conversion of factories. At the end of World War II, the United States government placed many of the factories it had built to produce war goods into either a Departmental Reserve category (run by the Department of Defense) or a National Industrial Reserve category. Those in the latter category were sold, but only under the stipulation that they had to be maintained so as to allow the government to reconvert them to military production within 120 days.[56] Out of 438 plants, 354 were reconverted during 1950–51.[57] The delivery of end-items and construction activity went from a half-billion dollars per month before Korea, to $1.5 billion per month by June 1951, to $4 billion per month by June 1952.[58] The rate of orders coming in exceeded the output of finished goods from late 1950 until 1952.[59] Between the fourth quarter of 1950 and the third quarter of 1951, manufacturers' shipments of military transportation equipment more than doubled, shipments of electrical machinery to the military increased by more than 600 percent, shipments of fabricated metal products to the military increased more than 900 percent, and shipments of nonelectrical machinery to the military increased by more than 1,000 percent.[60]

By June 1951, the ODM could claim that "the Department of Defense has programmed nearly $6 billion for additional plant expansion. Of this amount, about $2.5 billion is sponsored by the Army, $1.6 billion by the Navy, and $1.8 billion by the Air Force. Nearly half the planned expansion of facilities under this program is to serve for the production of aircraft, nearly 20 per cent for tank-automotive production, and the remainder is for producing guided missiles, weapons, ammunition, and other items."[61]

The average workweek in aircraft plants increased from 40 to 45 hours,[62] but this increase still wasn't enough to catch up to new orders. New plants were created. Production worker employment in the aircraft and aircraft parts industry increased from 185,000 to 350,000 in the first 11 months of the Korean War.[63] Deliveries increased by two-thirds in the first year of the war, and had to be tripled in the second year of the war just to catch up to demand.[64] In the month of June 1952 alone, the aircraft industry delivered 768 warplanes.[65]

These were not just any warplanes. Jet engines, electronics, and new alloys had revolutionized aircraft construction. The F-86 had more than 700 percent more horsepower than the P-51, one of the best fighter aircraft of World War II. Whereas the P-51 had a maximum speed of 440 miles per hour, weighed 9,340 pounds, and could climb to a maximum altitude of 36,491 feet, the F-86 had a maximum speed of more than 671 miles per hour, weighed 13,885 pounds, and could climb to approximately 50,000 feet.[66] The average airframe weight of a warplane in 1940 was 3,850 pounds, while in 1951 the average weight was approximately 9,000 pounds.[67]

Other commonly produced warplanes were the air force's F-84 fighter bomber, and navy fighters such as the F10F, which came into production in early 1953.[68] The new fighters replaced the solid F-80, which was responsible for the majority of enemy kills in the first six months of the Korean War,[69] when the Communist forces relied heavily on swarms of inferior Soviet-made Yak fighters.[70] The twin-jet F7U Cutlass was one of the primary carrier-based fighters.[71] Another jet-powered, carrier-based fighter, the Phantom, was designed during the Korean War arms build-up and went into production shortly afterward.[72] The first supersonic American fighter planes, the F-101 and the F-102, were designed during this time and put into production in 1954.[73] Aircraft manufacturers also researched using titanium to replace steel, [74] and, because airborne operations were thought to be likely in a future major war, introduced the C-119. It could carry 64 fully equipped paratroopers and had a range of more than 2,000 miles with a 9-ton load.[75] Even bigger transports were in the works by 1951.[76]

Besides aircraft, tank production was another big item. In the early stages of the Korean War, the U.S. Army felt it suffered from a paucity of armored vehicles. The only operational tanks in East Asia were M-24 Chaffee reconnaissance tanks, which did not have effective guns[77] and which were destroyed in large numbers by the Soviet T-34's.[78] These tanks were soon augmented by World War II-era M-4A3E8 Sherman medium tanks that army ordnance in Tokyo hurriedly rebuilt.[79] Some M-26 Pershing medium tanks and M-46 Patton tanks were shipped to the front in July and August 1950,[80] bringing the total number of U.S. battle tanks in Korea to a little more than 500 by the end of August 1950.[81] While this was enough to give the UN forces tank superiority in the theater (the M-46 Pattons were particularly good at destroying the T-34),[82] it meant a serious depletion of all American tanks elsewhere. It was obvious to the administration that if the nation was to engage in the arms build-up and worldwide deployment that was planned, tanks would have to be one of the first items specified for production.

By March 1951, three months ahead of schedule, the first tanks ordered in the aftermath of the outbreak of hostilities came off the production line.[83] The plan was for a 1,600 percent increase in tank production in the two years following June 1950.[84] The T-41 light tank, designed to destroy the enemy's medium tanks, came into production in July 1951, with a 76mm gun, and a maximum speed of 35 miles per hour.[85] For medium tanks, the M-47, one of the main production line tanks, was replaced by the T-48, which first came off the assembly line in May 1952.[86] The T-48, for which the Chrysler Corporation was the main producer, had heavier armor, an improved turret, longer cruising range, and a lower silhouette than the M-47.[87] The tank, in the beginning, had a weight of 45 tons and mounted a 90mm gun.[88] For heavy tanks, work on a 55-ton model, with a 120mm gun, began during the war.[89] New improvements gave all tanks greater fire control.[90]

There were scores of other developments in conventional forces. One was the use of helicopters on a regular basis. A January 1951 *Wall Street Journal* article described the growth of the helicopter production business: "Before Korea, U.S. manufacturers hadn't built more than 1,000 of these planes all told-including all the military 'copters produced in World War Two. Today producers have orders for close to 600 of them and there's talk of hundreds more. Producers had a $20 million a year business just before the Korean fighting started. Since then well over $150 million of orders have blossomed on their books."[91] The main helicopters produced during the period were the Bell H-13, Hiller H-23, Sikorsky HRS-1, and Sikorsky HO3S-1.[92] Approximately one in seven American casualties in the Korean War was evacuated by helicopter,[93] and the so-called choppers also rescued downed pilots from behind enemy lines or in the water.[94] The navy ordered its first purpose-designed submarine-spotting helicopters in the early Korean War period.[95]

Another development was the expansion in the use of napalm (an acronym for naphthenic and palmitic acids), a jellied gasoline. Before Korea, napalm had been used in flamethrowers and only rarely in bombs or in antitank combat, but during the arms build-up its use and production were made common. According to one history, "During the course of the [Korean] war Far East Air Force alone expended 32,257 tons of napalm,"[96] mostly as part of the massive strategic bombing campaign that killed perhaps hundreds of thousands of North Koreans.[97]

Given the focus the Soviets were thought to be placing on armored attacks, antitank warfare was critical. Two weeks before the Korean campaign, the first production of ammunition for the new 3.5-inch bazooka began.[98] This weapon went into mass production with the beginning of the war, replacing the 2.36-inch model that had proved ineffective at stopping tanks. Despite the larger barrel size, the new bazooka weighed less,[99] had an effective firing range of 450 yards against tanks, could penetrate 6 to 8 inches of armor, and still be easily operated by one man.[100] The 105mm recoilless rifle, another tank-killer, replaced the 75mm model.[101]

There were also many smaller advances. A new entrenching tool replaced the shovel, and a new body armor, using plastic armor plates made of laminated layers of glass cloth filaments bonded under pressure to form a hard surface, called Doron, was produced, although its use was limited.[102]

The navy began an immense warship-building program. In the second half of 1950 alone, the navy commissioned 2 battleships, 2 heavy cruisers, 2 light aircraft carriers, 4 heavy aircraft carriers, 6 submarines, 7 escort carriers, 8 oilers, 13 frigates, 42 minesweepers, 54 destroyers, and a large number of transports, cargo ships, and landing craft,[103] in addition to commissioning vessels from the reserve fleet.[104] In the period from June 24 to October 3, 1950, alone, the navy recommissioned 62 vessels.[105] During the Korean War, construction began on a new class of super carriers, beginning with the 76,000-ton USS *Forrestal*.[106]

There were other major navy projects. Research began for an atomic-powered submarine during the arms build-up,[107] and by the spring of 1952, Truman was able to celebrate the laying of the keel at a Groton, Connecticut, shipyard.[108] The navy also researched a sonar system for mine location, automatic diving and depth control systems for submarines, a gyrocompass that could be used in latitudes above 70 degrees, improved electrical power systems on aircraft carriers, and a new anti-submarine torpedo to be launched from helicopters, named the Mark 43.[109] In a multinational effort involving the Canadians and the British, the U.S. Navy also worked toward creating antitorpedo devices, which included research of towed explosives and noise-making decoys.[110] The navy increased production of existing jet aircraft, such as the F3D-1 Skyknight, the F9F-4 Panther, and the F9F-2 Banshee,[111] and worked toward equipping all its carriers with jet aircraft.[112]

In addition to funding all the new combat forces, the U.S. arms build-up financed new early warning systems and a vast expansion and consolidation of the military's signals intelligence.

The Truman administration developed the Radar Defense Organization (RDO), designed to protect the United States from air attack. Although the Soviets did not yet have bases near enough or bombers with range enough to attack the United States (Alaska was not yet a state), both the military and the general public were concerned about the future. The RDO had barely developed beyond the planning stage before the Korean War, but by the end of 1950, 13 aircraft control and warning groups, each with radar, were in service.[113] To coordinate the efforts of these groups, and to give greater priority at the planning level to radar alert and interception of enemy aircraft, the air force created the Air Defense Command on January 1, 1951.[114] Not to be outdone, the army soon created its own antiaircraft command.[115]

In 1952, the Truman administration decided to construct a Distant Early

Warning (DEW) line of radar installations across Alaska and northern Canada.[116] Although the air force was not optimistic about its ability to destroy incoming planes, the DEW line would, according to plan, give enough warning to enable bombers to take off and disperse, maintaining a strong nuclear retaliatory capability.[117]

During the Korean War, the inability of American intelligence personnel to integrate into Korean society, combined with the clever use of disinformation by the North Koreans, made human intelligence-gathering of limited use. In its place, the military funded improved technical spying abilities, in fields such as radio interception and aerial photo reconnaissance. Because of the need to coordinate this growing empire and the need to prevent bickering among the services, the Armed Forces Security Agency (AFSA), which was supposed to help the services cooperate but had little authority, was remodeled into a new organization, the National Security Agency (NSA).[118] The NSA, the existence of which was secret, began operations on November 4, 1952, a date intentionally chosen since it was election day, when the attention of the press would be elsewhere.[119]

THE EXPANSION OF THE AMERICAN NUCLEAR ARSENAL AND DELIVERY SYSTEMS

During the arms build-up coinciding with the Korean War, the United States increased its stockpile of nuclear weapons, invested large sums in improving the means to deliver them, enhanced the quality of existing atomic weapons by making more productive use of fissionable materials, and, as a result of the hydrogen bomb research program that had been an ongoing concern since before the Korean War, detonated the first experimental fusion bomb.

As we have seen, Truman approved large spending increases for the nuclear establishment. Two major increases in the first year of the Korean War totaled more than $3.5 billion.

Two new major plants were built: a $500 million gaseous diffusion plant in Paducah, Kentucky, and a $1.2 billion Savannah River production plant in South Carolina.[120] The construction of the two plants required 11 percent of annual U.S. nickel production, 33 percent of annual U.S. hydrofluoric acid production, and 34 percent of annual U.S. stainless steel production.[121] The two plants consumed more electricity than the Tennessee Valley Authority and the Hoover and Grand Coulee Dams could have provided had they been devoted to the purpose.[122] To make use of the plants, the United States made arrangements with foreign producers of uranium, such as Canada, South Africa, and the Belgian Congo, and subsidized mineral exploration, helping produce extraordinary new quantities of weapons-grade uranium domestically and in Canada.[123] The American stockpile of nuclear weapons, which consisted of 250 bombs at the end of 1949, grew to 298 bombs in 1950; 832 in 1952; 1,161 in 1953; 1,630 in 1954; and 2,422 in 1955.[124] By 1962, the number would be 27,100.[125]

The first successful American laboratory test of fusion occurred on May 8, 1951.[126] The first successful American test of a boosted fission weapon occurred just 16 days later,[127] and the first fusion explosion, the MIKE test, done at Eniwetok Atoll in the central Pacific, occurred on November 1, 1952.[128] By March 1, 1954, with the CASTLE test of the Bravo bomb, the United States had a hydrogen weapon small enough to be loaded into a bomber.

The military believed that improving the means of delivering atomic weapons to the site of attack was just as important as augmenting the destructiveness of atomic weapons. Means already existed in some quantity, since the strategic bombing fleet had received more attention than any other part of the American military in the period from Hiroshima to the beginning of the Korean War, when American military doctrine gave primary emphasis to atomic weapons. However, the fleet was judged insufficient for the new nuclear capabilities, and a modernization of the SAC fleet began.

In early 1950, the air force had 3 bomber groups equipped with B-36s, 12 bomber groups with either B-29s or B-50s, and 5 strategic reconnaissance groups.[129] The B-29 was the oldest bomber, and its 4,000-mile range would have limited its ability to attack sites deep in the interior of the Soviet Union in the event of war; the B-50, derived from the B-29, was little better.[130] Only the B-36 bomber was considered suitable, given its 8,000-mile range.[131] Its development was the achievement of a long effort to create a true intercontinental bomber. That effort began early in World War II, when American planners were concerned about the possibility of a German conquest of Britain and the rest of Europe, which might have necessitated transoceanic sorties.[132] The number of B-36s in SAC grew from 38 at the end of 1950 to 185 by the end of 1953.[133] The air force, however, disliked the B-36 because of the altitude at which it flew.[134]

In 1951, the B-36s began to be replaced by B-47s,[135] which would be the main medium-range American bomber of the 1950s. By the end of 1952, the United States was producing B-47s at the rate of one per day, and assembly lines in two new plants were nearing completion.[136] By the end of 1953, SAC had 329 B-47s,[137] and by 1959 there were more than 2,500 in service, constituting the vast majority of the SAC fleet.[138] The design of the B-47 began in 1945, but development was slow until the Korean War, when it was rushed into mass production. It was the first all-jet bomber,[139] and its introduction truly marked the beginning of a new era, in which the World War II-era bombers and their derivatives were replaced by aircraft of a new level of expense and technology. One ODM report asserted that:

A B-47 is made up of some 72,000 parts exclusive of nuts, bolts, and rivets. The B-47 requires 40 miles of wiring compared to 10 miles for the B-29. A B-47 contains over 1,500 electrical tubes. The wing skin must be tapered in thickness throughout its entire length from five-eighths inch at the body joint to three-sixteenths inch at wing tip. The first B-47 plane required 3,464,000 engineering man-hours compared to 85,000 man-hours for the first production model of the B-17. Equipment and material in the new planes are tested to operate in temperatures ranging from 65 degrees below zero to 160 degrees above.[140]

Three other important bombers were created during the arms build-up. One was the supersonic B-58, which would eventually surpass the B-47 in performance.[141] The B-57, a British-designed bomber, came into American production in 1953.[142] The B-52, which would eventually become a principal long-range bomber of the American fleet, and was still an important part of operations during the Iraq War in 2003, was conceived during the Truman administration and deployed in June 1955.[143] It was a high-altitude bomber propelled by eight jet engines, and was distinguished by its in-flight refueling capacities.

SAC grew into a juggernaut during the arms build-up. At the end of 1950, SAC had 16 permanent bases, all in the United States.[144] By the beginning of 1952, SAC had 19 bases domestically and 1 abroad, and by the end of that year SAC was using 30 bases domestically and 11 abroad.[145] The number of SAC bombers would leap from 668 at the end of 1951 to 2,500 bombers in the mid-1950s, to more than 3,000 by 1959.[146] Personnel numbers grew from 85,473 at the end of 1950 to 170,982 by the end of 1953.[147] Aerial refueling measures had been perfected by 1950.[148] During the Korean War era, SAC engaged in a never-ending effort to keep bombers in the sky at all times. The air force claimed that this was done to minimize the possibility that an enemy would believe that it could destroy the atomic capabilities of the United States in a series of sudden strikes. Potential enemies, according to the air force, would know that even in the event of an atomic attack on the United States, the Americans would still possess the ability to retaliate with weapons of mass destruction. Critics of the air force, such as the other two major services, claimed that the air force favored strategic bombing because it allowed them to play first fiddle, rather than engage in support actions for other services.[149]

The desire of the older services to prevent themselves from becoming outmoded, combined with the development of technologies enabling the miniaturization of atomic weapons, led to new means of delivering atomic weapons. The navy created an atomic bomb so small that it could be carried by a single-seat navy Douglas A4D-1 Skyhawk attack jet.[150] It also produced atomic depth charges.[151] The army, also seeking its own niche in nuclear affairs, designed and constructed a 280mm cannon capable of firing nuclear projectiles, which it successfully tested in the Nevada desert in May 1953.[152] Although the cannon was deployed to Germany, it never became a critical part of America's nuclear delivery capabilities, partly because it was so unwieldy that it occasionally tipped over.[153] The army also developed the Davy Crockett, described by one historian as "essentially an atomic hand grenade."[154] However, the real wave of the future for all the services, and the greatest beneficiary from the development of small warheads, was to be rocketry.

In 1950, the Department of Defense created the director of guided missiles position, to advise the military on improvements in missile research, production, and development.[155] By September 1951, the U.S. military was experimenting with guided missiles,[156] and by June 1952, the first three American guided missiles were in assembly line production: the Nike, a liquid-fuel-powered surface-to-air missile; the Corporal, a liquid-fuel-powered surface-to-surface missile; and the Matador, a jet-engine-powered surface-to-surface missile.[157] The connection to the improvements in nuclear energy was obvious. Tactical use of rockets with atomic warheads was possible after the miniaturization of fission weapons, and strategic use of rockets would be feasible after the production of fusion warheads. A rocket's high average distance from the target meant that most atomic weapons would fall miles away from their designated targets. The enormous cost and slow schedules involved in atomic bomb production led the military to prefer bombers to missles in the era before work progressed on the hydrogen bomb. But even before the fusion weapon was created, analysts realized that the enormous killing radius of the H-bomb made it possible to miss a target by 10 miles and still destroy it.[158] Consequently, the United States produced intermediate-range nuclear-capable missiles in the mid-1950s and intercontinental-range ballistic missiles in 1958 (a year after the Soviets). The United States also produced the USS George Washington, a Polaris submarine equipped with 144 nuclear missiles that could be launched from under the ocean surface, and had it at sea in 1960.

The American military also continued to improve its understanding of operations in a nuclear battlefield. This insight was sometimes gained at the expense of significant, if delayed, health hazards, such as when soldiers were exposed to atomic blasts from measured distances during experimental nuclear tests in the Nevada desert in November 1951.[159]

1953–54: EISENHOWER AND RESTRICTIONS ON MILITARY SPENDING

Eisenhower, after resigning from the military in the summer of 1952, was elected president in November 1952, inaugurated in January 1953, and was commander in chief at the time of the final armistice in Korea in July 1953.

When working for the Truman administration, Eisenhower's positions on military funding had been quite moderate. As we have seen, he had been quite willing to work for the Truman administration in cutting defense budgets during 1948–49, with the exception of some minor disagreement over one of Truman's 1950 ceilings. He had followed the general consensus on spending.[160] After Korea began, Eisenhower again seems to have been a part of the consensus. He fully supported the build-up that he supervised in Europe. In a letter that he wrote for Truman but never sent, Ike even recommended an expansion of conscription and consideration of direct controls, which had not yet been implemented.[161] According to his aide, General Andrew Goodpaster, the only thing in NSC-68 that Eisenhower disagreed with was the contention that there would be a year of maximum danger in the early 1950s.[162]

There was little in the presidential campaign that could reliably predict Eisenhower's attitude toward military armaments. On the one hand, Ike pleased the Old Guard Republicans by making a campaign promise that became known as the Morningside agreement. It was a pledge with Senator Taft to reduce the defense budget by $5 billion a year.[163] On the other hand, Ike's team, during the same campaign, used rhetoric indicating that an Eisenhower administration would consider the use of a rollback strategy of removing Soviet influence from eastern Europe.[164]

Once in office, the Eisenhower administration fashioned the New Look foreign policy. The New Look, theoretically, was different from the Truman policy of containing Soviet influence through the maintenance of a large standing army deployed globally. The New Look was based on building more cost-effective nuclear weapons instead of armies, and entailed a willingness to threaten the use of nuclear weapons in virtually any situation. In its reliance on a nuclear deterrent, the New Look was similar to certain policies from the days of the American atomic monopoly.

The desire for a de-emphasis on standing armies was not novel. During the Korean era arms build-up, some analysts, such as Senator McMahon, chairman of the Senate Atomic Energy Committee; General Curtis LeMay, head of SAC; and Thomas Finletter, secretary of the air force, had advocated such a stance. McMahon had gone so far as to claim, in 1951, that if atomic weapons were mass-produced, the cost of each would be less than that of a medium tank, and that concentration on nuclear production could lead to savings of $30 billion per year by the end of a three-year period.[165] The idea of a larger nuclear deterrent had even been part of the Truman administration's policy, as we have seen. The difference between Eisenhower and Truman, in their attitudes toward the role of nuclear weapons, lay in clarity and emphasis. The new president was more amenable to their use in a wider variety of situations.[166] Throughout the post-Nagasaki period of the Truman administration, the military planned to use atomic weapons in the event of a major war with the Soviets. However, the issue of exactly when they would be brought into use in other situations was never clearly decided, which has led historian John Lewis Gaddis to comment that "the President and his advisors were as uncertain about what they could actually do with nuclear weapons when they left office in 1953 as they had been in 1949," the year the American atomic monopoly ended.[167] Gaddis sees Truman as confused between a "war fighting" strategy of constructing tactical nuclear weapons so as to enable the United States to initiate the use of nuclear weapons without threatening nuclear annihilation, and a "war avoidance" strategy of planning for nuclear overkill in order to deter any conflict. Eisenhower chose the latter.[168] His NSC authorized the Joint Chiefs of Staff to plan for war on the assumption that nuclear weapons, both tactical and strategic, were to be used wherever it was convenient to do so.[169] The new administration considered the use of nuclear weapons in Korea (1953),[170] Indochina (1954),[171] and even in response to any change in status of the Quemoy and Matsu islands.

A problem with the Truman version of containment, or so the new administration saw it, was that it allowed the Soviets, secure in the knowledge that the Americans would not initiate the nuclear phase of a war, to pursue bold foreign policy gambits wherever they had conventional superiority. Furthermore, the deployment of U.S. troops to many points along the vast border between the Sino-Soviet bloc and the rest of the world was vastly expensive. As John Foster Dulles, now the secretary of state, explained it: "we cannot build a 20,000 mile Maginot line or match the Red Armies, man for man, gun for gun and tank for tank at any particular time or place their general staff selects. To attempt that would mean real strength nowhere and bankruptcy everywhere."[172] What the Eisenhower administration was going to do, according to Dulles, was engage in a scaling back of deployed forces and the adaptation of a first-use nuclear policy. Thus, the administration could respond to Soviet threats in an asymmetrical manner, choosing not only the time and place but also the degree of the American response. The Truman administration had responded to a conventional attack by a Soviet ally with conventional force. It is not clear that the Eisenhower administration would have done the same. This concept of containment, based on a nuclear threat to the enemy's homeland, was termed massive retaliation by Dulles.[173]

To what extent did the new team carry out these reforms? Dulles and Eisenhower engaged in much rhetoric to convince the Soviets that massive retaliation was a genuine statement of policy, as seen by Eisenhower's claim that "where these [nuclear] things can be used on strictly military targets and for strictly military purposes, I see no reason why they shouldn't be used just exactly as you would use a bullet or anything else."[174] Eisenhower even hinted that he was considering the use of nuclear weapons as a means of inducing the Chinese to reach a settlement at Korea.[175] However, it appears that the Eisenhower team wasn't as successful in reorienting military policy as they said they wanted to be.

The Eisenhower administration's military policy was really not that different from Truman's. This fact became apparent to those in the administration as early as the summer of 1953, with the conclusion of Operation Solarium. Solarium was conducted, on Eisenhower's orders, at the National War College and in the basement of the White House. Three teams were created to debate three policy options and present them to the president: a continuation of Truman's containment (ironically, this team was headed by Kennan, who had resigned because his ideas of containment differed from the Truman administration), a deterrence strategy of massive retaliation in the event of any negative change in the spheres of influence, and a rollback strategy, dependent on propaganda and covert activity and designed to shrink the Soviet sphere of influence.[176] The last option was dumped entirely,[177] although some members of the public did not become aware of this change until the events in Hungary in 1956. Eisenhower combined the first two, and modified them with an insistence on lowering costs. Some of the means but virtually none of the ends of the Truman administration were altered. The goal of lower costs was given a high priority, but could not be pursued as vigorously as it had been before the Korean conflict, given that the administration would not forfeit the deployment of large American conventional forces in Europe and Korea that had occurred in the last three years of the Truman administration.

Although the administration wanted reductions in troops, it does not seem to have pursued a withdrawal of U.S. troops from Europe with any vigor. The Eisenhower National Security Council's first blueprint, entitled "Basic National Security Policies and Programs in Relation to Their Costs,"[178] stated: "The national security programs for Fiscal 1954 and Fiscal 1955 will provide greater force strength than we have today—in the United States, in NATO, and in the Far East." A planned reduction in personnel was limited to slightly more than 250,000, the most the administration considered possible without sacrificing its ability to live up to the commitments it had chosen.[179]

The small efforts the administration did make towards replacing troops with nuclear power were heavily resisted, in Congress, in the military establishment (General Maxwell Taylor, a member of the Joint Chiefs of Staff, even published a book in 1957 criticizing the massive retaliation strategy)[180], and, most importantly, by the NATO allies. The European members of NATO preferred reliance on conventional forces to reliance on a first-use nuclear policy. In response to a recommendation in June 1954 to make a stronger and clearer commitment to a first-use atomic policy, Dulles replied, "If we do so, very few of our allies will follow us . . . the tide is running against us in the channel of this tough policy. If we are to continue to pursue it we shall lose many of our allies, and this in itself compels a reappraisal of our policy."[181] The discovery in August 1953 that the Soviets had developed a thermonuclear device, at a time when the Americans hadn't yet downsized their own to be a working bomb, put a damper on plans to rely primarily on the nuclear deterrent.[182]

There were some savings that resulted from the end of the Korean War and the replacement of conventional forces with nuclear weapons. The fiscal year 1961 military budget, the last one created in the Eisenhower administration, was smaller, in real terms, than the fiscal year 1953 military budget, which was Truman's last. In inflation-adjusted terms, the savings were significant.

However, it would be a mistake to view the New Look as a radical alteration of policy. Although American planners continually talked about eventually withdrawing the army from Europe, the four extra divisions sent to Europe in the winter of 1950–51 would remain there long after the Eisenhower presidency.[183] The massive retaliation idea didn't change the existence of large conventional forces in Germany and Korea, only the scope. The increasing reliance on the nuclear component in NATO strategy may have actually made an American withdrawal of conventional forces from Europe less possible.[184] Before the nuclear build-up, NATO allies could assume that the United States would come to their aid, in the event of a grand war, with large conventional forces from North America. Once a large nuclear defense had been created, the Europeans feared that the United States would be too quick to rely on nuclear weapons, and they were therefore opposed to the withdrawal of American forces. In order to avoid disrupting the Atlantic alliance, the United States continued to maintain large deployments in Europe.

1953–54: SOVIET MILITARY EXPANSION AFTER STALIN

Similar to the United States, the Soviet Union, after a change in leadership (in this case because of Stalin's death on March 5, 1953) and the end of the Korean War, engaged in military reform without reverting to what would have been considered normal peacetime defense spending by most nations. Although accurate information is difficult to come by, it seems that the Soviets reduced the manpower of their military to pre-Korean War levels in the mid-1950s.[185] However, the costs of new weapons development kept military spending on an upward trajectory, slowly closing the gap between American and Soviet military expenditure that was created during the Korean War era.[186]

In a June 26, 1953, Presidium meeting, a group of armed generals and party figures, acting in large part on the orders of Nikita Khrushchev and Minister of Defense Nikolay Bulganin, and led by Marshal Zhukov, arrested Laventri Beria, who had assumed vast powers after Stalin's death. After this episode, the military-industrial complex found itself in a greater position of power than at any time in Soviet history. It immediately set about gaining control of nuclear weapons, for the first time, and reorganizing itself.[187]

Khrushchev and his military allies in the coup had strong ideas on increasing the pace of Stalin's military modernization program. The plan was to lessen the number of troops in uniform, and use the savings to improve mobility, nuclear weapons, nuclear delivery systems, air defenses, and the navy. The changes introduced were so bold that the 1953–60 period would come to be known as the "Revolution in Military Affairs" within the Soviet military establishment.[188]

In the army, Khrushchev's reforms brought about a more technologically advanced force. Unarmored trucks that transported the infantry in the armored and mechanized divisions were increasingly replaced with armored personnel carriers.[189]

The hydrogen bomb project, which began in 1948, even before the first successful Soviet A-bomb test, was completed.[190] Soviet Premier Georgi Malenkov informed the world on August 8, 1953, that the Soviets were capable of fusion, and the Soviets successfully tested the device on August 12 at Semipalatinsk. The 400-kiloton explosion, 20 times greater than that of the first Soviet atomic bomb, created a 5 kilometer-wide lake of glazed earth.[191] The bomb's radioactive fallout was such that the American government was rapidly made aware that the Soviets had indeed detonated a thermonuclear device of significant magnitude (the Americans guessed 500 kilotons).[192] The Soviet hydrogen explosion convinced mathematician John Von Neumann, a member of the American atomic research establishment, that "from 1945 to 1949 there was a uniform time lag of about four years between us and the Soviets in our favor . . . This time lag seems to me to be now hardly more than one year."[193]

Although the Soviets had a limited stockpile of fission bombs, perhaps fewer than fifty,[194] the Soviet hydrogen bomb may have given Moscow near parity with the United States in nuclear weapons, at least for a few months. The Soviet H-bomb was only 400 kilotons, less than either the 500-kiloton American fission weapon detonated at the IVY test of November 1952 and much less than the 10,000-kiloton American hydrogen weapon used in the MIKE test. But the Soviet bomb, based on lithium deuteride, was small enough that, with a few months of simple redesigning, it could be loaded on to a bomber and dropped, whereas the American fusion weapon, was too large to be placed in an aircraft.[195] The United States would not achieve a lithium deuteride explosion until the CASTLE test of March 1, 1954.[196] The Soviet nuclear arsenal grew to 1,050 weapons by 1959 and 3,100 by 1962.[197]

Like the Americans, the Soviets worked to improve their methods of delivering atomic weapons. The Tu-16 bomber and the Tu-95 bomber, nicknamed Badger and Bear, respectively, by the Americans, possessed heavier load capacities and greater range than the Tu-4, and were part of the fleet by 1955.[198] The Tu-95 had intercontinental range.[199] In the event of war, Soviet bomber forces may have been helped by a NATO friend or foe device, enabling radar operators to differentiate incoming planes, which Soviet spies had persuaded a Dutch air force officer stationed at NATO headquarters to turn over.[200]

By December 1953, the Presidium had approved the development of three strategic missile projects to help deliver atomic warheads: the R-5 and two versions of the R-11, one for the navy and one for the army (Americans termed the R-5 the SS-3, the R-11 navy missile the SS-N-3, and the R-11 army missile the SCUD).[201] The R-5 had a range of more than 1,000 kilometers, approaching that of the first intercontinental ballistic missile, which the Soviets would develop by 1957.[202]

Missile development was not limited to offensive applications. More than 3,000 R-113 antiaircraft missiles were deployed around Moscow, beginning in 1954.[203] The Soviets placed such a heavy emphasis on rockets and air defense that they created entirely new services to carry out these tasks. After the changes, the Soviets had five military services: army, navy, air force, strategic rocket force, and air defense.

As part of the doctrinal change, with its new emphasis on fighting a war in a nuclear age, the Soviets engaged in experiments and training to prepare for the nuclear battlefield. Beginning on September 14, 1954, at the Totskoe testing ground in the South Urals Military District, the Soviets simultaneously held exercises involving 44,000 troops while setting off an atomic detonation in the vicinity.[204] Once again, the comparison with the United States is obvious.

In another doctrinal change, Stalin's view that the navy was a defensive instrument was replaced by a more aggressive version. In a fateful decision reminiscent of the shipbuilding boom in the waning years of the Czars, the Soviets embarked on an expensive attempt to challenge the Western allies on the high seas. This plan involved building a navy that could send self-sustaining fleets on long missions far from home. It is possible to speak of quantity of combat vessels, but the numbers are not that important, considering that the Soviets always manufactured so many vessels. By 1955, not long after Stalin's death, the Soviet navy had 3 battleships, more than 25 cruisers, 135–150 destroyers and destroyer escorts, and 370–400 submarines (but the submarines varied in quality).[205] The important factor over the next two decades would be the improvement in performance with the use of missiles (both surface-launched and submarine-launched), nuclear-powered vessels, and antisubmarine warfare technologies. By the 1970s, the Soviets would introduce their first aircraft carrier, the *Kiev*, to help support these fleets, and by the early 1980s the Soviets would begin developing a new class of aircraft carriers that could handle larger, higher-performance aircraft.[206]

By the summer of 1953, the Soviets were also preparing covert networks abroad that could be called upon in war to sabotage Western nuclear weapons storage facilities and centers of communications, logistics, or supply.[207] These networks were sometimes run by veterans of the partisan war against the Germans in World War II.[208]

Conclusions

The American arms build-up of 1950–51 can only be understood as part of the larger shift toward a more assertive containment policy. Changes in American security obligations, changes in the status of German and Japanese military power, huge increases in American foreign aid, and the arms build-up were interrelated parts of an important alteration in American policies. How important? James Reston, the famous *New York Times* correspondent, called this shift "the decisive point in the politics of the twentieth century."[1] It was a momentous step in the direction of bipolarity, the domination by two superpowers that characterized international politics for the next 40 years. Although the European empires decayed only slowly, the American show of force in Korea, the deployment of troops around the world, and the new security treaties all indicated a future in which the United States would play a wider role. The dramatic shift, which was seen by the Americans as a counter to Soviet actions, was, to use poker terminology, seen and raised by the Kremlin, leading to an arms race that in scale, scope, and technology dwarfed previous arms races. Even after the end of the Cold War and its related arms race, the impact of the American arms build-up persists. The decisions of 1950–51 forged a political culture in which America sought to prevent possible repeats of the June 25 scenario by using deployments and alliances. This culture, despite much criticism, survives. There have been 11 American administrations since 1950, and not one of them has come close to ending American involvement in NATO or removing American troops from Europe or Korea.

This culture stemmed from the ideological and economic outlooks of decision-makers, but was shaped by the perceptions of events overseas. It is impossible to study the arms build-up without reference to both. The political culture that shaped, and was inhabited by, the decision-making elites was, as all cultures are, a culmination of many traditions, as well as a unique momentary phenomenon, in which people could be dominated by singular events and personalities. This book has attempted to give some sense of the political culture of the period, especially in reference to the existence of anti-Communist hysteria, and struggles over the appropriate role of American power abroad, as witnessed in the Great Debate. The Truman administration could try to influence, but not mold, the political culture, and had to make decisions regarding the arms build-up within that culture. Perceptions of events abroad must be added to this explanation of the domestic political scene. In terms of the arms build-up, the most critical perceptions were overwhelmingly those of Soviet capabilities and intentions. Specifically, to critique the arms build-up, one must ask two questions: whether a preponderance of Soviet military power actually existed, and whether such power, if in existence, needed to be addressed through a build-up of American forces abroad. In very general terms, historians can produce four possible answers: "yes" to both questions, "no" to both, "yes/no," and "no/yes." Since a "no" answer to the first question would settle the issue, the "no/no" and "no/yes" answers may be combined into one for purposes of investigation.

Consider a very rough grouping of historians into these three general schools of thought. One is the orthodox view, first espoused by the famous men of the day, such as Churchill, Acheson, and de Gaulle, who publicly warned of the threat of the Soviet military and advocated balancing it through military preparations. This view is now the common view among many in the military, who feel that the crushing losses of Task Force Smith, the first American force to land in Korea in the summer of 1950, should be used as a reminder of the danger of cuts in the U.S. defense budget. Most of all, the orthodox view is the domain of the Truman sympathizers, who are plentiful given the recent popularity of biographies of the man, such as those by Hamby and McCollough.[2]

In July 1951, Truman himself provided one of the first orthodox historical accounts of the arms build-up when he reminisced on events of the previous year, concluding that "never before have free men in such large numbers acted together in advance to prevent a supreme crisis. Never before on so vast a scale have free men assumed great risks voluntarily, so that even greater risks may not descend upon them involuntarily. Never before has there been so deep and widespread in the hearts of mankind the feeling that the price of peace is the willingness to fight for justice."[3] This message was repeated, in its essentials, for the rest of his life.

Another example of the group in favor of the arms build-up is the team of Allan Millett and Peter Maslowski, authors of *For the Common Defense: A Military History of the United States of America,* which concludes that

in two years [1951–1953] NATO had become at least the equal to the Soviet forces deployed in East Germany . . . Critics of this militarization of American diplomacy believed the rearmament policy was an exaggerated reaction to an overestimated Soviet threat. But the Russia of 1950–1953 was Stalin's domain, and conventional wisdom gave Moscow the power to control its Communist collaborators in Europe and Asia. The Truman administration, buffeted at home by its political enemies and growing disillusionment over the war, won a lasting victory for the Free World.[4]

A second school of thought refutes the belief that the Soviet military enjoyed a preponderance of power. This group is sometimes led by historians known as revisionists, who took the name during the Vietnam War era, and who are known for critiques of a lack of moral guidance in American foreign policy.[5]

A representative view is that of Matthew Evangelista, who, in his article, "Stalin's Army Reappraised," claims that:

It seems now that the Soviet military threat was considerably exaggerated during this period. Indeed, the notion of an overwhelmingly large Soviet Army facing only token western forces was inaccurate. Moreover, it appears that Soviet troops were not capable of executing the kind of invasion feared in the West during the late 1940's, due in part to strictly military considerations, and also the fact that many of them were engaged in nonmilitary tasks instead of in training for an offensive.[6]

A third school of thought argues that there was an overwhelming Soviet conventional preponderance of power in central Europe, but that various constraints, both internal and external, and both voluntary and involuntary, prevented the Soviets from ever using this force in the field of battle. The Soviets possessed the capabilities to overrun Western Europe, but, given the nature of the world system, lacked the intentions. This group does not argue against the existence of a large Soviet force in central Europe, but argues that this force was, in an age of atomic warfare and industrial battles, not a decisive factor in the real balance of power. An example is Kennan. In a February 1994 speech at the Council of Foreign Relations, he suggested that, in reacting to the existence of the Soviet military presence in central Europe, there were better options than creating a large NATO armed force. Kennan began by explaining his famous 1947 long telegram:

What I was then advocating for our government was a policy of 'containment' of Soviet expansionist pressures, a policy aimed at halting the expansion of Soviet power in Central and Western Europe.

I viewed this as primarily a diplomatic and political task, though not wholly without military implications. I considered that if and when we had succeeded in persuading the Soviet leadership that the continuation of these expansionist designs not only held out for them no hopes of success but would be, in many respects, to their disadvantage, then the moment would have come for serious talks with them about the future of Europe.

But when, some three years later [1950], this moment had arrived-when we had made our point with the Marshall Plan, with the successful resistance to the Berlin blockade and other measures- when the lesson I wanted to see us convey to Moscow had been successfully conveyed, then it was one of the great disappointments of my life to discover that neither our government nor our Western European allies had any interest in entering into such discussions at all. What they and the others wanted from Moscow, with respect to the future of Europe, was essentially "unconditional surrender." They were prepared to wait for it. And this was the beginning of the 40 years of cold war.

Those of my opponents of that day who have survived into the present age would say, I am sure: 'You see, we were right. The collapse of the Soviet system amounted to the unconditional surrender we envisaged- an involuntary one if you will, but surrender nevertheless. And we paid nothing for it.'

To which I should have to reply: 'But we did pay a great deal for it. We paid with 40 years of enormous and otherwise unnecessary military expenditures.'[7]

This outlook has been a relatively consistent view of Kennan's. Although he was careful, during the crises after the attack on South Korea, not to discount the possibility of a Soviet attack elsewhere,[8] he was also careful not to support military efforts to counter these possibilities, feeling that existing constraints of the nuclear deterrent and Western economic might were sufficient. In the 1994 article, Kennan also attempted to balance the costs of the arms build-up with the gains. However, he might underrate his opponents when he claims that they believed that America would pay nothing for the collapse of the Soviet Union. It was clear to nearly everyone that huge prices would have to be paid. What is important is whether the price could have been avoided.

Even the openings in access to Soviet archives following the collapse of the USSR have not produced, and shall not produce, a final answer. Although Russian scholars with access to Soviet documents can show that the Soviets were not planning a European counteroffensive to American actions in Korea,[9] the Soviet capacity to do so existed, and intentions, particularly in a state dominated by an elderly, unstable, paranoid, and violent man such as Stalin, could change far more rapidly than capabilities.

The Truman administration acted, understandably, on its understanding of Soviet capabilities. The cost of the arms build-up was undoubtedly high, but after June 25, 1950, Truman was convinced that the costs of not arming would be even higher.

A preponderance of Soviet power existed. This fact was one of overwhelming importance. Neither reliance on the American nuclear deterrent, nor reliance on America's economic ability to defeat the Soviets in a long war was considered sufficient to provide for America's defense.

The Soviets had blatantly used an ally to further their interests in a war in Korea, and the possibility that the Soviets would try this again, using East Germany, could not be discounted. The existence of American nuclear superiority had not been shown to have ameliorated Soviet behavior. Truman acted accordingly.

Ultimately, the decision rested with Truman, not his advisers. While it is important to emphasize the political culture that Truman had to operate within, it should also be said that, at the critical moments, it was he who had to provide the leadership, and that a different president might have led the nation toward a vastly different course of action. The bureaucracy failed to initiate the arms build-up when it wanted to do so, beginning in the fall of 1949 and reaching a crescendo with the completion of NSC-68 in April 1950. The president was firmly in control of his underlings, and Truman's famous "The Buck Stops Here" sign on his desk can be seen as symbolic of the decision-making apparatus in the Truman administration.[10]

But if the arms build-up was not an example of rule by bureaucracy, was it a perfect example of the immense powers over foreign policy formulation that, according to some political scientists, American presidents have had since World War II? Was it an example of the Imperial Presidency? Deploying troops to Korea in such rapid fashion, without asking for formal congressional approval, is surely one of the prime examples of presidential authority in the history of American foreign policy. But the arms build-up was different. It required a larger amount of cooperation with Congress and with all elements of the federal government. Above all, the scale of the build-up was possible only because of the vast support the public was willing to grant Truman once he committed forces to Korea. Had Truman tried to submit larger defense budgets to Congress before the Korean War, he may have had enough support to have them passed, but only if the increases were on a reasonable scale, and not the exponential scale that they were in 1950–52. The war presented the military with a window of opportunity for its enlargement, and it was only because of the war that Truman could accomplish his task of creating a monumental expansion of the American armed forces. At no other time during the Cold War was the American public so seized with anti-Communist fervor. One only has to scan the newspapers of the grim winter of 1950–51 to realize this mood. For example, consider the headlines over a two-day span, December 1 and 2, 1950, in the *New York Times*: "Greatest Peril for US: Western Civilization Faces Destruction if Threat From East Is Not Met Boldly," "Crisis Spurs City Defense Activity; Fear of New War Grips Populace,"

"President Warns of Atom Bomb In Korea If Soviet Vetoes Plan," "Feinberg Act Barring Red Teachers Upheld by State Court of Appeals," "US Casualties at 31,028," "House Bill Proposes Coordinator of Civil Defense With Wide Power," "Senators Battle Over Atomic Bomb Use," "Truman Asks 18 Billion For Arms; Reds Push Toward New UN Line; MacArthur Calls Curbs A Handicap," and "All Out War Force Sought By Truman."[11] These were the top stories in what was considered a generally liberal publication, one of the least sensationalist of the nation's major newspapers.

The rising tide of resentment toward the USSR already existed before the war, in part because of the perceived setbacks for American postwar plans, attributed to Soviet selfishness. The Soviets had already been viewed as potentially threatening, and the revelation of ideologically motivated spies within the American atomic establishment had already created a red scare of sorts. However, this fervor was turned toward the goal of an armed America by Truman's decisions, including the one to go to war in Korea, and the one to focus on Central Europe as the focal point of American diplomacy.

Truman led the move toward the arms build-up, only to find that the momentum behind it became so great that the administration soon found itself trailing in the wake of public opinion. Compared with both Republican opposition and American cultural institutions, the administration in the winter of 1950–51 appears, in hindsight, relatively calm. Truman's stance on military spending was, for a time, actually more restrained than that of Congress. In a period when the leader of American military forces in East Asia was recommending laying a belt of radioactive cobalt across the Korean peninsula to stop Communist advances, and when some Congressmen favored the use of the atomic bomb, and when being labeled sympathetic to Communism was tantamount to career suicide, the Truman budgets appeared modest to many.

Most Americans supported the arms build-up. Even among the minority opposed to the deployments abroad and the new alliance commitments, there was considerable support for increasing America's military power. Indeed, after Truman himself became grossly unpopular in the last two years of his administration because of corruption scandals among his cronies, the seeming futility of the peace talks in Korea, and the general lack of growth in living standards described earlier, the arms build-up remained popular. In December 1951, Truman's approval rating in polls sunk to just 23 percent,[12] and yet the primary domestic political opponent of the Truman arms build-up, Senator Taft, found himself losing his grip on his own party, which slowly abandoned him for Eisenhower's military credentials. Taft was not replaced by a new generation of antimilitary populists. The next three presidential elections, from 1952 to 1960, saw the major candidates trying to outdo each other in efforts to appear the most opposed to Communism.

Thus, the debate moved on. The issue of arming the United States to an unprecedented level in peacetime, and deploying that new force abroad, was settled. In its place were arguments about whether and how to use that force to contain Soviet power. The dispute over creating combat forces was replaced, in the next two decades, by disputes over whether to use those forces in the Straits of Taiwan, Lebanon, Laos, Cuba, and Vietnam. The Cold War had come of age, and the race for victory was on.

Notes

INTRODUCTION

1. Charles E. Bohlen, *Witness to History, 1929–1969* (New York: W. W. Norton, 1973), p. 303. If anything, Bohlen was underestimating. There were 22 nations outside Latin America that the United States was allied to by the mid-1950s. Constance Coblenz, Morton Kaplan, and William Reitzel, *United States Foreign Policy, 1945–1955* (Washington, D.C.: The Brookings Institution, 1956), p. 365.

2. NARA, record group 273, National Security Council Mill 9, "United States Foreign and Domestic Policy in Furtherance of National Security," 25 February 1948, p. 12.

3. While this book deals strictly with the arms build-up, the Truman administration placed almost equal weight on military aid during this era. The United States spent more on military aid in the two-year period of 1950–51 than it had on the entire Marshall Plan from its creation.

4. Other treaty commitments made during this era, such as the Australia, New Zealand and United States security pact (ANZUS), the Southeast Asian Treaty Organization (SEATO), the Japanese-American security arrangement, and the Philippine-American security treaty, were also significant, and would make any future roll-back of military power difficult.

5. Truman quote: Truman's mid-year Economic Report to Congress, 23 July 1951, text contained in PRO FO 371 90951, AU 1104/3.

6. Interview of Truman by Carleton Kent, *The Washington Sun-Times,* January 16, 1953; for a discussion of the admission of Turkey to NATO, see Melvyn Leffler, "Strategy, Diplomacy, and the Cold War: The United States, Turkey, and NATO, 1945–1952," *Journal of American History* (March 1985).

CHAPTER 1: DEMOBILIZATION

1. Dewey predicted that the Democrats would keep troops in the army to continue New Deal projects and to avoid unemployment. President Roosevelt was careful to also promise demobilization.

2. FDRL, The Papers of Alexander Sachs, box 163, folder entitled "Reports, Studies, and Memoranda on War Progress, June 1945." For a series of detailed charts on past and projected munitions production, see a pamphlet entitled "Delayed Economic Reflection of Military Reverses in Belgium and Subsequent Prefatory Readjustments for One Front War."

3. FDRL, Map Room Files, box 157, MR 401(4), Section 1.

4. FDRL, The Papers of Harold Smith, box 3, folder on conferences with the president, 1943–45.

Smith's notes on his conferences with Roosevelt indicate that the president favored rapid disarmament, but that the slow pace of the campaign in Europe delayed larger cutbacks. The two did agree on a $15 to $17 billion reduction in war expenditures for fiscal year 1946 (July 1, 1945–June 30, 1946), from a total of $86 billion the previous year.

5. David McCollough, *Truman* (New York: Simon and Schuster, 1992), p. 468.

6. Examples of the public pressures to demobilize included the formation of more than 200 Bring back Daddy clubs, composed of servicemen's wives lobbying Congress and the president for a quick return of troops, and the writing of "No boats, no votes" letters by service members to Congress when a shortage of transport developed in the Pacific that stalled their return. Deborah Welch Larson, *Origins of Containment: A Psychological Explanation* (Princeton: Princeton University Press, 1995), p. 240.

7. McCollough, *Truman*, p. 469.

8. John B. Rae, *Climb to Greatness: The American Aircraft Industry, 1920–1960* (Cambridge: MIT Press, 1968), p. 173.

9. Herbert S. Parmet, *The Democrats: The Years After FDR* (New York: Oxford University Press, 1976), p. 60.

10. John Lewis Gaddis, *Strategies of Containment: A Critical Appraisal of Postwar American National Security Policy* (Oxford: Oxford University Press, 1982), p. 359.

11. Jack Holl and Terrence Fehner, "Truman," *The Harry S. Truman Encyclopedia,* ed. Richard Kirkendall (Boston: G. K. Hall, 1989), p. 238.

12. Gaddis, *Strategies*, p. 359.

13. James A. Huston, *Outposts and Allies: U.S. Army Logistics in the Cold War, 1945–53* (Cranbury, N.J.: Associated University Presses, 1988), p. 16.

14. Melvyn Leffler, *A Preponderance of Power: National Security, the Truman Administration, and the Cold War* (Stanford, Calif.: Stanford University Press, 1992), p. 111.

15. William Manchester, *The Glory and the Dream: A Narrative History of America, 1932–1972* (New York: Bantam Books, 1990), p. 531.

16. February 1945: FDRL, Map Room Files, box 157, folder MR 401(4); 1948: Clay Blair, *The Forgotten War* (New York: Times Books, 1987), p. 8.

17. Blair, *Forgotten War*, p. 9.

18. CSQ, *Congress and the Nation, 1945–64* (Washington, D.C.: 1965), p. 265. 1945

air force: *The World Almanac, 1993,* p. 694. At that time, the personnel were members of the Army Air Corps.

19. William Cunningham, "Postwar Developments and the Location of the Aircraft Industry in 1950," *The History of the American Aircraft Industry: An Anthology,* ed. G. R. Simonson (Cambridge: MIT Press, 1968), pp. 181, 185.

20. Harry S. Truman, *Memoirs: 1945, Year of Decisions* (New York: Signet, 1955), p. 509.

21. Manchester, *Glory,* p. 531.

22. Jan van der Harst, "From Neutrality to Alignment: Dutch Defense Policy, 1945–51," *NATO: The Founding of the Atlantic Alliance and the Integration of Europe,* ed. Francis Heller and John Gillingham (London: Palgrave Macmillan, 1992), p. 29.

23. William P. Snyder, *The Politics of British Defence Policy, 1945–62* (Columbus, Ohio: Ohio State University Press, 1964), p. 193.

24. In 1947, the Defence Committee of the British Cabinet concluded that the possibility of a major war in the next five years was remote and that the situation was unlikely to become dangerous in the next ten years. Eric Grove, *Vanguard to Trident: British Naval Policy Since World War II* (London: The Bodley Head, 1987), p. 39.

25. Peter Slowe, *Manny Shinwell: An Authorized Biography* (London: Pluto Press, 1993), p. 233; Leffler, *Preponderance of Power,* p. 286.

26. Slowe, *Shinwell,* p. 233.

27. A. W. DePorte, *Europe Between the Superpowers: The Enduring Balance* (New Haven: Yale University Press, 1979).

28. James H. Hansen, *Correlation of Forces: Four Decades of Soviet Military Development* (New York: Praeger, 1987), p. 9.

29. David Holloway, *Stalin and the Bomb: The Soviet Union and Atomic Energy, 1939–1956* (New Haven: Yale University Press, 1994), p. 151.

30. Jeffrey A. Richelson, *A Century of Spies: Intelligence in the Twentieth Century* (New York: Oxford University Press, 1995).

31. 80,000 soldiers: ibid., p. 246. Lithuanian partisans later claimed that the Soviets lost between 80,000 and 100,000 Soviet soldiers from 1945 to 1952. 100,000 soldiers: Matthew A. Evangelista, "Stalin's Post-War Army Reappraised," *International Security* (winter 1982/83).

32. Richelson, *Century of Spies,* pp. 226–27.

33. David Martin, *Wilderness of Mirrors* (New York: Ballantine Books, 1980); Richelson, *Century of Spies.*

34. Holloway, *Stalin and the Bomb,* p. 153. Klaus Fuchs, a British nuclear scientist spying for the Soviets for ideological reasons, was a Soviet informant on this matter; Richelson, *Century of Spies,* p. 227; six-bomb statistic: Robert Dorr, "Thermonuclear Legacy," *Military History* (August 1995): p. 63.

35. Dmitri Volkogonov, *Stalin: Triumph and Tragedy* (New York: Grove Wiedenfield, 1992), p. 504, except for the statistic on bridges, which comes from Evangelista, "Stalin's Post-War Army Reappraised," p. 122, and the statistics on livestock, oil wells, and coal pits, which come from Douglas Botting, *In The Ruins of the Reich* (London: Grafton Books, 1985), p. 135.

36. The Soviets began the demobilization process for troops in Europe on May 21, 1945, less than two weeks after V-E Day. Antiaircraft and cavalry forces were demobilized first, followed by 40 to 60 percent of the infantry units. Demobiliza-

tion for units in Asia began in September, after the war against Japan ended. The manpower of the Red Army was reduced from 11.365 million in May to approximately 8 million by the end of the year. By the end of 1947, the armed forces had been reduced to 2.874 million troops.

Holloway puts Soviet defense budgets at 137.8 billion rubles in 1944, 128.2 billion in 1945, 73.6 billion in 1946, and 66.3 billion in 1947 (at 1946 prices it would have been 55.2 billion). In February 1948, the Soviet press published statistics indicating that Soviet military spending in 1947 and 1948 was 66.1 and 66.4 billion rubles respectively, much lower than wartime levels.

Volkogonov, *Stalin*, p. 504; Hansen, *Correlation*, p. 7; Holloway, *Stalin and the Bomb*, p. 152; FRUS, 1948, vol. 4, telegram by the U.S. Ambassador to the Soviet Union (Smith) to the Secretary of State (Marshall), 3 February 1948, pp. 802–803.

37. Hansen, *Correlation*, pp. 7, 12.

38. Volkogonov, *Stalin*, p. 504.

CHAPTER 2: CONSOLIDATION

1. Paul Y. Hammond, "NSC-68: Prologue to Rearmament," in *Strategy, Politics, and Defense Budgets*, ed. Warner Schilling, Paul Hammond, and Glenn Snyder (New York: Columbia University Press, 1966), p. 277.

2. For one of many possible examples of the administration's conviction that the Soviets were working to enlarge their sphere of influence, see HSTL, B file, Ideological Foundations of the Cold War, folder number 7, document entitled "Soviet Foreign Policy: A Summation."

3. The air force would not become a service of its own until 1947.

4. The manuscript was titled *A Strategic Chart of Certain Russian and Manchurian Urban Areas*. Richard Rhodes, *Dark Sun: The Making of the Hydrogen Bomb* (New York: Simon and Schuster, 1995), p. 24.

5. A paucity of bombs made some of these plans unrealistic and led to the outright replacement of FLEETWOOD. PDDE, vol. 10, p. 367.

6. James H. Hansen, *Correlation of Forces: Four Decades of Soviet Military Development* (New York: Praeger, 1987), p. 14.

7. Omar Bradley, *A General's Life: An Autobiography* (New York: Simon and Schuster, 1983), p. 474. Bradley seems to have felt that he was at least partially responsible for that situation, admitting that he supported the president on the budget-cutting decisions.

8. Keyserling, who argued that significant amounts of deficit-based spending could drive an economy to full capacity without controls and eventually pay off the resulting debts with the resulting tax revenues, became chairman of the Council of Economic Advisers in early 1950. See John Lewis Gaddis, *Strategies of Containment: A Critical Appraisal of Postwar American National Security Policy* (Oxford: Oxford University Press, 1982), pp. 93–94, and Daniel Yergin, *Shattered Peace: The Origins of the Cold War and the National Security State* (Boston: Houghton Mifflin, 1977), p. 404.

9. One of Truman's biggest acts as a county judge had been to streamline procurement, and track and destroy fraud and waste, in order to reduce the county

debt by $700,000. Deborah Welch Larson, *Origins of Containment: A Psychological Explanation* (Princeton: Princeton University Press, 1995), p. 132.

10. While a senator, his proposals led to the creation, in February 1941, of the Senate Committee on Defense Production and Procurement, designed to oversee the build-up of forces that the Roosevelt administration had initiated as the wars in Europe and Asia had grown. The committee was chaired by Truman, who later claimed to have saved the nation $15 billion in this capacity. It was this job that propelled Truman into the headlines and may have led to his consideration for the job of vice president. Clay Blair, *The Forgotten War* (New York: Times Books, 1987), p. 5.

11. Alonzo Hamby, "American Interpreters of American History: U.S. Political History," *American Cold War Strategy: Interpreting NSC 68*, ed. Ernest May (Boston: Bedford Books, 1993), p. 157.

12. Harry S. Truman, *Public Papers of the Presidents of the United States: Harry S. Truman, 1950* (Washington D.C.: GPO, 1965). Truman spoke on this matter during a radio and television address to the country following the signing of the Defense Production Act, September 9, 1950.

13. HSTL, quoted by Keyserling in the Oral History with Leon Keyserling, p. 117. Keyserling at least had the president's ear, which he got by going through presidential assistant Clark Clifford. Nourse was so out of the policymaking loop that he resigned. See HTSL, Oral History of Edwin G. Nourse, p. 60.

14. HSTL, Oral History of Edwin G. Nourse, p. 26.

15. Harry S. Truman, *Memoirs: Years of Trial and Hope, 1946–1952* (New York: Signet, 1956), p. 36.

16. The debt had risen from $16.1 billion in 1930 and $43 billion in 1940.

17. Truman, *Trial and Hope*, p. 38.

18. The debt figures are from the Bureau of Public Debt, Department of the Treasury, as quoted in *The World Almanac, 1993*, p. 128. The gross national product figures are from Gaddis, *Strategies*, p. 359.

19. Truman, *Trial and Hope*. This was after Congress had already supported three small tax bills during the war.

20. At no point of Truman's administration did the comparable figure slip below 30 percent. Bureau of the Census, *Historical Statistics of the United States, Colonial Times to 1970* (Washington, D.C., 1975), pp. 224, 1116. As quoted in Gaddis, *Strategies*, p. 359.

21. HSTL, Papers of Harry S. Truman, president's secretary's files, subject file on Bureau of the Budget, box 150, folder on Bureau of the Budget, fiscal year 1951, memorandum for the president from Frank Pace, "Basic Policies with Respect to 1951 Budget Ceilings." Spending on items other than debt and international policy amounted to a smaller proportion of the national income than they had ten years previously. Address at the Jefferson-Jackson Day Dinner, Truman, *Public Papers, 1950*.

22. Truman began using the term *Fair Deal* in January 1949.

23. Blair, *Forgotten War*, p. 4.

24. Truman often commented that military history was his hobby. He liked to give examples of battles in ancient Rome or in the American Civil War when discussing military matters. For some examples, see *Public Papers of the Presidents: Harry S. Truman, 1950*, Rear Platform and Other Informal Remarks (Baker,

Oregon), 10 May 1950; Remarks at the Armed Forces Dinner, 19 May 1950; Remarks at the U.S. Marine Corps Base, Quantico, Virginia, 15 June 1950; Address at Valley Forge, 30 June 1950.

25. Ed Cray, *General of the Army: George C. Marshall, Soldier and Statesman* (New York: Norton, 1990), p. 663. The statement was made in late March 1948.

26. Terrence J. Gough, *US Army Mobilization and Logistics in the Korean War: A Research Approach* (Washington, D.C.: Army Center of Military History, 1987), p. 23.

27. Yergin, *Shattered Peace*, p. 399.

28. As opposed to Dewey, one of Truman's campaign positions was to cap military spending. Richard Norton Smith, *Thomas E. Dewey and His Times* (New York: Simon and Schuster, 1984), p. 31.

29. Russell Weigley, *History of the United States Army* (London: B. T. Batsford, 1967), appendix.

30. Smith, *Dewey*, p. 302.

31. Paul Kennedy, *The Rise and Fall of the Great Powers: Economic Change and Military Conflict, 1500–2000* (London: Fontana, 1989), p. 382.

32. Ibid., p. 429. Military expenditure did not begin to increase until calendar year 1940, when it was 3.9 percent of the gross national product, and then calendar year 1941, when the naval rearmament and war status of the year's last few weeks brought the comparable figure up to 13.1 percent of the gross national product.

33. DDEL, Eisenhower Pre-Presidential Papers, Name Files, box 13.

34. FRUS, 1949, vol. 1, Views of the Joint Chiefs of Staff on Military Rights in Foreign Territories, undated, pp. 302–11, enclosed with Johnson memorandum of 19 May 1949; Melvyn Leffler, *A Preponderance of Power: National Security, the Truman Administration, and the Cold War* (Stanford, Calif.: Stanford University Press, 1992), pp. 56–59, especially map on p. 57.

35. Marc Trachtenberg, "The Nuclearization of NATO and US-West European Relations," *History and Strategy*, ed. Marc Trachtenberg (Princeton: Princeton University Press, 1991).

36. PRO FO 371/90989, AU 1225/1, "Annual Report for 1950 on the US Air Force, Prepared by the Air Attaché," 5 March 1951. Later, during the Korean War, the air force would reorganize itself, trying to improve on its weaknesses in tactical air support by making the Tactical Air Command an independent command, directly responsible to the air force chief of staff.

37. Certain sections of the air force went so far as to advocate a preventive atomic bombing of the Soviet Union. According to historians Russell Buhite, Christopher Hamel, and Marc Trachtenberg, these views were shared by the air force chief of staff, General Nathan Twining; the commander of SAC, General George Kenney; the future commander of SAC, Curtis LeMay; the deputy commander of the Army Air Force, Lieutenant General Ira Eaker; and the senior Army Air Force officer on the Joint War Plans Committee, Brigadier General Frank Everest. Twining and Kenney: Marc Trachtenberg, "A Wasting Asset: American Strategy and the Shifting Nuclear Balance, 1949–1954," *History and Strategy*, ed. Marc Trachtenberg (Princeton: Princeton University Press, 1991), p. 106; Everest, LeMay, and Eaker: Russell Buhite and W. Christopher Hamel, "War for Peace: The Question of an American Preventive War Against the Soviet Union, 1945–55," *Diplomatic History* (summer 1990): p. 373.

The preventive war argument was based on the premises that war with the

Soviets was nearly inevitable, that waiting until the eventual war broke out might allow the American monopoly on nuclear weapons to lapse, and that a nuclear bombardment would lead to a quick Soviet surrender. The Truman administration didn't believe the first assertion, despite the fact that it considered the second to be true, and commissioned surveys, the Harmon and Hull reports, to gauge the accuracy of the third premise. As will be seen in a later section, these reports found air force claims for effectiveness to be exaggerated.

38. The battle became so heated that air force generals issued an order to not allow any navy personnel to enter a B-36 bomber. Robert Dorr, "Thermonuclear Legacy," *Military History* (August 1995): p. 64.

39. Ibid. The Navy succeeded in building the Lockheed P2V-3C, which could take off from an aircraft carrier but not land on one.

40. Ibid. Critics pointed out that the map assumed that navy carriers would be in the Black Sea, an unlikely proposition at the beginning of a war, and in the Caspian Sea, an impossible proposition.

41. It was acting, in part, on a December 1947 report by Truman's own Air Policy Commission (also known as the Finletter Commission in reference to its chairman, Thomas K. Finletter). The Finletter Commission posited that the USSR would acquire atomic weapons, and that 1953 was the year of greatest danger for the United States. It recommended an extra $1.5 billion spent on the air force annually for five years. The money was to be used to support a 70-group air force instead of the current 55, with 12,400 modern aircraft instead of the current 10,800. There were to be no major changes in the funding of the other services. Warner Schilling, "The Politics of National Defense: The Fiscal 1950 Defense Budget," *Strategy, Politics, and Defense Budgets,* ed. Warner Schilling, Paul Hammond, and Glenn Snyder (New York: Columbia University Press, 1962), p. 37. John B. Rae, *Climb to Greatness: The American Aircraft Industry, 1920–1960* (Cambridge: MIT Press, 1968), p. 193.

42. Aaron Friedberg, "Why Didn't the United States Become a Garrison State," *International Security* (spring 1992): p. 126.

43. Samuel Huntington, *Common Defense: Strategic Programs in National Politics* (New York: Columbia University Press, 1961), p. 240.

44. Friedberg, "Garrison State," p. 125.

45. Ibid., p. 126. Congress eventually did pass a UMT bill, but only in 1951, during the Korean War, and only in a version that accepted the principle of UMT but made no plans for its implementation. UMT has still not, and might never be, implemented. Weigley, *United States Army,* p. 500.

46. Schilling, "The Politics of National Defense," p. 41.

47. Doris M. Condit, *The Test of War, 1950–1953,* vol. 2 of *History of the Office of Secretary of Defense* (Washington, D.C.: Office of the Secretary of Defense, 1988), p. 4.

48. Buhite and Hamel, "War for Peace."

49. Lloyd Gardner, "From Liberation to Containment, 1945–53," *From Colony to Empire: Essays in the History of American Foreign Relations,* ed. William Appleman Williams (New York: John Wiley & Sons, 1972), p. 359.

50. Ibid.

51. Buhite and Hamel, "War for Peace."

52. Robert Norris, "Estimated U.S. and Soviet/Russian Nuclear Stockpiles," *The Bulletin of Atomic Scientists* (November/December 1994), pp. 58–59.

53. Arnold Rogow, *James Forrestal: A Study of Personality, Politics, and Policy* (New York: MacMillan, 1963), p. 207. The air force was still in the experimental stage in trying to develop in-flight refueling capabilities for the B-29. Schilling, "The Politics of National Defense," p. 43. The August 1948 edition of *Aviation Week* mentioned that B-29's were not atomic-capable.

54. Brad Westerfield, *The Instrument of America's Foreign Policy* (Westport, Conn.: Greenwood, 1980), p. 178.

55. PRO FO 371/89978, WU 1197/2, "Memorandum for Minister of State for the Cabinet Defence Committee Concerning US Air Force Groups Based in the UK," 31 December 1949.

56. Leffler, *Preponderance of Power*, p. 285.

57. Blair, *Forgotten War*, p. 9.

58. Ibid., p. 8.

59. FRUS, 1949, vol. 1, Memorandum by the Secretary of Defense to the Executive Secretary of the National Security Council, 17 March 1949, pp. 286–87; Leffler, *Preponderance of Power*, p. 287.

60. FRUS, 1949, vol. 1, Views of the Joint Chiefs of Staff on Military Rights in Foreign Territories, undated, pp. 302–11, enclosed with memorandum from Johnson of 19 May 1949.

61. PRO FO 371/81692, AU 11917/11, Memorandum from Sir Oliver Franks, 28 July 1950.

62. Jonathan Helmreich, *Belgium and Europe: A Study in Small Power Diplomacy* (The Hague: Mouton, 1976), p. 386.

63. Ibid., p. 387.

64. C. J. Bartlett, *The Global Conflict: The International Rivalry of the Great Powers, 1880–1970* (Harlow, Essex: Longman Group, 1984), p. 275. The remark was made on 3 March 1948.

65. Peter Boyle, "Oliver Franks and the Washington Embassy, 1948–52," *British Officials and British Foreign Policy, 1945–50*, ed. John Zametica (Leicester: Leicester University Press, 1990) p. 193.

66. Peter Slowe, *Manny Shinwell: An Authorized Biography* (London: Pluto Press, 1993), p. 242.

67. There were 12 signatory nations: Belgium, Canada, Denmark, France, Iceland, Italy, Luxembourg, the Netherlands, Norway, Portugal, the United Kingdom, and the United States. They each ratified the treaty by 24 August 1949.

68. Slowe, *Shinwell*, p. 235.

69. Ibid., p. 239.

70. Ibid., p. 239.

71. van der Harst, "Dutch Defense," p. 33.

72. Ibid., p. 31.

73. During the Senate's ratification hearings for the treaty, the administration attempted to temper fears of an entangling alliance by emphasizing that article five of the treaty gave each nation the right to decide whether to declare war. Truman thereby claimed that the United States was not necessarily committing itself to war ahead of time. While this was technically true, the administration continued to use operational plans proposing the nuclear bombing of the USSR

in the event of conflict with the USSR in Europe, and it was a virtually unquestioned assumption of American officials that the United States would fight in the event of such a war.

74. This was a prime reason for the participation of some European nations in the alliance. For example, see the Danish government's request, FRUS, 1949, vol. 4, Memorandum of Conversation, by the Assistant Secretary of State for Congressional Relations, pp. 206–9.

75. van der Harst, "Dutch Defense," p. 35.

76. PRO FO 371/89979, WU 1197/13, Memorandum from the Colonial Office, 28 December 1949; PRO FO 371/89979, WU 1197/16, Memorandum from Sir N. Charles, in Ankara, 28 December 1949.

77. The treaty also did nothing on the issue of German rearmament. The European powers were split on the issue, and it was intentionally left out of the treaty.

78. Phil Williams, *The Senate and US Troops in Europe* (London: Macmillan, 1985), pp. 36–37.

79. United Kingdom Paper P.M.M. (48)1, *Documents in Contemporary History: British Defence Policy Since 1945*, ed. Ritchie Ovendale (Manchester: Manchester University Press, 1994), pp. 69–71.

80. BLHC, Records of the Joint Chiefs of Staff, Part 2, Europe and NATO, Microfilm Reel 5.

81. Lawrence Kaplan, *NATO and the United States: The Enduring Alliance* (Boston: Twayne Publishers, 1988), p. 37.

82. Lawrence Kaplan, "The Office of Secretary of Defense and NATO, 1948–1951" (unpublished conference presentation at the Army Center of Military History Conference on the Early Years of the Cold War, 1945–1958, Arlington, Va., June 1996), p. 6.

83. Ibid., p. 5.

84. Ibid., p. 6.

85. Ibid., p. 1.

86. Robert J. Donovan, *Tumultuous Years: The Presidency of Harry S. Truman, 1949–53* (New York: W. W. Norton, 1982), p. 59.

87. Michael J. Hogan, *A Cross of Iron: Harry S. Truman and the Origins of the National Security State, 1945–1954* (Cambridge: Cambridge University Press, 1998), p. 267.

88. Condit, *Test of War*, p. 14.

89. PDDE, Memorandum for the Record to the Military Sub-Committee of the Appropriations Committee of the Senate, 28 March 1950, pp. 1041–46.

90. Ibid., pp. 104–46.

91. Leffler, *Preponderance of Power*, p. 273.

92. Ibid.

93. Ibid., p. 275.

94. Ibid., p. 304.

95. Ibid., p. 309.

96. It seems that Pace was very much influenced by Nourse in his recommendations. Edwin Nourse, *Economics in the Public Service* (New York: Harcourt Brace & Co., 1953), pp. 485–95.

97. Leffler, *Preponderance of Power*, p. 304.

98. Ibid.

99. PDDE, Memorandum for the Record to the Military Sub-Committee of the Appropriations Committee of the Senate, 28 March 1950, pp. 1041–46.

100. Leffler, *Preponderance of Power*, p. 276.

101. For the 104 cities statistic: Hansen, *Correlation*, p. 19.

102. Leffler, *Preponderance of Power*, pp. 273–74.

103. Ibid., pp. 273,276.

104. Condit, *Test of War*.

105. Leffler, *Preponderance of Power*, pp. 276,286.

106. Kaplan, "Secretary of Defense."

107. PDDE, vol. 10, p. 371.

108. Robert Ferrell, "The Formation of the Alliance, 1948–1949," *American Historians and the Atlantic Alliance*, ed. Lawrence Kaplan (Kent, Ohio: Kent State University Press, 1991), p. 27.

109. "US Fiscal Deficit $3,122 Million, $2,411 Million Under Truman's Prediction," *The Wall Street Journal*, 5 July 1950, p. 2.

110. HSTL, Papers of Harry S. Truman, President's Secretary's Files, Subject File on Bureau of the Budget, box 150, Folder on Bureau of the Budget and the Military, 1945–53, Memorandum for Secretary Johnson from Assistant Secretary McNeil, 5 July 1950.

111. FRUS, 1949, vol. 5, Despatch from the Ambassador in the Soviet Union (Kirk) to the Secretary of State (Acheson), 1 October 1949, pp. 659–64.

112. Leffler, *Preponderance of Power*, p. 149.

113. Ibid., pp. 307–8.

114. Ibid.

115. BLHC, Records of the Joint Chiefs of Staff, Part 2, Europe and NATO, microfilm reel 5, "Intelligence Guidance for the US Representatives on the Regional Planning Groups of the North Atlantic Treaty Organization," 16 February 1950. The Attlee government also considered 175 to be the minimum number of Soviet divisions. CA, Winston Churchill Papers, box 5/36, Mr. Churchill's Speech in Debate on Defence, 27 July 1950.

116. Buhite and Hamel, "War for Peace."

117. Ibid.

118. BLHC, Records of the Joint Chiefs of Staff, Part 2, Europe and NATO, microfilm reel 5, "Intelligence Guidance for the US Representatives on the Regional Planning Groups of the North Atlantic Treaty Organization," 16 February 1950.

119. Ibid.

120. Ibid.

121. Leffler, *Preponderance of Power*, p. 306.

122. BLHC, Records of the Joint Chiefs of Staff, Part 2, Europe and NATO, microfilm reel 5, "Intelligence Guidance for the US Representatives on the Regional Planning Groups of the North Atlantic Treaty Organization," 16 February 1950.

123. Leffler, *Preponderance of Power*, p. 307.

124. BLHC, Records of the Joint Chiefs of Staff, Part 2, Europe and NATO, microfilm reel 5, "Intelligence Guidance for the US Representatives on the Regional Planning Groups of the North Atlantic Treaty Organization," 16 February 1950.

125. Ibid.

126. Leffler, *Preponderance of Power,* p. 306.

127. BLHC, Records of the Joint Chiefs of Staff, Part 2, Europe and NATO, microfilm reel 5, "Intelligence Guidance for the US Representatives on the Regional Planning Groups of the North Atlantic Treaty Organization," 16 February 1950.

128. Ibid.

129. Ibid.

130. FRUS, 1949, vol. 5, The Charge in the Soviet Union (Kohler) to the Secretary of State (Acheson), 6 April 1949. See the enclosure entitled "Report on Soviet Intentions Prepared by the Joint Intelligence Committee, American Embassy, USSR, April 5, 1949," pp. 603–9.

131. ACMH, Historical Resources Center, file 384.1, folder entitled "Geog.M Germany-Causes."

132. 800,000 man statistic: Matthew Evangelista, "Stalin's Postwar Army Reappraised," *International Security* (winter 1982/1983): pp. 118–19. Evangelista gives the following manpower statistics:

Germany and Austria		Home Armies	
U.K.:	140,000	France:	270,000
US:	126,000	Netherlands:	108,000
France:	80,000	Belgium:	50,000
Belgium	24,000	Denmark:	22,000
Norway:	4,400		
Denmark:	4,000		

Evangelista's sources are the Joint Intelligence Committee Report of 2 December 1948, and *The New York Times,* 12 May 1947.

133. NATO Information Service, *NATO: Facts and Figures* (Brussels: 1971), p. 195.

134. CA, Winston Churchill Papers, box 5/36, Mr. Churchill's speech in debate on defense, 27 July 1950, p. 4. Churchill includes, in his total, two British, two American, seven French, and one Belgian division, but U.S. army records indicate that only one U.S. division was in Europe.

135. ACMH, Army Directory and Station List, May 1950. Divisions at this time could be undermanned. To meet budgetary ceilings and still provide the required divisions, the army, under General Collins, had eliminated one battalion in three in each division's three infantry regiments, and one of three firing battalions in each of the four divisional artillery battalions. Omar Bradley, *A General's Life: An Autobiography* (New York: Simon & Schuster, 1983).

136. Blair, *Forgotten War.*

137. BLHC, Records of the Joint Chiefs of Staff, Part 2, Europe and NATO, microfilm reel 5, "Report By the Joint Strategic Plans Group to the Joint Strategic Plans Committee on Availability of Military Forces for Short-Term Planning, North Atlantic Regions."

138. Hammond, "Origins of NSC-68," p. 289.

139. CA, Winston Churchill, box 5/36, Mr. Churchill's speech in debate on defense, 27 July 1950, p. 5.

140. Bartlett, *Global Conflict*, p. 304.

141. BLHC, Official Conversations and Meetings of Dean Acheson (1949–1953), Memorandum 0507, 11 April 1950.

142. Ibid.

143. Kaplan, "Secretary of Defense," p. 1.

144. Samuel J. Wells, "The First Coldwar Buildup: Europe in United States Strategy and Policy, 1950–1953," *Western Security: The Formative Years; Atlantic and European Defence, 1950–1953*, ed. Olav Riste (Oslo: Norwegian University Press, 1985), p. 182.

145. CA, Winston Churchill Papers, box 5/36, Mr. Churchill's speech in debate on defense, 27 July 1950, p. V.

146. BLHC, Official Conversations and Meetings of Dean Acheson (1949–1953), Memorandum of Conversation, 24 April 1950.

147. Development from Fat Man: Dorr, "Legacy," p. 63; David Callahan, *Dangerous Capabilities: Paul Nitze and the Cold War* (New York: Harper Collins, 1990).

148. Alonzo Hamby, *Man of the People: A Life of Harry S. Truman* (New York: Oxford University Press, 1995), p. 524.

149. FRUS, 1949, vol. 5, The Charge in the Soviet Union (Kohler) to the Secretary of State (Acheson), 6 April 1949, pp. 603–9. See the enclosure entitled "Report on Soviet Intentions Prepared by the Joint Intelligence Committee, American Embassy, USSR, April 5, 1949."

150. Dr. Donald Steury, interview by author, CIA Historical Office, 12 September 1995.

151. Leffler, *Preponderance of Power*, p. 306.

152. Ibid.

153. Ibid.

154. BLHC, Records of the Joint Chiefs of Staff, Part 2, Europe and NATO, microfilm reel 5, "Intelligence Guidance for the US Representatives on the Regional Planning Groups of the North Atlantic Treaty Organization," 16 February 1950.

155. Albert and Joan Seaton, *The Soviet Army: 1918 to the Present* (London: The Bodley Head, 1986), p.160, for the 2.5 million figure; Nikita Khrushchev, *Khrushchev Remembers* (Boston: Little Brown, 1970) claims that there were 2.8 million personnel; John Erickson, Lynn Hansen, and William Schneider, *Soviet Ground Forces: An Operational Assessment* (Boulder, Colo.: Westview Press, 1986), p. 21, for the 2.874 million figure.

156. For 100 division statistic, see Seaton, *Soviet Army*, p. 160; for 175 division statistic, see Malcolm Mackintosh, *Juggernaut: A History of the Soviet Armed Forces* (New York: Macmillan, 1967), p. 271.

157. Robert Kilmarx, *A History of Soviet Air Power* (London: Faber and Faber, 1962), p. 226.

158. Ibid., p. 227.

159. Hansen, *Correlation*, p. 10.

160. Alexander Boyd, *The Soviet Air Force Since 1918* (London: MacDonald and Jane's, 1977), pp. 205–6.

The United States also benefited from German scientists. Toward the end of World War II, Werner von Braun, one of the leaders of the German rocket programs that launched the V-1 and V-2 weapons, among other things, transported some men and equipment from eastern Germany toward the West so he could avoid falling into Soviet hands. He was given control of a rocket program in Alabama by the Americans, but this did not receive priority funding or attention until the 1950s.

161. Ibid., p. 207.

162. Ibid., pp. 212–14; Allan R. Millett, and Peter Maslowski, *For the Common Defense: A Military History of the United States of America* (New York: Free Press, 1984), p. 500.

The greatest challenge to the Mig-15 came from the American F-86 Sabrejet, which, according to USAF claims, had an eight-to-one kill ratio over the Mig-15 during the Korean War. The Russians, however, have countered that this extraordinary ratio was because of the inexperience of the Chinese and North Korean pilots flying the Migs. The Soviets claim a two-to-one kill ratio in their advantage for those incidents over Korea in which Soviet-piloted Mig-15s encountered F-86s.

After a North Korean pilot defected to South Korea in a Mig-15 in 1953, the Americans ran a large number of tests on the captured aircraft. They concluded that it was difficult to ascertain whether the F-86 or the Mig-15 was better, particularly because of their different firing mechanisms (the Mig-15's two guns fired a larger caliber round that was less accurate but more destructive than the F-86's six machine guns). Nevertheless, the Mig-15 did lead in certain measurable flying categories.

Dale Trapp, "During the Korean War, A Brief Incident Near Vladivostock Pitted Grumman F9F-5s Against MiG-15s," *Military History* (April 1996): p. 70; The Discovery Channel, "Korean War Duel," *Wings Over the Red Star Series*, 25 August 1997.

163. Dr. Donald Steury, interview by author, CIA Historical Office, 12 September 1995. The wing layout of the Mig-15 may have been based on that of the Ta183, a German aircraft that was in the final stages of design at the time of the collapse of Nazi Germany.

164. Hansen, *Correlation*, pp. 8,31.

165. David Holloway, *Stalin and the Bomb: The Soviet Union and Atomic Energy, 1939–1956* (New Haven: Yale University Press, 1994), pp. 242–43.

166. Kilmarx, *Soviet Air Power*, pp. 223, 226, and 230.

167. Holloway, *Stalin and the Bomb*, p. 243.

168. Hansen, *Correlation*, p. 8.

169. Kilmarx, *Soviet Air Power*, p. 234.

170. Hansen, *Correlation*, p. 8.

171. Vladislav Zubok and Constantine Pleshakov, *Inside the Kremlin's Cold War* (Cambridge: Harvard University Press, 1996), p. 76.

172. Erickson, Hansen, and Schneider, *Soviet Ground Forces*, p. 20.

173. "The Soviet Army," *Times* (London), 6 October 1950, p. 7.

174. Ibid.

175. Seaton, *Soviet Army*, p. 155.

176. "The Soviet Army," p. 7.

177. Seaton, *Soviet Army*, p. 155.

178. "The Soviet Army," p. 7.

179. Seaton, *Soviet Army*, p. 153.

180. Mackintosh, *Juggernaut*, p. 224.

181. "The Soviet Army," p. 7.

182. Ibid.

183. P. H. Vigor, *Soviet Blitzkrieg Theory* (London: MacMillan, 1983), pp. 122–24. The Manchurian campaign also saw the greatest use of armored warfare in the entire Pacific War. Gerhard Weinberg, *A World At Arms: A Global History of the Second World War* (Cambridge: Cambridge University Press, 1994), p. 540.

184. Hansen, *Correlation*, p. 10.

185. Earl Ziemke and Magna Bauer, *Moscow to Stalingrad: Decision in the East* (New York: Military Heritage Press, 1988).

186. Holloway, *Stalin and the Bomb*, p. 242.

187. Ibid., p. 8, for Breslau; Weinberg, *World At Arms*, p. 559, for Dyhernfurth.

188. Hansen, *Correlation*, p. 8.

189. Weinberg, *World At Arms*, p. 560.

190. Mackintosh, *Juggernaut*, p. 281.

191. Hansen, *Correlation*, p. 9.

192. Michel Garder, *A History of the Soviet Army* (London: Pall Mall Press, 1966), p. 129, points out that despite these precautions, as many as 75,000 men may have deserted from Soviet occupation forces in Germany and Austria in the immediate postwar years.

193. Holloway, *Stalin and the Bomb*, p. 241.

194. Ibid.

195. Ibid.

196. Ibid.

197. Khrushchev, *Khrushchev Remembers*.

198. Holloway, *Stalin and the Bomb*, p. 241.

199. "The Soviet Army," p. 7. It was thought that a British division had an administrative tail approximately 15 percent larger, proportionate to the size of the division, than that of the Soviet division.

200. Seaton, *Soviet Army*, p. 155.

201. 300 divisions: Ibid., pp. 153, 160; 500 divisions: Mackintosh, *Juggernaut*, p. 269.

202. Evangelista, "Stalin's Postwar Army Reappraised."

203. Some Western analysts have criticized Soviet navy strategy. The USSR was the dominant continental power, spanning the heart of Eurasia, and its strongest rivals in the immediate postwar period were on the fringes of Eurasia or across the seas. Thus, the enemy's sea lines of communications and transportation (SLOC) were vulnerable to submarines, whereas the Soviet SLOC were not. The Soviets could have invested in the construction of Soviet attack submarines capable of long-range oceanic missions. But the Soviets, during Stalin's life, instead focused on using submarines as defensive weapons and on building surface ships. Soon after the war, the Soviets had between 150 and 200 submarines, but these were not of very high quality.

ACMH, History Resources Center 091, folder on Soviet Union, article from the United States Naval Institute Proceedings, June 1955, by Rear Admiral E. M. Eller, titled "Soviet Bid for the Sea," p. 622; and Dr. Donald Steury, interview by author, CIA Historical Office, 12 September 1995.

204. Officially, the USSR had four fleets (Arctic, Baltic, Black, and Pacific) and one flotilla (Caspian).

205. The Soviets probably would have captured all of Spitzbergen within a day of the start of a European war as a means of protecting the Soviets' northern flank. John Teal Jr., "Europe's Northernmost Frontier," *Foreign Affairs* (January 1951).

206. Richard Crockatt, *The Fifty Years War: The United States and the Soviet Union in World Politics, 1941–1991* (London: Routledge, 1995), p. 86.

207. Michel Heller and Aleksandr Nekrich, *Utopia in Power: A History of the USSR From 1917 to the Present*, trans. Phyllis Carlos (London: Hutchinson, 1985), p. 476.

208. *Current Digest of the Soviet Press*, "Elections to Local Soviets," 9 December 1950 (translation of a Pravda article of 26 October 1950).

209. Heller and Nekrich, *Utopia in Power*, p. 476.

210. David Martin, *Wilderness of Mirrors* (New York: Ballantine Books, 1980), p. 89. This knowledge would come from the May 1955 tapping of a major East Berlin underground communications cable.

211. Evangelista, "Stalin's Postwar Army Reappraised."
These partisan bands were composed primarily of local anti-Communists, but some members were German soldiers who had refused to surrender to the Soviets on V-E Day and had instead joined the resistance. Douglas Botting, *In the Ruins of the Reich* (London: Grafton Books, 1985), p. 137.

212. Heller and Nekrich, *Utopia in Power*, p. 495.

213. PRO FO 371/87478, Memorandum entitled "Information Received from the Turkish Military Attache concerning Russian military equipment movements into the satellites and Bulgarian troop movements," March 1950.

214. Stalin received a report from his embassy in Japan concluding that the atomic bombing of Hiroshima and Nagasaki had not been as effective as outsiders were led to believe, and another report, by physicist Peter Kapitsa, that claimed that the blasts in Japan were so destructive because the Japanese lived in crowded "cardboard houses." Kapitsa added that protective measures could reduce damage. Stalin often indicated his belief that atomic weapons would not prove decisive in a general war, a strategy that seems to have been critical in leading the Soviets to maintain a preponderance of conventional military force in central Europe. Holloway, *Stalin and the Bomb*, pp. 226–27 for reports; same chapter for examples of remarks Stalin made disdaining atomic weapons.

215. Holloway, *Stalin and the Bomb*, p. 151.

216. PRO FO 371/87465, Memorandum from the Chancery, Moscow, to the Foreign Office's Northern Department, 4 April 1950, see the included translation of an *Isvestiya* article from 31 March 1950.

217. Jeffrey A. Richelson, *A Century of Spies: Intelligence in the Twentieth Century* (New York: Oxford University Press, 1995), p. 216.

218. Paul Adair, *Hitler's Greatest Defeat: The Collapse of Army Group Centre, June 1944* (London: Brockhampton Press, 1996), p.63.

219. Martin, *Wilderness*, p. 54.

220. Ibid.

221. Richelson, *Century of Spies*, p. 217; Hansen, *Correlation*, p. 19.

222. Martin, *Wilderness*, p. 57.

223. Ibid., p. 62.

224. Richelson, *Century of Spies*, p. 218.

225. Angelo Codevilla, *Informing Security: Intelligence for a New Century* (New York: The Free Press, 1992), p. 86.

226. Ibid., p. 87.

227. Ibid., p. 99. According to Codevilla, in 1952, GRU (Soviet Military Intelligence) Major Vladimir Popov initiated contact with the CIA in Vienna, becoming the first penetration of the Soviet government the United States ever had.

228. Walter Isaacson and Evan Thomas, *The Wise Men: Six Friends and the World They Made* (London: Faber and Faber, 1986), p. 499.

229. Martin, *Wilderness*, p. 68.

230. Richelson, *Century of Spies*, p. 248.

231. Christopher Andrew, *For the President's Eyes Only: Secret Intelligence and the American Presidency from Washington to Bush* (New York: Harper Collins, 1995), p. 181.

232. Dr. Donald Steury, interview by author, CIA Historical Office, 12 September 1995.

233. Harry G. Summers Jr., *Korean War Almanac* (New York: Facts on File, 1990), p. 89. It was only in 1961 that the CIA moved to Langley, Virginia, its present location.

234. Richelson, *Century of Spies*, p. 218.

235. Ibid., pp. 219–20, for information on operations LEOPARD, RICKRACK, STONEWORK, and OVERCALLS; Rhodes, *Dark Sun*, for information on 1950s operations.

236. Richelson, *Century of Spies*, p. 222, see information on SIGINT station in Alaska.

237. Adair, *Hilter's Greatest Defeat*, p. 57.

238. For example, BLHC, Confidential U.S. State Department Central Files, The Soviet Union: Foreign Affairs, 1950–54, Foreign Service Memorandum from Embassy in Moscow, 5 January 1950; Incoming Airgram, 16 January 1950.

239. James Brooke, "Russia Reopens Its Cosmopolitan Door to the Pacific," *New York Times*, 8 August 1996.

CHAPTER 3: RECONSIDERATION

1. Paul Y. Hammond, "NSC-68: Prologue to Rearmament," in *Strategy, Politics, and Defense Budgets*, ed. Warner Schilling, Paul Hammond, and Glenn Snyder (New York: Columbia University Press, 1966), p. 293.

2. Robert J. Donovan, *Tumultuous Years: The Presidency of Harry S. Truman, 1949–53* (New York: W. W. Norton, 1982), p. 62. Donovan got this information in an interview with William J. Bray, a one-time head of the Democratic National Committee.

3. Ibid., p. 159.

4. FRUS, 1949, vol. 1, Record of Discussions at the Meeting of the Senate Foreign Relations Committee, Washington, 21 April 1949, pp. 288–91.

5. Johnson was used to battles: he had, ironically enough, been a proponent of increased military funding during his stint as Roosevelt's assistant secretary of war, under the isolationist secretary of war, Harry Woodring. Hammond, "NSC-68." Alonzo Hamby, *Beyond the New Deal: Harry S. Truman and American Liberalism* (New York: Columbia University Press, 1973), p. 356.

6. CSQ, *Congress and the Nation, 1945–64* (Washington, D.C.: 1965), p. 253.

7. Walter Poole, 1950–1952, vol. 4 of *History of the Joint Chiefs of Staff* (Wilmington, Del.: Michael Glazier, 1980).

8. Lawrence Kaplan, "The Office of Secretary of Defense and NATO, 1948–1951" (unpublished conference presentation at the Army Center of Military History Conference on the Early Years of the Cold War, 1945–1958, Arlington, Va., June 1996), p. 3.

9. PRO FO 371/81692, AU 11917/4, Memorandum from Sir O. Franks, 13 March 1950.

10. CSQ, *Congress and the Nation*, p. 253; Doris M. Condit, *The Test of War, 1950–1953*, vol. 2 of *History of the Office of Secretary of Defense* (Washington, D.C.: Office of the Secretary of Defense, 1988), p. 15. The B-36 was also the nation's first intercontinental bomber.

11. HSTL, Papers of Harry S. Truman, President's Secretary's Files, B File: Development of Atomic Weapons Program, box 1, folder 2, Memorandum for the President from the Director of the Bureau of the Budget (Pace), 5 April 1949.

12. John B. Rae, *Climb to Greatness: The American Aircraft Industry, 1920–1960* (Cambridge: MIT Press, 1968), p. 196.

13. Donovan, *Tumultuous Years*, p. 302.

14. Rae, *Climb to Greatness*, pp. 184, 195.

15. Ibid., p. 195.

16. Condit, *Test of War*, p. 16. Royall resigned in April 1949, Sullivan left in May 1949, and Gray and Symington left in April 1950.

17. Harry Truman told his staff in August 1949 that Johnson wanted to run for president. Brigadier General Louis Renfrow, Johnson's assistant, said the same. Donovan, *Tumultuous Years*, p. 62.

18. Secretary of State Marshall, like Forrestal, had sharply differed with Truman over the creation of Israel in 1948. This discord, combined with his poor health, led Marshall to resign.

19. Melvyn Leffler, *A Preponderance of Power: National Security, the Truman Administration, and the Cold War* (Stanford, Calif.: Stanford University Press, 1992), pp. 269–70.

20. FRUS, 1949, vol. 5, The Charge in the Soviet Union (Kohler) to the Secretary of State (Acheson), 6 April 1949, pp. 603–9. See the enclosure entitled "Report on Soviet Intentions Prepared by the Joint Intelligence Committee, American Embassy, USSR, April 5, 1949."

21. Dean Acheson, *Present at the Creation: My Years at the State Department* (New York: W. W. Norton, 1969), p. 376.

22. *Department of State Bulletin*, 23 January 1950, p. 114.

23. Paul Nitze, "NSC-68 and the Soviet Threat," *International Security* (spring 1980).

24. Walter Isaacson and Evan Thomas, *The Wise Men: Six Friends and the World They Made* (London: Faber and Faber, 1986), p. 489.

25. Major General Sir Ian Jacob, "Principles of British Military Thought," *Foreign Affairs* (January 1951): pp. 219–28; Anthony Eden, "Britain in World Strategy," *Foreign Affairs* (January 1951): pp. 341–50, divulges that British troop commitments at the time of the writing of the article were: Korea, 12,000; Austria and Trieste, 10,000; Germany 50,000; Great Britain, 230,000; Middle East, 45,000; Malaya, 17,000; Hong Kong 20,000; and bases other than Singapore and Hong Kong, 20,000.

26. Constance Coblenz, Morton Kaplan, and William Reitzel, *United States Foreign Policy, 1945–1955* (Washington, D.C.: The Brookings Institution, 1956), p. 333.

27. PRO FO 371/89951, Western Union Secretariat, 1112/95, note from the Foreign Office to Sir Gladwyn Jebbs.

28. Leffler, *Preponderance of Power*, p. 277; Dean Rusk and Richard Rusk, *As I Saw It* (New York: Penguin, 1990), p. 165; Isaacson and Thomas, *Wise Men*, p. 475.

29. Acheson, *Creation*, p. 374.

30. [George Kennan], "The Sources of Soviet Conduct," *Foreign Affairs* (July 1947).

31. Jerald A. Combs, "The Compromise That Never Was: George Kennan, Paul Nitze, and the Issue of Conventional Deterrence in Europe, 1949–1952," *Diplomatic History* (summer 1991).

32. Ibid.

33. Ibid.

34. Kaplan, *NATO*, p. 34.

35. Isaacson and Thomas, *Wise Men*, p. 488.

36. FRUS, 1949, vol. 1, Minutes of the 148th Meeting of the Policy Planning Staff, Tuesday, 11 October 1949, pp. 399–403.

37. George Kennan, *Memoirs, 1925–1950* (Boston: Little Brown, 1967), p. 464.

38. FRUS, 1949, vol. 1, Minutes of the 148th Meeting of the Policy Planning Staff, Tuesday, 11 October 1949, pp. 399–403.

39. Combs, "Compromise."

40. Nitze, "NSC-68," p. 171.

41. Combs, "Compromise"; John Lewis Gaddis. *Strategies of Containment: A Critical Appraisal of Postwar American National Security Policy* (Oxford: Oxford University Press, 1982), chapter 3. Kennan's belief that a united, demilitarized Germany was possible represented a change from what he thought in 1944–46. Daniel Yergin, *Shattered Peace: The Origins of the Cold War and the National Security State* (Boston: Houghton Mifflin, 1977), p. 75.

42. Hammond, "NSC-68," p. 287.

43. Ibid.

44. Ibid.

45. FRUS, 1949, vol. 1, Minutes of the 171st Meeting of the Policy Planning Staff, Friday, 16 December 1949, pp. 413–16.

46. Ibid.

47. John Lewis Gaddis, *The United States and the End of the Cold War: Implications, Reconsiderations, and Provocations* (Oxford: Oxford University Press, 1994), p. 29.

48. FRUS, 1949, vol. 1, Minutes of the 148th Meeting of the Policy Planning Staff, Tuesday, 11 October 1949, pp. 399–403.

49. FRUS, 1949, vol. 1, Minutes of the 171st Meeting of the Policy Planning Staff, Friday, 16 December 1949, pp. 413–16.

50. FRUS, 1949, vol. 1, Minutes of the 148th Meeting of the Policy Planning Staff, Tuesday, 11 October 1949, pp. 399–403.

51. Isaacson and Thomas, *Wise Men*, p. 489.

52. FRUS, 1949, vol. 1, Minutes of the 171st Meeting of the Policy Planning Staff, Friday, 16 December 1949, pp. 413–16.

53. Douglas Brinkley, *Dean Acheson: The Cold War Years, 1953–71* (New Haven: Yale University Press, 1992), p. 92.

54. David Callahan, *Dangerous Capabilities: Paul Nitze and the Cold War* (New York: Harper Collins, 1990), p. 71.

55. FRUS, 1949, vol. 1, Record of the Under Secretary's Meeting, Department of State, 15 April 1949, pp. 283–84.

56. FRUS, 1949, vol. 1, Minutes of the 148th Meeting of the Policy Planning Staff, Tuesday, 11 October 1949, pp. 399–403; FRUS, 1949, vol. 1, Minutes of the 171st Meeting of the Policy Planning Staff, Friday, 16 December 1949, pp. 413–16.

57. Callahan, *Nitze*; Thomas and Isaacson, *Wise Men*.

58. Christopher Andrew, *For the President's Eyes Only: Secret Intelligence and the American Presidency from Washington to Bush* (New York: Harper Collins, 1995), p. 177.

59. Richard Rhodes, *Dark Sun: The Making of the Hydrogen Bomb* (New York: Simon and Schuster, 1995), p. 241.

60. FRUS, 1948, vol. 1, part 2, Memorandum of Conversation, by Mr. Edmund A. Gullion, Special Assistant to the Under Secretary of State, 27 January 1948, p. 508.

61. Gregg Herken, *Cardinal Choices: Presidential Science Advising from the Atomic Bomb to SDI* (New York: Oxford University Press, 1992), p. 38. There was wide variation in the numerous American predictions made on Soviet atomic capabilities. For one of the worst, see CIA Intelligence Memorandum 225, 20 September 1949, which predicted that the Soviets could not achieve fission before mid-1950. Michael Warner, ed., *CIA Cold War Records: The CIA Under Harry Truman* (Washington, D.C.: CIA, 1994).

62. Jeffrey A. Richelson, *A Century of Spies: Intelligence in the Twentieth Century* (New York: Oxford University Press, 1995), p. 222.

63. Rhodes, *Dark Sun*, p. 366.

64. Ibid., p. 367.

65. Ibid., p. 364.

66. Hammond, "NSC-68," p. 290.

67. Alonzo Hamby, *Man of the People: A Life of Harry S. Truman* (New York: Oxford University Press, 1995), p. 525.

68. Callahan, *Nitze*.

69. FRUS, 1949, vol. 5, Telegram from the Ambassador in the Soviet Union (Kirk) to the Secretary of State (Acheson), 29 September 1949, p. 658.

70. Paul Boyer, *By the Bomb's Early Light: American Thought and Culture at the Beginning of the Atomic Age* (New York: Pantheon, 1985), p. 337.

71. FRUS, 1949, vol. 1, Minutes of the 148th Meeting of the Policy Planning Staff, Tuesday, 11 October 1949, pp. 399–403.

72. David Lilienthal, *The Atomic Energy Years, 1945–1950*, vol. 2 of *The Journals of David Lilienthal* (New York: Harper and Row, 1964), pp. 580–81.

73. In retrospect, this meeting was a partial step away from the overwhelming

reliance on strategic bombing that characterized American security policy in the immediate post-Hiroshima era. It suggested that the path ahead might lie in a twin commitment to conventional and nuclear deterrence, in which the United States would not abandon the principle of first use, but would attempt to construct another alternative. This was what American policy would be for several decades, but no one at the time could be certain of such an outcome.

74. FRUS, 1949, vol. 1, Report to the President by the Special Committee of the National Security Council on the Proposed Acceleration of the Atomic Energy Program, p. 562.

75. Callahan, *Nitze*, p. 78.

76. HSTL, President's Secretary's Files, B File: Development of Atomic Weapons, box 1, folder 2, Report to the President by the Special Committee of the National Security Council on the Proposed Acceleration of the Atomic Energy Program, 10 October 1949.

77. Ibid.

78. Ibid.

79. Ibid.

80. Lilienthal, *Atomic Energy Years*, p. 577; 10 and 29 October 1949, pp. 580–81.

81. A Joint Chiefs of Staff study submitted to the National Security Council on 1 February 1950 estimated that the Soviets would possess 10–20 atomic bombs by the middle of that year and 70–135 by mid-1953. The CIA completed a report on 10 February 1950 concluding that the Soviets would have 100 atomic bombs by 1953 and 200 by the end of 1955. The CIA report also included the prediction that 200 atomic weapons delivered on proscribed targets "might prove decisive in knocking the United States out of the war," although it did not predict that the Soviets would feel that their superiority was great enough to take such action until 1956 or 1957. Samuel Wells, "Sounding the Tocsin: NSC-68 and the Soviet Threat," *International Security* (fall 1979).

82. Soviet bomb: David Holloway, *Stalin and the Bomb: The Soviet Union and Atomic Energy, 1939–1956* (New Haven: Yale University Press, 1994), p. 306; American bomb: Paul Nitze, *From Hiroshima to Glasnost* (London: Weidenfield and Nicholson, 1989), p. 92.

83. FRUS, 1949, vol. 1, Minutes of the 148th Meeting of the Policy Planning Staff, Tuesday, 11 October 1949, pp. 399–403.

84. Ibid.

85. FRUS, 1949, vol. 1, Minutes of the 171st Meeting of the Policy Planning Staff, Friday, 16 September 1949, pp. 413–16.

86. NARA, record group 273, NSC-68, 11 April 1950.

87. PDDE, Volume 10, p. 569, footnote #2.

88. Combs, "Compromise."

89. The Harmon Report, quoted in David Alan Rosenberg, "American Atomic Strategy and the Hydrogen Bomb Decision," *Journal of American History* (June 1979).

90. Combs, "Compromise."

91. Holloway, *Stalin and the Bomb*, p. 240.

92. PDDE, p. 569.

93. *The New York Times*, October 16, 1949.

94. Lilienthal, *Atomic Energy Years*, 31 December 1949, pp. 616–17.

95. Marc Trachtenberg, "A Wasting Asset: American Strategy and the Shifting Nuclear Balance, 1949–1954," *History and Strategy,* ed. Marc Trachtenberg (Princeton: Princeton University Press, 1991), p.109.

96. Aaron Friedberg, "Why Didn't the United States Become a Garrison State," *International Security* (spring 1992): p. 126.

97. Ibid., p. 11.

98. Holloway, *Stalin and the Bomb,* p. 299.

99. Herken, *Cardinal Choices,* p. 35.

100. Hammond, "NSC-68," p. 290

101. Herken, *Cardinal Choices,* p. 37.

102. Callahan, *Nitze,* p. 73.

103. Hammond, "NSC-68," p. 290.

104. Lawrence Freedman, *The Evolution of Nuclear Strategy* (New York: St. Martin's Press, 1983), p. 68.

105. Hammond, "NSC-68," p. 291.

106. Ibid., p. 293.

107. Lilienthal, *Atomic Energy Years,* 25 December 1949.

108. Harry S. Truman, *Memoirs: Years of Trial and Hope, 1946–1952* (New York: Signet, 1956), p. 309.

109. Lilienthal, *Atomic Energy Years,* 25 December 1949, pp. 613–14.

110. Ibid., 26 January 1950, p. 620; Hammond, "NSC-68."

111. Nitze, *Hiroshima to Glasnost,* p. 91. Later, Johnson would claim that he had not been informed of the writing of the review and that the whole exercise had been a conspiracy arranged behind his back by Nitze and General Truman Landon, who was the liaison between the team writing the review and the Joint Chiefs of Staff.

112. Discussion with Acheson: Lilienthal, *Atomic Energy Years,* 26 January 1950, p. 620; writing of the directive: Hammond, "NSC-68."

113. Hammond, "NSC-68," p. 292.

114. Ibid., p. 303.

115. Pearson and *The New York Times*: Callahan, *Nitze,* p. 84; Murrow and Baruch: Lilienthal, *Atomic Energy Years,* 28 and 29 January 1950.

116. Hamby, *Man of the People,* p. 526.

117. George H. Gallup, *The Gallup Poll: Public Opinion, 1935–71, Volume 2* (New York: Random House, 1972), p. 888.

118. Callahan, *Nitze,* p. 84.

119. Donovan, *Tumultuous Years,* p. 155, claims that Truman had made up his mind at least 10 days before the meeting.

120. Holloway, *Stalin and the Bomb,* p. 299.

121. Nitze, *Hiroshima to Glasnost,* p. 91.

122. Statement by the President on the Hydrogen Bomb, Harry S. Truman, *Public Papers of the Presidents of the United States: Harry S. Truman, 1950* (Washington, D.C.: GPO, 1965), p. 138.

123. Isaacson and Thomas, *Wise Men,* p. 499. Although the team at first planned to make large parts of their report public, and therefore referred to the project as Operation CANDOR, Acheson decided during its creation that it would be more useful to write it as a top-secret internal memorandum.

124. Nitze, *Hiroshima to Glasnost,* p. 94.

125. Hammond, "NSC-68."

126. Ibid.

127. Judging by those meetings whose minutes are in FRUS, 21 men partici-
pated in the exercise. From NSC: James Lay Jr. (executive secretary of NSC) and
S. Everett Gleason (deputy executive secretary of NSC). From PPS: Paul Nitze,
George Butler, Carlton Savage, Harry Schwartz, Robert Tufts, and R. Gordon Ar-
neson. Other State participants: Adrian Fisher (legal adviser) and Joseph Chase
(staff member, Office of the Undersecretary of State). From Defense: James Burns,
Truman Landon, Najeeb E. Hallaby (director, Office of Foreign Military Affairs),
Robert LeBaron (atomic energy adviser to the secretary of defense), and Lt. Colonel
William Burke. As consultants, six men were brought in for one meeting each:
physicists J. Robert Oppenheimer and Ernst Lawrence, AEC member Henry
Smyth, Chester Barnard (former consultant to the State Department's Committee
on Atomic Energy), James Conant (former head of the Manhattan Project), and
Robert Lovett (former assistant secretary of war and former undersecretary of
state). Only three of these men, Nitze, Arneson, and Landon, attended all the
meetings. FRUS, 1950, vol. 1, Records of Meetings of the State-Defense Policy
Review Group, 27 February, 2 March, 10 March, 16 March, and 20 March 1950.

128. It seems possible that the draft Nitze asked John Paton Davies, of the PPS,
to write on 2 February, concerning the probability of war with the USSR, made a
substantial contribution. FRUS, 1950, vol. 1, Record of the Eighth Meeting (1950)
of the Policy Planning Staff of the Department of State, 2 February 1950,
pp. 142–43. Nitze, *From Hiroshima to Glasnost,* p. 94, credits Davies and Robert
Hooker, as well as Tufts, all from PPS, with helping write NSC-68.

129. Hammond, "NSC-68," p. 299.

130. Ibid.

131. Nitze, *Hiroshima to Glasnost,* p. 94.

132. Acheson, *Creation,* pp. 374–75.

133. Isaacson and Thomas, *Wise Men,* p. 497.

134. Nitze would later defend the language used in a 1975 interview by explaining that "Today, I think you would write that question about the freedom of
the individual, and the freedom of states to develop as they want, somewhat
differently . . . One goes back to the period of '49-'50. This was really a passionate
belief on the part of those of us who were working on this statement, on the part
of Mr. Truman. I think there's less of that today." HSTL, Oral History #454 (Paul
Nitze), vol. 2, p. 253.

135. NARA, record group 273, NSC-68, 14 April 1950.

136. Ibid.

137. Ibid.

138. Ibid.

139. Ibid.

140. Ibid.

141. Ibid.

142. Ibid.

143. Ibid.

144. Ibid.

145. Ibid.

146. Ibid.

147. Ibid.

148. Ibid.

149. Ibid.

150. Ibid. NSC-68's hostility to negotiating with the Soviet leadership seems to have coincided with Truman's thoughts on the matter. In a 20 April 1950 meeting with Trygve Lie, the secretary general of the United Nations, Truman was asked by Lie to consider talking with Stalin. Truman responded that the experience of Potsdam had left him completely disillusioned about the usefulness of such meetings. After Lie persisted, Truman relented only to the extent that he would allow Stalin to come to Washington, insisting that he would not attend a meeting anywhere else. Truman probably knew that any trip he took outside of the United States might create the perception that he was appeasing the Soviets, a situation of which his domestic political opponents could eagerly take advantage. He may also have known that Stalin was loath to travel without a division of troops to protect him, and that it was very unlikely that he would visit Washington. Stalin never did. BLHC, Official Conversations and Meetings of Dean Acheson (1949–53), Memorandum of Conversation with the President and Mr. Lie, 20 April 1950.

151. NARA, record group 273, NSC-68, 14 April 1950.

152. Ibid.

153. Ibid.

154. Ibid.

155. FRUS, 1952–54, vol. 2, 14 July 1952, p. 59.

156. Nitze, *Hiroshima to Glasnost*, p. 96.

157. FRUS, 1950, vol. 1, Record of Meeting of the State-Defense Policy Review Group, Department of State, 27 February 1950, pp. 168–75.

158. Callahan, *Nitze*, p. 66.

159. NARA, record group 273, NSC-68, 14 April 1950. What NSC-68 failed to mention was that the arms build-up for World War II occurred under special circumstances. The Depression was almost as bad in 1940 as it had been at the start of the decade, and capacity in all private sectors, was generally so underutilized that vast increases in armaments production could occur without necessarily dampening consumer power. Even under those special circumstances, World War II still led to many shortages and, in certain cases, price controls merely led to decrease in the quality of consumer goods.

160. Callahan, *Nitze*, p. 67.

161. NSC 20/4 makes similar assumptions about Soviet aggressive intent.

162. For example, see FRUS, 1949, vol. 1, Basic US Security Resource Assumptions, 1 June 1949, pp. 339–45; FRUS, 1950, vol. 4, Memorandum Prepared in the Department of State: Recent Soviet Moves, 8 February 1950, pp. 1099–1101.

163. NARA, record group 273, NSC-68, 14 April 1950.

164. FRUS, 1950, vol. 1, Records of Meetings of the State-Defense Policy Review Group, 27 February, 2 March, 10 March, 16 March, and 20 March. Of particular interest are Nitze's comments to Barnard and Smyth in 10 March meeting. Ernest May, "NSC-68: The Theory and Politics of Strategy," in *American Cold War Strategy: Interpreting NSC 68* (Boston: Bedford Books, 1993).

165. Nitze, *Hiroshima to Glasnost*, pp. 94–95; Acheson, *Creation*, p. 373; Isaacson and Thomas, *Wise Men*, p. 500; Hammond, "NSC-68," pp. 322–23; Poole, *JCS*, p. 8.

166. Acheson, *Creation*, p. 374.

167. Nitze, *Hiroshima to Glasnost*, p. 95.

168. The Alsops maintained their advantage in gaining scoops by dining with high-ranking officials, including Secretary of the Army Frank Pace, Justice Felix Frankfurter, and Assistant Secretary of State Dean Rusk, any of whom might have been willing to help attack Johnson's budgeting policies. Rusk and Rusk, *As I Saw It*, p. 161.

The Alsops' first column opposing the budgeting must have touched a raw nerve in Johnson, for the day after its publication, he passionately defended himself, claiming that he would work to achieve economies in defense "if it takes me to my dying breath," and stating that the economies he was creating were based on elimination of waste and duplication, as shown by the dismissal of 157,542 civilian department employees who, he said, were unnecessary. PRO FO 371/81692, AU 11917/4, Memorandum from Sir O. Franks, 13 March 1950.

169. Leffler, *Preponderance of Power*, p. 358, claims that NSC-68 was so vague that Johnson might have approved it because he wasn't aware that Nitze was thinking in terms of funding increases on such a vast scale.

170. May, "NSC 68."

171. May, "NSC 68," p. 13; Kennan's report from the trip is in FRUS, 1950, vol. 1, and is also summarized in his *Memoirs, 1925–1950*, although in neither does he accuse Acheson of planning the trip to remove him from the country. Kennan's quote about drastic measures is from Isaacson and Thomas, *Wise Men*, p. 496.

172. Charles E. Bohlen, *Witness to History, 1929–1969* (New York: W. W. Norton, 1973), p. 290.

173. Leffler, *Preponderance of Power*, p. 357.

174. FRUS, 1950, vol. 1, memorandum by Schaub to Lay, 8 May 1950, pp. 298–306.

175. Michael J. Hogan, *A Cross of Iron: Harry S. Truman and the Origins of the National Security State, 1945–1954* (Cambridge: Cambridge University Press, 1998), p. 303.

176. Hamby, *Man of the People*, p. 514.

177. *Public Papers of the Presidents: Harry S. Truman, 1950*, The President's News Conference of 4 May 1950, p. 286.

178. HSTL, Frederick Lawton Papers, Box 6, Folder on Meetings with the President, Memorandum for the Record, 23 May 1950.

179. *Public Papers of the Presidents: Harry S. Truman, 1950*, The President's News Conference of 25 May 1950, p. 440.

180. Isaacson and Thomas, *Wise Men*, p. 504.

181. "Peace and the High Cost Thereof," *Newsweek*, June 12, 1950.

182. Leffler, *Preponderance of Power*, p. 358.

183. *Public Papers of the Presidents: Harry S. Truman, 1950*, The President's News Conference of 22 June 1950, p. 487.

184. CSQ, *Congress and the Nation*, p. 265.

185. The Department of Defense, as quoted in CSQ, *Congress and the Nation*, p. 265.

186. Poole, *JCS*, p. 39.

187. *The World Almanac 1993*, p. 693.

188. BLHC, Official Conversations and Meetings of Dean Acheson (1949–53), Memorandum of Conversation, 24 April 1950.

189. PRO FO 371/90987, AU 1213/1, Naval Attaché's Annual Report on the U.S, Navy for the Year 1950.

190. "Combat Airplanes Increasing In Size," *The New York Times*, June 25, 1950, p. 17.

191. Rusk and Rusk, *As I Saw It*, p. 166.

192. HSTL, President's Secretary's Files, box 207, folder on 55th meeting, Letter from Truman to Lay, 12 April 1950.

193. HSTL, President's Secretary's Files, box 207, Minutes of the 55th Meeting of the National Security Council, 20 April 1950. The committee consisted of senior representatives designated by each NSC member, as well as the secretary of the treasury, the Economic Cooperation Administrator, the director of the Bureau of the Budget, and the chairman of the Council of Economic Advisers. This group was, with the exception of two people (Gleason and Lay), different from the one that had written NSC-68. They produced, with much help from the Department of Defense, a document that, unlike NSC-68, was detailed in its budgetary estimates. It became known, upon its completion in September, as NSC 68/1, and later was updated by revisions known as NSC 68/2, NSC 68/3, and so on.

194. Nitze, *Hiroshima to Glasnost*, p. 83; Rusk and Rusk, *As I Saw It*, p. 155; Bohlen, *Witness to History*, p. 301; Deborah Welch Larson, *Origins of Containment: A Psychological Explanation* (Princeton: Princeton University Press, 1995) provides a psychological explanation of Truman's desire to make decisions swiftly.

195. Ernest Lindley, "Is There Real Danger of War?" *Newsweek*, 15 May 1950; Ernest Lindley, "A Long Cold War," *Newsweek*, 22 May 1950.

196. May, "NSC 68," p. 14.

197. Ibid.

198. For example, Melvyn Leffler, *The Specter of Communism: The United States and the Origins of the Cold War, 1947–1953* (New York: Hill and Wang, 1994), p. 93, refers to NSC-68 as "one of the most important national security documents of the Cold War." For another example, see Gaddis, *Strategies*, chapter 4.

199. $3 billion statistic: Samuel F. Wells, "The First Cold War Buildup: Europe in United States Strategy and Policy, 1950–1953," *Western Security: The Formative Years; European and Atlantic Defence, 1947–53*, ed. Olav Riste (Oslo: Norwegian University Press, 1985), p. 183. The judgment on Truman's likely behavior is my own.

200. For an alternative view of Truman's reactions to NSC-68, see Samuel P. Huntington, *The Soldier and the State: The Theory and Politics of Civil-Military Relations* (Cambridge, Mass.: Belknap Press, 1957), p. 384. Huntington suggests that Truman believed in the recommendations of NSC-68, but did not allow Congress to be informed of NSC-68 because he felt that an arms build-up was not politically feasible at the time. Thus, Huntington concludes, "in the spring of 1950 the Administration, in effect, had two defense policies: a public one embodied in the thirteen billion dollar defense budget recommended for the next fiscal year and a private one embodied in NSC-68. This duality was ended only by the outbreak of the Korean War." Huntington gives no sources for this argument, nor does he

mention that it was Truman who was the bigger cost-cutter than Congress, having opted not to spend money that Congress had authorized for the air force the previous year. Nor does Huntington explain the logic of Truman opting to ask for extra cuts in the defense budget in May 1950.

201. BLHC, Public Statements of the Secretaries of Defense, Part 1: The Truman Administration, microfilm reel 215, Selective Service Extension Act of 1950 and Manpower Registration and Classification Act, Hearings Before the Committee on Armed Services, United States Senate, 1, 5, and 8 June 1950, p. 40.

202. Acheson, *Creation*, p. 374.

203. HSTL, Papers of Harry S. Truman, President's Secretary's Files, Box 209, Minutes of the 68th Meeting of the National Security Council, 29 September 1950.

204. Isaacson and Thomas, *Wise Men*, p. 503.

205. Acheson, *Creation*, p. 377–78.

206. BLHC, Public Statements by the Secretaries of Defense, Part 1: The Truman Administration, microfilm reel 215, "Selective Service Extension Act of 1950 and Manpower Registration and Classification Act," 1 June 1950, p. 666.

207. Bohlen, *Witness to History*, p. 291.

208. Norman Graebner, "NSC 68," *The Harry S. Truman Encyclopedia*, pp. 261–62.

209. DDEL, Eisenhower Pre-Presidential Papers, box 62, Louis Johnson folder, memo of 26 August 1949.

210. NARA, record group 330, entry 80, fiscal year 1951 file, memorandum from the Bureau of the Budget to the Secretary of Defense (Johnson), 16 December 1949.

211. FRUS, 1949, vol. 1, Report by the National Security Council; Government Programs in National Security and International Affairs for the Fiscal Year 1951, 29 September 1949, pp. 386–93.

212. NARA, record group 330, fiscal year 1951 budget folder, letter for the director of the Bureau of the Budget from the Office of the Assistant Secretary of Defense, Comptroller, 15 September 1949.

213. NARA, record group 330, entry 80, fiscal year 1951 file, memorandum from the Bureau of the Budget to the Secretary of Defense (Johnson), 16 December 1949.

214. HSTL, Frederick Lawton Papers, box 5, folder entitled "Budget, National, FY 1951," Memorandum of Mr. Lawton's Telephone Conversation with Mr. Pace from Key West, Florida, on 9 and 10 December 1949.

215. NARA, record group 330, entry 80, box 32, fiscal year 1951 file, letter by Loftis to Johnson, 16 December 1949.

216. Condit, *Test of War*, p. 224; Poole, *JCS*, p. 20.

217. BLHC, Public Statements by the Secretaries of Defense, Part 1: The Truman Administration, microfilm reel 215, "Selective Service Extension Act of 1950 and Manpower Registration and Classification Act."

218. PRO FO 371/ 90989, AU 1225/1, "Annual Report for 1950 on the US Air Force, Prepared by the Air Attaché," 5 March 1951.

219. Ibid.

220. Poole, *JCS*, p. 21.

221. Ibid., p. 23.

222. Hogan, *Cross of Iron*, p. 289.

223. Ibid.

224. Condit, *Test of War*, p. 224.

225. Poole, *JCS*, p. 25.

226. Condit, *Test of War*.

227. NARA record group 330, CD 380, memorandum from Secretary Johnson to the service secretaries, 22 February 1950, as cited in Condit, *Test of War*.

228. Condit, *Test of War* p.nbsp;244.

229. NARA memorandum from the Secretary of Defense to service Secretaries, record group 330, Assistant to Secretary of Defense and Deputy Secretary of Defense files, NSC-68 folder, 25 May 1950.

230. Water's edge quote from Walter LaFeber, *The American Age: U.S. Foreign Policy at Home and Abroad, 1750 to the Present* (New York: W. W. Norton, 1994), p. 504.

231. H. Bradford Westerfield, *Foreign Policy and Party Politics, Pearl Harbor to Korea* (New Haven: Yale University Press, 1955), p. 371.

232. Ibid., p. 372.

233. *The New York Times,* January 9, 1950.

234. Taft in letter of 18 September 1949, quoted in Walter LaFeber, "NATO and the Korean War: A Context," *Diplomatic History* (fall 1989).

235. Ronald Caridi, *The Korean War and American Politics: The Republican Party as a Case Study* (Philadelphia: University of Pennsylvania Press, 1968).

236. Hogan, *Cross of Iron*, p. 289.

237. Isaacson and Thomas, *Wise Men*, p. 475. The China Lobby and the Asia First lobby were most popular in the Midwest and West. Supporting the Nationalist Chinese may have been a means for getting back at the perceived bias of the State Department, the composition of which was widely considered to be East Coast men with cultural and business connections to Europe, who did not share the antipathy many in the United States felt toward Europe and toward Communism. Many Democrat foreign policy leaders (including Acheson, Nitze, Forrestal, Bohlen, Kennan, and Harriman, though not Truman, Byrnes, or Marshall), were seen as representing both East Coast commercial interests in Europe and a culture of Europhilia obtained at East Coast universities or in New York. The large aid projects to Europe, which occurred simultaneously with the end of aid to Chiang, were seen as proof of this phenomenon.

238. Robert Griffith, "Old Progressives and the Cold War," *Journal of American History* (September 1979).

239. Rhodes, *Dark Sun*, p. 422.

240. Associated Press, "Syracuse Chemist Arrested on Spy Charge," *Washington Post*, 16 June 1950, p. 1.

241. The other members of the Tydings Committee were Theodore Francis Green (Democrat, Rhode Island), Bourke B. Hickenlooper (Republican, Iowa), Henry Cabot Lodge Jr. (Republican, Massachusetts), and Brien McMahon (Democrat, Connecticut).

242. Donovan, *Tumultuous Years*, p. 168. Wherry had been in the funeral service business before entering elected office.

243. Ibid.

244. Ibid., p. 169.

245. Statement by the President Announcing Steps Taken to Develop a Bipartisan Approach to Foreign Policy, *Public Papers of the Presidents: Harry S. Truman, 1950*, p. 273.

246. Harry S. Truman, *Public Papers of the Presidents, Harry S. Truman, 1950*; Donovan, *Tumultuous Years*, p. 175.

247. Donovan, *Tumultuous Years*, p. 176.

CHAPTER 4: TRANSFORMATION

1. *The New York Times*, June 26, 1950, see map on p. 2 with accompanying captions; or see map on p. 59 of James F. Schnabel and Robert Watson, *The History of the Joint Chiefs of Staff: The Joint Chiefs of Staff and National Policy*, vol. 3, part 1 of *The Korean War* (Wilmington, Del.: Michael Glazier, 1979).

2. Matthew Ridgway, *The Korean War* (New York: DaCapo, 1967), p. 17. The ROK air force had requested its first combat aircraft from the United States, but these had not yet arrived. Schnabel and Watson, *Joint Chiefs and National Policy*, p. 42.

3. *Current Digest of the Soviet Press*, "People of South Korea Greet People's Army Soldiers," 22 July 1950 (translation of a Pravda article of 28 June 1950).

4. NARA, record group 273, National Security Council Mill 9, "United States Foreign and Domestic Policy in Furtherance of National Security," 25 February 1948, p. 7.

5. Harry G. Summers Jr., "The Korean War: A Fresh Perspective," *Military History* (April 1996): p. 24, and William O'Neill, *American High: The Years of Confidence, 1945–1960* (New York: MacMillan, 1986), p. 115.

6. Summers, "The Korean War: A Fresh Perspective," p. 25.

7. Robert J. McMahon, "Credibility and World Power: Exploring the Psychological Dimension in Postwar American Diplomacy," *Diplomatic History* (Fall 1991); Melvyn Leffler, *The Specter of Communism: The United States and the Origins of the Cold War, 1947–1953* (New York: Hill and Wang, 1994), p. 100; Dean Acheson, *Present at the Creation: My Years at the State Department* (New York: W. W. Norton, 1969), p. 405.

8. Harry S. Truman, *Memoirs: Years of Trial and Hope, 1946–1952* (New York: Signet, 1956), p. 333.

9. Michael Schaller, *Douglas MacArthur: The Far Eastern General* (New York: Oxford University Press, 1989), p. 185; Walter Isaacson and Evan Thomas, *The Wise Men: Six Friends and the World They Made* (London: Faber and Faber, 1986), p. 508.

10. The minutes of most of these meetings are in BLHC, Official Conversations and Meetings of Dean Acheson, Memorandum of Conversation, Subject: Korean Situation, 26 June 1950.

11. "Beyond Subversion," *Time*, July 3, 1950, p. 7. The Seventh Fleet consisted of one aircraft carrier, two cruisers, 12 destroyers, and four submarines. On the first day of the invasion, MacArthur began sending fighter planes to the South Korean air force. "War in Asia," *Time*, July 3, 1950, p. 14. Truman mentioned, but never implemented, the possibility of "taking Formosa back as part of Japan and putting it under MacArthur's command." BLHC, Official Conversations and

Meetings of Dean Acheson, Memorandum of Conversation, Subject: Korean Situation, 26 June 1950.

12. For Johnson: Robert J. Donovan, *Tumultuous Years: The Presidency of Harry S. Truman, 1949–53* (New York: W. W. Norton, 1982), p. 198; Doris M. Condit, *The Test of War, 1950–1953*, vol. 2 of *History of the Office of Secretary of Defense* (Washington, D.C.: Office of the Secretary of Defense, 1988), p. 49; "Johnson Gives Witness Cues," *Washington Post*, June 28, 1950, p. 4

For Nitze: HSTL, Oral History #454 (Paul Nitze), p. 262. Nitze claimed that although he was obviously in favor of the arms build-up, he was "less enthusiastic about reacting" to the attack than others because of the work he had done with the JCS showing America's inadequacy to fight a conflict beyond what was considered its perimeter of action. He did approve of involving the UN in the conflict.

For Bradley and Pace: BLHC, Official Conversations and Meetings of Dean Acheson (1949–53), Item 0643, Memorandum of Conversation, 25 June 1950.

13. Alonzo Hamby, *Man of the People: A Life of Harry S. Truman* (New York: Oxford University Press, 1995), p. 536.

14. O'Neill, *Years of Confidence*, p. 116.

15. Speech by Robert Taft in the Senate, 28 June 1950, text in *Vital Speeches of the Day*, 1950, pp. 613–17. Acheson had a series of conversations with senators in the days after the invasion to inform them of events, but made sure that decision-making authority stayed with the president. BLHC, Official Conversations and Meetings of Dean Acheson.

16. Clayton Knowles, "Congressmen Back Moves Made By US," *New York Times*, 26 June 1950, p. 1; Associated Press, "Members of Congress Surprised by Invasion," *Los Angeles Times*, 26 June 1950, p. 2.

17. "Strange Bedfellows," *The Economist*, July 8, 1950.

18. "Comments by Press of Nation on Korean Situation," *The New York Times*, June 27, 1950, p. 16, has excerpts from 16 newspapers from across the nation.

19. United Press, "Where American Forces Are Stationed in Orient," *The Los Angeles Times*, June 25, 1950, p. 1

20. Schaller, *MacArthur*, p. 185.

21. Summers, "The Korean War: A Fresh Perspective," p. 25. Summers was one of those soldiers.

22. July 10 1950 edition; quoted in Geoffrey Perrett, *A Dream of Greatness: The American People, 1945–1963* (New York: Coward, McCann, and Geoghegan, 1979), p. 163.

23. Walter LaFeber, "NATO and the Korean War: A Context," *Diplomatic History* (fall 1989).

24. Schaller, *MacArthur*, p. 187.

25. Truman, *Years of Trial and Hope*, p. 341.

26. Walter Poole, *History of the Joint Chiefs of Staff, Volume 4: 1950–1952* (Wilmington, Del.: Michael Glazier, 1980), p. 48.

27. Charles E. Bohlen, *Witness to History, 1929–1969* (New York: W. W. Norton, 1973), p. 304.

28. FRUS, 1950, vol. 1, Draft Report by the National Security Council, 1 July 1950, pp. 331–38.

29. FRUS, 1950, vol. 1, Statement by the Chairman of the National Security

Resources Board (Symington) to the National Security Council, 6 July 1950, pp. 338–41.

30. Associated Press, "Bulgarian Troops Near Yugoslavia," *Los Angeles Times*, 24 June 1950, p. 1.

31. FRUS, 1950, vol. 1, Memorandum of National Security Council Consultants' Meeting, Thursday, 29 June 1950, pp. 324–26. According to historian Richard Crockatt, Stalin cancelled plans to conquer Yugoslavia in July 1950 after the U.S. intervention in Korea convinced him that the Soviets might meet an armed response. Richard Crockatt, *The Fifty Years War: The United States and the Soviet Union in World Politics, 1941–1991* (London: Routledge, 1995).

32. FRUS, 1950, vol. 1, Memorandum of National Security Council Consultants' Meeting, Thursday, 29 June 1950, pp. 324–26.

In another NSC Consultants' Meeting (pp. 327–31) that day, Kennan added, and the other participants agreed, that present NSC policy in the event of a Soviet attack on Yugoslavia was only to provide limited assistance to Tito. However, various participants at the meeting commented that an attack on Yugoslavia, Iran, or Germany might be the first step should the Soviets decide to launch World War III.

Bohlen and Kennan both claimed, in their memoirs, *Witness to History* and *Memoirs, 1950–1963*, that together they lobbied against the prevailing belief that Korea represented the first event in a new phase of Soviet foreign policy. However, Kennan, as cited above, was worried about Soviet military action at this time. According to Walter Isaacson and Evan Thomas, both Kennan and Bohlen hedged their bets, writing that they thought Soviet military action was unlikely, but, lacking the confidence in this belief to say it categorically, warning that it was possible. Isaacson and Thomas, *Wise Men*, p. 512.

33. Associated Press, "Bulgarian Troops Near Yugoslavia," Los Angeles Times, 24 June 1950, p. 1.

34. *Current Digest of the Soviet Press*, May 20 1950, p. 27 (translation of a Pravda article of 1 April 1950).

35. BLHC, Official Conversations and Meetings of Dean Acheson (1949–53), Item 0673, Memorandum of Conversation, 26 June 1950.

36. FRUS, 1950, vol. 1, Draft Report of the National Security Council, 1 July 1950, pp. 334–35.

37. For discussions on perceptions of Soviet intentions in the immediate aftermath of the North Korean attack, see FRUS, 1950, vol. 1, Memorandum of National Security Council Consultants' Meeting, Thursday, 29 June 1950, p. 324-26d FRUS, 1950, vol. 1, Draft Report of the National Security Council, 1 July 1950, pp. 331–38.

38. BLHC, Official Conversations and Meetings of Dean Acheson, Statement Before the Cabinet on Korean Crisis, 14 July 1950.

39. Ibid.

40. Ibid.

41. Acheson, *Creation*, p. 420.

42. David S. McLellan and John W. Reuss, "Foreign and Military Policies," *The Truman Period as a Research Field*, ed. Richard Kirkendall (Columbia: University of Missouri Press, 1967), p. 75.

43. Melvyn Leffler, *A Preponderance of Power: National Security, the Truman Ad-*

ministration, and the Cold War (Stanford, Calif.: Stanford University Press, 1992), p. 370.

44. Ibid.

45. Ibid., p. 363. Another new trend was begun when the service secretaries began meeting in informal meetings to discuss international political affairs. PRO FO 371/81692, AU 11917/11, Memorandum from Sir Oliver Franks, 28 July 1950.

46. Leffler, *Preponderance of Power*, p. 363; Smith had been publicly mentioned as a candidate to replace Hillenkoetter even before the war, Harry S. Truman, *Public Papers of the Presidents of the United States: Harry S. Truman, 1950* (Washington, D.C.: GPO, 1965). See The President's News Conference of June 1, 1950; for Symington: PRO FO 371/81692, AU 11917/11, Memorandum from Sir Oliver Franks, 28 July 1950.

47. Daniel Yergin, *Shattered Peace: The Origins of the Cold War and the National Security State,* (Boston: Houghton Mifflin, 1977), p. 405.

48. FRUS, 1950, vol. 4, Memorandum by Mr. Charles E. Bohlen, Minister to France, Temporarily in Washington, 13 July 1950, pp. 1220-21. See the enclosure entitled "US Actions Required to Minimize the Likelihood of Soviet Aggression or of New Soviet-Inspired Aggression and to Deal With Such Aggression if it Occurs."

49. Ibid. Note: italics in first paragraph are mine, while others are in the original. Dean Acheson apparently was so impressed with the wording of this memorandum that he used part of it in his declaration on the Korean Crisis to the Cabinet the next day. BLHC, Official Meetings and Conversations of Dean Acheson, Statement Before the Cabinet, 14 July 1950.

50. BLHC, Official Conversations and Meetings of Dean Acheson, Memorandum of Conversation, Subject: Korean Situation, 25 June 1950.

51. HSTL, The Papers of Stephen Springarn, box 28, folder entitled "Defense Production Act of 1950." See the 19 July speech for examples of how Truman tried, in public, to make the situation on the peninsula seem better than it was. Truman also claimed in his memoirs that the performance of the U.S. forces constituted "a glorious chapter in the history of the American Army," but most contemporary accounts show otherwise. Truman, *Years of Trial and Hope*, p. 345.

52. Russell Weigley, *History of the United States Army* (London: B. T. Batsford, 1967), p. 502; Harry G. Summers Jr., *Korean War Almanac* (New York: Facts on File, 1990) pp. 223–24, 235.

53. Weigley, *United States Army*, pp. 503, 507. This is the standard view of the initial stages of the Korean conflict. For an alternative view, see Schaller, *MacArthur*, which claims that the United States always had superiority of men and equipment, but that MacArthur's use of them in the initial stages of the war was questionable.

54. "Angry U.S. Girds for Rough War," *Newsweek*, July 24, 1950.

55. Douglas MacArthur, *Reminiscences* (New York: McGraw Hill, 1964), p. 337.

56. "Commercial Airlines To Fly Men, Supplies To Korea For US," *The Wall Street Journal*, July 6, 1950, p. 1.

57. For air force's tactical bombing: PRO FO 371/90987, AU 1213/1, Naval Attache's Annual Report on the US Navy for the Year 1950; reconnaissance and maps: William Stueck, *The Korean War: An International History* (Princeton: Princeton University Press, 1995), p. 128.

58. Ridgway, *Korean War*, p. 34.

59. Paul Y. Hammond, "NSC-68: Prologue to Rearmament," in *Strategy, Politics, and Defense Budgets*, ed. Warner Schilling, Paul Hammond, and Glenn Snyder (New York: Columbia University Press, 1966), p. 289.

60. Bruce Cumings and Jon Halliday, *Korea: The Unknown War* (London: Viking, 1988), claims that up to two million North Koreans may have died as the result of the American strategic bombing offensive.

61. "Rough War," *Newsweek*, July 24, 1950; Summers, *Korean War Almanac*, p. 290. For information on the reasons each of the UN nations had for sending troops, see Stueck, *Korean War*.

62. Summers, "The Korean War: A Fresh Perspective," p. 26.

63. Ridgway, *Korean War*, p. 27.

64. Ibid.

65. Merle Gulick, "Korea Strife to Cost US Taxpayer Billions; Pentagon Staff Starts Totting Up New Expenses," *Wall Street Journal*, 10 July 1950, p. 2.

66. Poole, *JCS*, p. 41.

67. "What It Takes," *Time*, July 17, 1950, p. 11.

On the issue of air force planes in storage, this article claims that there were 4,600 combat planes in reserve, and Robert Lovett, in his OSDH Oral History, claimed that there were seas of parked aircraft stored at bases in the American West. However, neither of these sources mentions that most of these were World War II leftovers whose usefulness in modern combat varied widely.

68. Anna Kasten Nelson, "President Truman and the Evolution of the National Security Council," *Journal of American History* (September 1985): p. 373; Truman, *Years of Trial and Hope*, p. 348.

69. "What It Takes," *Time*, July 17, 1950, p. 11.

70. Terrence J. Gough, *US Army Mobilization and Logistics in the Korean War: A Research Approach* (Washington, DC: Army Center of Military History, 1987), p. 3.

71. Ibid., p. 4.

72. Poole, *JCS*, p. 42.

73. Truman, *Years of Trial and Hope*, p. 348.

74. Department of Defense, *Semiannual Report of the Secretary of Defense, July 1 to December 31, 1950*, p. 1.

75. *Public Papers of the Presidents: Harry S. Truman, 1950*, Statement by the President Upon Approving an Increase in U.S. Forces in Western Europe, September 9, 1950.

76. Condit, *Test of War*, p. 468.

77. Ibid.

78. FRUS, 1950, vol. 1, Memorandum by the Executive Secretary of the National Security Council to the Secretary of State, the Secretary of Defense, and the Chairman of the United States Atomic Energy Commission, 8 August 1950, p. 570.

79. Condit, *Test of War*, p. 469.

80. Ibid.

81. Ibid.; Richard Rhodes, *Dark Sun: The Making of the Hydrogen Bomb* (New York: Simon and Schuster, 1995), p. 561, claims that there was a January 1952 program bigger than the October 1950 one.

82. Leffler, *Preponderance of Power*, p. 373.

83. John Lewis Gaddis. *Strategies of Containment: A Critical Appraisal of Postwar American National Security Policy* (Oxford: Oxford University Press, 1982), p. 359.

84. Martin Walker, *The Cold War* (London: Vintage, 1994), p. 139.

85. PRO FO 371/90951, AU 1104/3, Truman's mid-year Economic Report to Congress, 23 July 1951.

86. Ibid. Truman claimed that the increase had been approximately $30 billion, whereas the World War II buildup, in 1951 prices, had amounted to approximately $75 billion.

87. John Swomley, *The Military Establishment* (Boston: Beacon Press, 1964), p. 101. Standard Oil of New Jersey would later develop into Exxon.

88. Ibid., p. 102.

89. "Arms and More Arms," *Newsweek*, June 19, 1950.

90. Samuel F. Wells, "The First Cold War Buildup: Europe in United States Strategy and Policy, 1950–1953," *Western Security: The Formative Years; European and Atlantic Defence, 1947–53*, ed. Olav Riste (Oslo: Norwegian University Press, 1985), p. 185.

91. For the Truman quote, see PRO FO 371 90951, AU 1104/3, Truman's mid-year Economic Report to Congress, 23 July 1951.

92. Interview of Truman by Carleton Kent, *The Washington Sun-Times*, 16 January 1953.

93. NARA, record group 273, National Security Council Paper 68/1, 21 September 1950, p. 1.

94. FRUS, 1950, vol. 4, Paper Prepared by the United States High Commissioner for Germany (McCloy), the Commander in Chief, Europe (Handy), and the United States Commander, Berlin (Taylor), 29 August 1950, pp. 867–88, (quote from p. 884).

95. B-50 bomber: PRO FO 371/90989, AU 1225/1, "Annual Report for 1950 on the US Air Force, Prepared by the Air Attaché," 5 March 1951, see Appendix C.

Note that this appendix clearly shows that fighter and reconnaissance aircraft were overwhelmingly more likely to be in the Far Eastern air force than in Europe at the end of 1950.

C-124 transport: Robert Dorr, "Thermonuclear Legacy," *Military History* (August 1995), p. 66.

96. MacArthur, *Reminiscences*, p. 337.

97. Ibid.

98. David Martin, *Wilderness of Mirrors* (New York: Ballantine Books, 1980), p. 76.

99. The sum of annual military budgets is listed in Gaddis, *Strategies*, p. 359. He uses information from the Statistical Abstract of the United States.

The $50 billion estimate comes from Alan R. Millett and Peter Maslowski, *For the Common Defense: A Military History of the United States of America* (New York: Free Press, 1984), p. 504. Millett and Maslowski also estimate that "the administration eventually spent 60 percent of the FY 1951–1953 defense budgets on general military programs and 40 percent on waging the war," p. 490.

100. FRUS, 1950, vol. 7, Acheson meeting with the Joint Chiefs of Staff and the Secretary of Defense, 3 December 1950, p. 1326.

101. NARA record group 273, National Security Council Paper 68/1, 21 September 1950, p. 13 for estimates of cost, p. 14 for prediction on Korea.

102. NARA record group 273, National Security Council 68/3, 8 December 1950, p. 14.

103. HSTL, Papers of Harry S. Truman, White House Central Files; Confidential Files, box 16, folder on the Second Quarterly Report to the President by the Office of Defense Mobilization, preliminary draft of 20 June 1951, p. II-1.

104. Stephen Ambrose, *Rise to Globalism: American Foreign Policy Since 1938* (New York: Penguin Books, 1988), p. 130.

105. Condit, *Test of War,* p. 225.

106. PRO FO 371/90989, AU1225/1, "Annual Report on the US Air Force, Prepared by the Air Attaché," 5 March 1951.

107. Condit, *Test of War,* p. 224.

108. HSTL, Papers of Frederick Lawton, box 6, Folder on Meetings with the President, Memorandum for the Record, 6 September 1950.

109. PRO FO371/81692.

110. Condit, *Test of War,* p. 225.

111. *Department of State Bulletin,* 31 July 1950. The quote was from a 21 July press conference.

112. Condit, *Test of War,* p. 227.

113. Testimony by Secretary of Defense Louis Johnson in Congress, 25 July 1950. House Committee on Appropriations, *The Supplemental Appropriation Bill for 1951: Hearings,* 81st Cong., 2d session, 25 July 1950, pp. 4, 8. PRO FO 371/90989, AU 1225/1, "Annual Report for 1950 on the US Air Force, Prepared by the Air Attache," 5 March 1951.

114. Condit, *Test of War,* p. 227.

115. Ibid.

116. HSTL, White House Bill File, box 81, Senate "Calendar No. 2571," p. 2.

117. Ibid., pp. 18–21.

118. Condit, *Test of War,* p. 227.

119. HSTL, White House Bill File, box 81, Senate "Calendar No. 2571," pp. 1–2.

120. PRO FO 371/90989, AU 1225/1, "Annual Report for 1950 on the US Air Force, Prepared by the Air Attache," 5 March 1951.

121. Condit, *Test of War,* p. 227.

122. NARA, memorandum from the secretary of the army for the secretary of defense, 24 August 1950, record group 330, CD 111; also a memo from the assistant secretary of the army for the assistant secretary of defense (Comptroller), 7 September 1950, record group 330, CD 111 (1951).

123. NARA, memorandum from the Joint Chiefs of Staff to the secretary of defense, 22 September 1950, record group 218, CCS 370.

124. NARA memorandum from the Joint Chiefs of Staff to the secretary of defense, 13 November 1950, record group 330, CD 111 (1951).

125. PRO FO 371/90989, AU 1225/1, "Annual Report for 1950 on the US Air Force, Prepared by the Air Attache," 5 March 1951.

126. HSTL, Papers of Harry S. Truman, White House Bill File, box 84, folder on bill files, 4–6 January 1951, Senate Calendar No. 2679, chart on p. 2.

127. *Public Papers of the Presidents: Harry S. Truman, 1950*, Special Message to the Congress Requesting Additional Appropriations for Defense, 1 December 1950.

128. House, Second Supplemental Appropriations Bill, 1951, 81st Cong., 2d sess., 1951, H. Rept. 3193, as contained in PRO FO 371/90963.

129. Ibid.

130. Ibid.

131. Ibid.

132. Ibid.

133. *Public Papers of the Presidents; Harry S. Truman, 1950*, Radio and Television Report to the American People on the National Emergency, 5 December 1950.

134. HSTL, Papers of Harry S. Truman, White House Bill File, box 84, folder on bill files, 4–6 January 1951, Senate Calendar No. 2679, pp. 15–16.

135. Condit, *Test of War*, p. 239.

136. HSTL, Papers of Harry S. Truman, White House Bill File, box 84, folder on bill files, 4–6 January 1951, Senate Calendar No. 2679, chart on p. 2. "What's News World Wide," *Wall Street Journal*, 3 January 1951, p. 1.

137. Ibid.; "Washington Checklist," *Wall Street Journal*, 3 January 1951, p. 9.

138. HSTL, Papers of Harry S. Truman, White House Bill File, box 84, folder on bill files,4–6 January 1951, Truman's message to Congress on 6 January 1951, p. 1.

139. Condit, *Test of War*, p. 240.

140. PRO FO 371/90904, AU 1013/25, Weekly Political Summary by Sir Oliver Franks, 2 June 1951.

141. PRO FO 371/90929, AU 1052/11, Memorandum from Everson on Visit of American Senators, 9 July 1951.

142. Ibid.

143. Ibid.

144. For the total sum, there is a discrepancy. *The World Almanac 1952*, p. 223, gives the statistic used here. Sir Oliver Franks, the British ambassador to the United States, claims in PRO FO 371/90904, AU 1013/25, weekly political summary, 2 June 1951, that the actual total was $6.438 billion.

On the amount dedicated to the Department of Defense, there is agreement, from Franks, as cited above, and Condit, *Test of War*, p. 240, although Condit rounds the figure to $6.380 billion.

The AEC figure is from Franks, as cited above.

145. *The World Almanac 1952*, p. 223.

146. Ibid.; Condit, *Test of War*, p. 241, claims that the total fiscal year appropriations were actually $48.182 billion, a slightly lower figure than the one given here.

147. Condit, *Test of War*, p. 240.

148. PRO FO 371/90987, AU 1213/1.

149. Paul Nitze, *From Hiroshima to Glasnost* (London: Weidenfield and Nicholson, 1989), p. 105.

150. NARA memorandum from the secretary of defense for service secretaries, record group 330, CD 381, 10 August 1950.

151. NARA memorandum from the secretary of defense to the service secretaries, record group 330, assistant to the secretary of defense and deputy secretary of defense files, "Supplemental Approval July and December 1950" folder, 13 September 1950.

152. NARA memorandum from the Joint Chiefs of Staff for the secretary of defense, record group 218, CCS 370, 22 September 1950.

153. Condit, *Test of War*, p. 245.

154. NARA memorandum from the Joint Chiefs of Staff to the secretary of defense, record group 330, CD 111 (1951), 13 November 1950.

155. NARA, record group 273, NSC-68/2 and NSC-68/4, 1950.

156. FRUS, 1950, vol. 1, pp. 474–77, 6 December 1950 memorandum attached to the 14 December 1950 memo from Marshall to the president.

157. FRUS, 1950, vol. 1, 14 December 1950, p. 474.

158. Wells, "Buildup," p. 185.

159. Ibid.

160. NARA, record group 330, CD 111 (general), 20 December 1950.

161. NARA, record group 330, CD 111 (1952), letter from the director of the Bureau of the Budget to the secretary of defense, 23 April 1951.

162. PRO FO 371/90951, AU1104/3, Truman's mid-year Economic Report to Congress, 23 July 1951.

163. PRO FO 371/90905, AU 1013/40, Weekly Political Summary by Ambassador Sir Oliver Franks, 8–14 September 1951.

164. PRO FO 371/90905, AU 1013/44, Weekly Political Summary by Ambassador Sir Oliver Franks, 6–12 October 1952.

Note that Millett and Maslowski, *For the Common Defense*, claim that the fiscal year 1952 budget appropriated $20.6 billion for the air force, $13.2 billion for the army, and $12.6 billion for the navy, p. 494. Condit, *Test of War*, p. 258, claims that the budget was for $55.5 billion.

165. Millett and Maslowski, *For the Common Defense*, p. 494.

CHAPTER 5: GLOBALIZATION

1. BLHC, Official Conversations and Meetings of Dean Acheson, Memorandum of Conversation, Subject: Meeting of the NSC in the Cabinet Room at the White House, 28 June 1950.

Associated Press, "Korea War Shakes Democratic World," *Los Angeles Times*, 27 June 1950, p. 2; Associated Press, "Dutch Ministers Confer on Korea Invasion Crisis," *Los Angeles Times*, 26 June 1950, p. 6.

2. PRO FO 371/84058, Foreign Office Memorandum of 26 June 1950.

3. The British commitment to maintain four divisions in NATO came later, in 1954, as part of the settlement reached with the French on the issue of German rearmament.

4. Bruce Cumings and Jon Halliday, *Korea: The Unknown War* (London: Viking, 1988), p. 204.

5. John Lewis Gaddis, *We Now Know: Rethinking Cold War History* (New York: Oxford University Press, 1997), p. 124.

6. Jack Raymond, "Germans Warned On Russian Move," *New York Times*, 28 June 1950, p. 9.

7. BLHC, Official Conversations and Meetings of Dean Acheson, Memorandum of Conversation, Subject: Korean Crisis, 30 June 1950.

8. Raymond, "Russian Move," p. 9.

9. "Test Case," *The Economist*, July 1, 1950.

10. William Stueck, *The Korean War: An International History* (Princeton: Princeton University Press, 1995), p. 345; for similar fears, also see "Italians Alarmed About Korean War; Fear New Conflict," *Los Angeles Times*, June 26, 1950, p. 2.

11. Charles E. Bohlen, *Witness to History, 1929–1969* (New York: W. W. Norton, 1973), p. 304.

12. PRO FO 371/85087, C2436, "Report and Comment on the Attitude in the Dutch Parliament on the Rearmament of Germany," from Sir P. Nicholls, 4 April 1950.

13. PRO FO 371/85087, C3360, "Notes From Which M. Stikker Spoke on May 13th 1950 at the Meeting of the 3 Foreign Ministers," 13 May 1950.

14. Melvyn Leffler, *A Preponderance of Power: National Security, the Truman Administration, and the Cold War* (Stanford, Calif.: Stanford University Press, 1992), chapter 8.

The United States publicly denied it was considering German rearmament in this era. For an example, see PRO FO 371, 85048, C3183G, "Draft Brief on German Defence Question for the Secretary of State at the Foreign Ministers Talks," 11 May 1950.

The British government had been considering admitting Germany to NATO even before the Korean War.

PRO FO 371, 85048, C3136G, 28 April 1950; also see, in the same folder, C2416, 4 April 1950, by the British Chiefs of Staff Committee, which recommended that "the Chiefs of Staff should inform the Foreign Office of the military advantages of creating a German Army."

15. PRO FO 371/85087, C3856, "General Bradley's Attitude Towards Re-Arming Western Germany," 7 June 1950.

16. PRO FO 371/85087, C2093, "Question and Answer By Mr. McCloy on Mr. Churchill's Statement Supporting a German Armed Force," 24 March 1950.

17. HSTL, President's Secretary's Files, box 208, Memorandum from the President to the Secretary of State, National Security Council Meeting 60, 16 June 1950.

18. Proposal for the enlistment of Germans into the U.S. Army, and the British *Volkspolizei* proposal are mentioned in Thomas A. Schwartz, "The 'Skeleton Key'—American Foreign Policy, European Unity, and German Rearmament, 1949–54," *Central European History* (December 1986), p. 374.

19. Ibid.

20. DDEL, The Pre-Presidential Papers of Dwight D. Eisenhower, box 75, McCloy folder, 29 January 1952 pamphlet entitled "German Evaluations of NATO," see especially p. 20 for general support for rearmament.

Despite this general support for rearmament, there was some concern that many younger Germans had become so pacifist after the war that they were opposed to conscription. PRO FO 371/85058, C679.

21. PRO FO 371, 85048, C3136G, 28 April 1950.

22. Schwartz, "Skeleton Key," p. 374.

23. Walter LaFeber, "NATO and the Korean War: A Context," *Diplomatic History* (fall 1989).

24. Howard Callender, "Big Four to Meet, Schuman Asserts," New York Times, 13 December 1950; "What's News World Wide," *Wall Street Journal*, 3 January 1951, p. 1.

25. Walter LaFeber, *The American Age: U.S. Foreign Policy at Home and Abroad, 1750 to the Present* (New York: W. W. Norton, 1994), p. 522.

26. PRO FO 371, 85048, C3183G, 11 May 1950. Quoted statement made 24 February 1950.

27. Stueck, *Korean War*, p. 71.

28. ACMH, Senior Officer Oral History Program, Frank Pace, section 1, p. 30, and section 3, p. 16.

29. Lawrence Kaplan, "The Office of Secretary of Defense and NATO, 1948–1951" (unpublished conference presentation at the Army Center of Military History Conference on the Early Years of the Cold War, 1945–1958, Arlington, Va., 1996), pp. 8, 10.

30. Schwartz, "Skeleton Key," p. 377.

31. Peter Slowe, *Manny Shinwell: An Authorized Biography* (London: Pluto Press, 1993), p. 252.

32. Ibid., pp. 252–53.

33. Manfred Jonas, *The United States and Germany: A Diplomatic History* (London: Cornell University Press, 1984).

34. The Bevin quote is from LaFeber, "NATO."

35. Kaplan, "Secretary of Defense," p. 8.

36. Ibid.

37. PRO FO 371/85058, C8126, "The Policy That Should Be Adopted Towards German Rearmament by His Majesty's Government," 8 December 1950.

38. Gerhard Wettig, "The Soviet Union and Germany in the Late Stalin Period, 1950–3," *The Soviet Union and Europe in the Cold War, 1945–53*, ed. Francesca Gori and Silvio Pons (London: St. Martin's Press, 1996).

39. These new fears were acute in France. In December, the assistant to Robert Schuman, the French foreign minister, asked an American official, "Do you really think we are going to be in war in three months?" Dean Acheson, *Present at the Creation: My Years at the State Department* (New York: W. W. Norton, 1969), p. 487.

General Charles de Gaulle, living in retirement, commented privately in November 1950 that "the war is spreading and will not stop. France will not recover in time, will be invaded, bombed ... there will be atomic attacks, hunger, deportation."

Jean LaCouture, *De Gaulle: The Ruler, 1945–70*, trans. Alan Sheridan (London: Harvill, 1992), p. 147. The statement was made to Georges Pompidou on 14 November 1950.

40. PRO FO 371/85058, C7996, "Dr. Adenauer's Conditions for the Participation of Germany in Western Defence," 12 December 1950.

41. Ibid.

42. Callender, "Big Four."

43. Clifton Daniel, "Atlantic Harmony on Bonn Complete," *New York Times*, 14 December 1950.

44. Ibid.

45. Ibid.

46. Clifton Daniel, "Britain For Speed in Arming Europe," *New York Times*, 15 December 1950.

47. Drew Middleton, "European Defense Faces New Hurdle," *New York Times*, 15 December 1950.

48. PRO FO 371/85058, C8057, 11 December 1950, conversation was on 8 December 1950.

49. "East-West Meeting," *The Wall Street Journal*, January 4, 1951, p. 6. Stalin's offer was a counterproposal to the Western powers' invitation for a conference on world affairs.

50. David Holloway, *Stalin and the Bomb: The Soviet Union and Atomic Energy, 1939–1956* (New Haven: Yale University Press, 1994), p. 286.

51. DDEL, Dwight D. Eisenhower Pre-Presidential Papers, box 116, Truman folder, note dated 19 December 1950.

52. NATO Information Service, *NATO: Facts and Figures* (Brussels: 1971), p. 196.

53. FRUS, 1951, vol. 3, notes on a 31 January 1951 meeting at the White House, p. 455. Doris M. Condit, *The Test of War, 1950–1953*, vol. 2 of *History of the Office of Secretary of Defense* (Washington, D.C.: Office of the Secretary of Defense, 1988), p. 340, claims that Ike wanted 20 divisions.

54. Pleven stated these views in a speech on 30 January at the National Press Club.

55. FRUS, 1951, vol. 4, Minutes of Truman-Pleven conversations, 30 January 1951, p. 319.

56. FRUS, 1951, vol. 4, Minutes of Truman-Auriol conversations, 29 March 1951, p. 366.

57. Leffler, *Preponderance of Power*, p. 410.

58. *The World Almanac 1952*, p. 225.

59. Harry G. Summers Jr., "The Korean War: A Fresh Perspective," *Military History* (April 1996): pp. 22–23. Summers includes the National Guard's Twenty-eighth and Forty-third Infantry Divisions as part of the 6 divisions. Summers adds that at peak strength, in July 1953, there were 302,483 American personnel in Korea (p. 25).

60. Leffler, *Preponderance of Power*, p. 412. In addition to all these arms build-ups, the Japanese one, perhaps, was most directly a result of American instigation. While still an occupied land (the formal power of the American military government was not terminated until 1952), Japan was rushed into remilitarization to meet the perceived Soviet threat. The U.S. military government ordered the creation of a National Police Reserve in early July 1950, composed of 75,000 personnel and designed to be a precursor for a genuine military establishment. The Japanese navy participated in the Korean War secretly, using minesweepers to clear harbors in the Sea of Japan in preparation for American amphibious attacks in 1950. K. Arakawa, "The Cold War and the Foundation of the Japanese Self Defense Force," presented at the Army Center of Military History Conference, Arlington, Virginia, June 1996, p. 1; Cumings and Halliday, *Korea: The Unknown War*.

61. Stueck, *Korean War*, p. 5.

62. Hastings L. Ismay, *NATO: The First Five Years* (New York: NATO, 1955), p. 102.

63. Alan R. Millett and Peter Maslowski, *For the Common Defense: A Military History of the United States of America* (New York: Free Press, 1984), p. 496.

64. FRUS, 1951, vol. 1, 11 January 1951 memorandum from W. Stuart Symington (Chairman of the National Security Resources Board) to the National Security Council (NSC), which filed it as NSC-100.

65. "A Special Wall Street Journal Report on 1951 Prospects," *The Wall Street Journal*, January 4, 1951, p. 1.

66. "Raid Shelters in New York," *The Times of London*, October 19, 1950, p. 3.

67. David Lilienthal, *The Venturesome Years, 1950–1955*, vol. 3 of *The Journals of David Lilienthal* (New York: Harper and Row, 1966), pp. 29–34.

68. Martin Walker, *The Cold War* (London: Vintage, 1994), p. 69.

69. The original telegrams can be read at the Truman Library.

70. PRO FO 371/90905, AU 1013/44, Weekly Political Summary by Ambassador Sir Oliver Franks, 6–12 October 1951.

71. C. P. Trussel, "Senators Battle on Atom Bomb Use," *New York Times*, 2 December 1950.

72. Associated Press, "2 Draft Aides Replaced," *New York Times*, 23 December 1950.

73. Books and the comic books: William Manchester, *The Glory and the Dream: A Narrative History of America, 1932–72* (New York: Bantam Books, 1990), chapter 18; movie: Walker, *Cold War*, p. 69.

74. Walker, *The Cold War*, p. 69.

75. Manchester, *Glory*, p. 567.

76. PRO FO 371/90951, AU 1104/3, Truman's mid-year Economic Report to Congress, 23 July 1951.

77. Department of Defense, *Semiannual Report of the Secretary of Defense, 1 July to 31 December 1950* (Washington, D.C.: GPO, 1951), p. 1.

78. quote by Congressman John Taber of New York, in Congressional Record of the House of Representatives, 1950, page 16816.

79. LaFeber, *American Age*, p. 523.

80. Sherman Kent, *Sherman Kent and the Board of National Estimates: Collected Essays*, ed. Donald Steury (Washington, D.C.: Central Intelligence Agency, 1994), p. 150.

Huebner had been commander of the First Infantry Division, the famous Big Red One at Normandy, and was deputy commander of U.S. occupation forces in Germany for a time, serving under General Lucius Clay.

ACMH, Senior Officer Debriefing Program, General Maxwell Taylor, section 3, p. 16.

81. DDEL, Pre-Presidential Papers of Dwight D. Eisenhower, box 60, Ismay folder, note of 3 January 1951.

82. Phil Williams, *The Senate and US Troops in Europe* (London: Macmillan, 1985), p. 44.

83. Raymond Daniel, "Acheson Influence in Europe Cut on Eve of Brussels Defense Talks," *New York Times*, 16 December 1950.

84. Ronald Powaski, *The Entangling Alliance: The United States and European Security, 1950–1993* (Westport, Conn.: Greenwood Press, 1994), p. 12.

85. Herbert Hoover, "Our National Policy In This Crisis," speech given 20 De-

cember 1950, *Vital Speeches of the Day* (January 1, 1951), pp. 165–67; The Soviets printed a full copy of this speech in Pravda. Holloway, *Stalin and the Bomb*, endnote #98, Chapter 13.

86. PRO, FO 371/90929, Memorandum from Sir Edward Plowden to Sir Roger Makins, 9 January 1951, see enclosed note by Lunn, p. 6.

87. Lippman and Krock: PRO FO 371/90903, AU 1013/1, Weekly Political Summary by Ambassador Sir Oliver Franks, 30 December 1950.

88. PRO FO 371/90903, AU 1013/2, Weekly Political Summary by Sir Oliver Franks, 6 January 1951.

89. Powaski, *Entangling Alliance*, p. 14.

90. Walter Millis, "Sea Power: Abstraction or Asset?" *Foreign Affairs* (April 1951): p. 371; Williams, *Senate and US Troops*, p. 53.

91. Williams, *Senate and US Troops*, p. 53.

92. Powaski, *The Entangling Alliance*, p. 15.

93. PRO FO 371/90903, AU 1013/4, Weekly Political Summary by Sir Oliver Franks, 13 January 1951.

94. Ibid.

95. Manchester, *Glory*, p. 557.

96. Williams, *Senate and US Troops*, pp. 40–41.

97. For Acheson's ideas on senators, see James Reston, *Deadline: A Memoir* (New York: Random House, 1991).

98. NARA, record group 330, CD 371, memorandum from JCS to secretary of defense (Marshall), 29 January 1951.

99. Millett and Maslowski, *Common Defense*, p. 496.

100. Powaski, *The Entangling Alliance*, p. 16.

101. Bridges claimed, in early January, that the choice lay between opening a second front against China and withdrawing from Korea. Wherry recommended in early January that if other member states of the UN did not send in more troops, the United States should pull out of Korea within 15 days. PRO FO 371/90903, AU 1013/2, Weekly Political Summary by Sir Oliver Franks, 6 January 1950.

102. Samuel F. Wells, "The First Cold War Buildup: Europe in United States Strategy and Policy, 1950–1953," *Western Security: The Formative Years; European and Atlantic Defence, 1947–53*, ed. Olav Riste (Oslo: Norwegian University Press, 1985), p. 193.

103. PRO FO 371/90947, AU 1075/1.

104. FO 371/90905, AU 1013/38, Weekly Political Summary by the Ambassador, Sir Oliver Franks, 25–31 August 1951.

105. Millett and Maslowski, *Common Defense*, p. 503.

106. George Herring, *America's Longest War: The United States and Vietnam, 1950–75* (New York: John Wiley & Sons, 1979), p. 45. Neutralist Burma, India, and Indonesia refused to join, and South Vietnam, Cambodia, and Laos were forbidden from joining by the terms of the Geneva Accords, which ended the French war in Indochina.

107. Stueck, *Korean War*, p. 73.

108. PRO FO 800, Herbert Morrison Papers, folder 660, Telegram from Foreign Office to Washington, 7 June 1951.

109. PRO FO 371/90904, AU 1013/21, Weekly Political Summary by Sir Oliver Franks, 12 May 1951.

110. Alonzo Hamby, *Man of the People: A Life of Harry S. Truman* (New York: Oxford University Press, 1995), p. 510.

111. Harry G. Summers Jr., *Korean War Almanac* (New York: Facts on File, 1990), p. 210.

112. PRO FO 371/90951, AU 1104/3, Truman's mid-year Economic Report to Congress, 23 July 1951.

113. What's News World Wide, *Wall Street Journal*, 1 July 1950, p. 1; Ray Cromley and Glenn Snyder, "Weapons for Asia: Secret Decision Made To Divert Arms From Europe to Far East," *Wall Street Journal*, 5 July 1950, p. 1.

114. HSTL, Papers of Harry S. Truman, White House Central Files; Confidential Files, box 16, folder containing the Report by the Office of Defense Mobilization to the President for the Second Quarter of 1951, preliminary draft of 20 June 1951, pp. VII–8.

115. Ibid.

116. Department of Defense, Semiannual Report of the Department of Defense, 1 July to 31 December 1950, p. 2.

117. PRO FO 371/90905, AU 1013/42 and AU 1013/44, Weekly Political Summaries by Ambassador Sir Oliver Franks, 22–28 September 1951 and 6–12 October 1951; PRO FO 371/90951, AU 1104/3, Truman, in his mid-year Economic Report to Congress, 23 July 1951, had asked for approximately $8.5 billion, but Congress had cut this sum.

118. HSTL, President's Secretary's Files, box 148, Report by the Director of Defense Mobilization to the President, 1 January 1953, p. 6.

119. Jeffrey A. Richelson, *A Century of Spies: Intelligence in the Twentieth Century* (New York: Oxford University Press, 1995), pp. 258–60.

120. Ibid., pp. 260–62.

121. Christopher Andrew, *For the President's Eyes Only: Secret Intelligence and the American Presidency from Washington to Bush* (New York: Harper Collins, 1995), p. 193.

122. Ibid.

123. Wells, "Buildup," p. 193.

124. Leffler, *Preponderance of Power*, p. 491.

125. Wells, "Buildup," p. 193.

126. Cumings and Halliday, *Unknown War*, p. 163.

127. Record of Conversation Between Comrade I. V. Stalin and Zhou Enlai, 20 August 1952, translated text in *Cold War International History Project Bulletin*, Issues 6–7, Winter 1995/1996, pp. 10–14.

128. Albert Seaton and Joan Seaton, *The Soviet Army: 1918 to the Present* (London: The Bodley Head, 1986), p. 161. Holloway, *Stalin and the Bomb*, p. 333, gives a figure, quoted from Khrushchev in 1960, of 5.7 million men in 1955.

129. Holloway, *Stalin and the Bomb*, p. 285.

130. David Martin, *Wilderness of Mirrors* (New York: Ballantine Books, 1980), p. 63.

131. Paul Kennedy, *The Rise and Fall of the Great Powers: Economic Change and Military Conflict, 1500–2000* (London: Fontana, 1989), pp. 28, 30.

132. Ibid., pp. 28, 32.

133. For example of Soviet press coverage of the U.S. arms build-up, see *Cur-*

rent *Digest of the Soviet Press,* December 16 1950, "US Economy Goes on Wartime Footing," p. 34 (translation of a Pravda article of 31 October 1950).

134. James H. Hansen, *Correlation of Forces: Four Decades of Soviet Military Development* (New York: Praeger, 1987), p. 30.

135. Ibid., p. 29.

136. Ibid.

137. Ibid., p. 31.

138. Holloway, *Stalin and the Bomb,* endnote #126 of Chapter 13.

139. Pavel Sudoplatov and Anatoli Sudoplatov, *Special Tasks: The Memoirs of an Unwanted Witness—A Soviet Spymaster* (Boston: Little, Brown and Company: 1995), p. 332.

140. Holloway, *Stalin and the Bomb,* pp. 286–87.

141. Ibid., p. 241.

142. Stueck, *Korean War,* p. 5.

143. Vladislav Zubok and Constantine Pleshakov, *Inside the Kremlin's Cold War: From Stalin to Khrushchev* (Cambridge: Harvard University Press, 1996), p. 72.

144. For example, see *Current Digest of the Soviet Press,* "Harold Stassen's Crooked Game," December 2, 1950.

145. "East-West Meeting," *The Wall Street Journal,* January 4, 1951, p. 6. Stalin's offer was a counterproposal to the Western powers' invitation for a conference on world affairs.

146. See translations of Soviet-Chinese discussions, *Cold War International History Project Bulletin,* Issues 6–7 (winter 1995/1996): pp. 94–119.

CHAPTER 6: ACTUALIZATION

1. For Truman's proposed tax increases, see Alonzo Hamby, *Man of the People: A Life or Harry S. Truman* (New York: Oxford University Press, 1995), p. 488.

2. Harry S. Truman, *Memoirs: Years of Trial and Hope, 1946–1952* (New York: Signet, 1956).

The tax increase passed in January 1951 raised the regular corporate tax rate two points to 47 percent and provided an effective excess profits tax rate of 77 percent. The *Wall Street Journal,* January 3, 1951.

The tax increase passed in October 1951 raised income taxes approximately 12 percent, and made further increases in the excess profits tax and in excise taxes. These tax increases added approximately $5.75 billion in revenue, making it the second largest tax increase in American history. PRO FO 371/90905, AU 1013/44, Weekly Political Summary by Ambassador Sir Oliver Franks, 6–12 October 1951.

3. Alonzo Hamby, *Beyond the New Deal: Harry S. Truman and American Liberalism* (New York: Columbia University Press, 1973), p. 442.

4. "Truman Was Handed His First Rebuff By the New 82nd Congress," *The Wall Street Journal,* January 4, 1951, p. 1.

5. Hamby, *Beyond the New Deal,* p. 442.

6. During the 1948 election campaign, Truman ordered the convening of a special session of Congress, which had a Republican majority, and dared them to pass legislation controlling consumer credit, prices, rents, and other elements of his Fair Deal legislation. This occurred on July 26, 1948. Nothing came of this campaign tactic. David McCollough, *Truman* (New York: Simon and Schuster, 1992), p. 651.

7. Hamby, *Man of the People*, p. 488.

8. For one example, see HSTL, President's Secretary's Files, box 144, folder entitled "Defense Production Act," 23 August 1951 message to Congress.

9. HSTL, The Papers of Stephen Springarn, box 28, folder entitled "Defense Production Act of 1950."

10. Hamby, *Beyond the New Deal*, pp. 415–18. A more radical example of government control over enterprise could be seen across the Atlantic, where a bill to nationalize the British steel industry passed approximately two weeks after the ESA introduced its wage and price freezes. Such controls represented the increased popularity of government management of economic affairs in the years following the New Deal, Keynes's growing popularity, and the seeming success of managed industry during World War II.

11. This Charles E. (Edward) Wilson is not the same man as Charles E. (Erwin) Wilson, who was head of General Motors and Eisenhower's secretary of defense.

12. HSTL, President's Secretary's Files, General File, box 131, folder entitled "National Advisory Board on Mobilization Policy," and President's Secretary's Files, box 142 .

13. See the many proposals on stockpiling, mobilization, managed production of commodities, and controls in HSTL, Papers of Harry S. Truman, White House Central File, Confidential Files, boxes 27 and 28, 10 folders on NSRB.

14. HSTL, President's Secretary's Files, box 131, folder entitled "National Security Resources Board," letter from Rusk (Chairman of HRAC) to the president, 22 September 1950.

15. HSTL, Papers of Harry S. Truman, White House Bill File, box 84, folder on bill, Senate Calendar No. 2679, 4–6 January 1951, p. 3.

16. Ibid.

17. HSTL, President's Secretary's Files, box 144, folder entitled "Defense Production Act," Truman message to Congress of 23 August 1951, p. 2.

18. Ibid., p. 3.

19. PRO FO 371/90951, AU 1104/3, HSTL, Truman's mid-year Economic Report to Congress, 23 July 1951; HSTL, President's Secretary's Files, Report to the president by the Director of Defense Mobilization, box 148, 1 January 1953, p. 7.

20. *The World Almanac 1952*, p. 220.

21. "Air Force Negotiating With GE," and "Lockheed to Reopen Bomber Plant," *The Wall Street Journal*, January 5, 1951, p. 16, "Helicopters Again: Rescue Jobs in Korea Boom Military Demand for 'Flying Windmills,'" January 5, 1951, p. 1.

22. John Rae, *Climb to Greatness: The American Aircraft Industry, 1920–1960* (Cambridge, Mass.: MIT Press, 1968), p. 197.

23. Ibid., p. 198.

24. Alan R. Millett and Peter Maslowski, *For the Common Defense: A Military History of the United States of America* (New York: Free Press, 1984), p. 493.

25. "Over $3 Billion of Vehicles, Parts Ordered in Detroit Since July, Army Ordnance Official States," *The Wall Street Journal*, January 5, 1951, p. 16, see squib on p. 1 for WW2 fact.

26. Rae, *Climb to Greatness*, pp. 196–97; Gerhard Weinberg, *A World At Arms: A Global History of World War Two* (Cambridge: Cambridge University Press, 1994), p. 494.

27. Rae, *Climb to Greatness*, chapter 9; Martin Walker, *The Cold War* (London: Vintage, 1994), pp. 139–40.

28. PRO FO 371/90989, AU 1225/1, "Annual Report for 1950 on the US Air Force, Prepared by the Air Attache," 5 March 1951, appendixes G and H.

29. "Production Cutbacks: Chrysler Production to Fall 20% . . . ," *The Wall Street Journal*, January 3, 1951, p. 16.

30. "What's News: Business and Finance," *Wall Street Journal*, January 4, 1951, p. 1.

31. *The World Almanac 1952*, p. 229.

32. PRO FO 371/90951, AU 1104/3, Truman's mid-year Economic Report to Congress, 23 July 1951.

33. HSTL, President's Secretary's Files, box 148, Report to the president by the Director of Defense Mobilization, 1 January 1953, p. 7.

34. Ibid.

35. "Trade Turnabout: 1951 May See 12 Month Imports Top Exports First Time Since 1893," *The Wall Street Journal*, January 3, 1951, p. 1.

36. Ibid.

37. PRO FO 371/90905, AU 1013/39, Weekly Political Summary by the Ambassador Sir Oliver Franks, 1–7 September 1951.

38. "Trade Turnabout: 1951 May See 12 Month Imports Top Exports First Time Since 1893," *The Wall Street Journal*, January 3, 1951, p. 1.

39. Ibid.

40. Ibid.

41. PRO FO 371 90951, AU 1104/2, Memorandum from Mr. Steel, in Washington, 2 March 1951.

42. HSTL, Papers of Harry S. Truman, box 16, White House Central File, Confidential Papers, folder for the Second Quarterly Report by the Office of Defense Mobilization to the President, preliminary draft, 20 June 1951, pp. VII-3.

43. "Trade Turnabout," p. 1.

44. Lawrence Davis, "US Seeks Import of Latin Workers," *New York Times*, 16 December 1950.

45. John Herling, "Labor Independence at Polls Hailed by Truman in Interview," *Washington Evening Star*, 14 January 1953. Murray did not mention that in 1946, Truman tried to draft striking railway workers into the army to break their resistance.

46. PRO FO 371, 90905, AU 1013/38, Weekly Political Summary by the Ambassador, Sir Oliver Franks, 25–31 August 1951.

47. Ibid.

48. PRO FO 371, 90905, AU 1013/39, Weekly Political Summary by the Ambassador, Sir Oliver Franks, 1–7 September 1951.

49. HSTL, President's Secretary's Files, box 148, Report to the president by the Director of Defense Mobilization, 1 August 1952.

50. Ibid.

51. Ibid.

52. HSTL, Papers of Harry S. Truman, White House Central File; Confidential Files, box 16, folder on Second Quarterly Report to the President by the Office of Defense Management, preliminary draft, pp. VII-1.

Western Europe was estimated to have 55 million tons per year of steel production, while the United States was estimated to have 108 million tons.

53. HSTL, President's Secretary's Files, box 148, Report to the president by the Director of Defense Mobilization, 1 August 1952.

54. Ibid., p. 2.

Note that in addition to the 10 divisions, the army, prior to 25 June 1950, also had 12 separate regimental-size units. However, the divisions, as of 1 January 1953, were at full strength, but may not have been as of 25 June 1950.

55. Ibid., see graph on p. 3.

56. HSTL, White House Central Files; Confidential Files, box 16, folder for the Second Quarterly Report by the Office of Defense Mobilization, preliminary draft of 20 June 1951, pp. II-6, II-7.

57. Ibid., pp. II-6, II-7.

58. Ibid., p. II-1.

59. Ibid., p. II-2.

60. HSTL, President's Secretary's Files, box 148, Report by the Director of Defense Mobilization to the President, 1 January 1952, see graph on p. 8.

61. HSTL, Harry S. Truman Papers, White House Central File, Confidential Files, box 16, folder on the Second Quarterly Report to the President by the Office of Defense Mobilization, preliminary draft of 20 June 1951, p. II-7.

62. Ibid., p. II-3.

63. Ibid., p. II-3.

64. Ibid., pp. II-2, II-3.

65. HSTL, President's Secretary's Files, box 148, Report to the President by the Office of Defense Mobilization, 1 August 1952, p. 9.

66. HSTL, President's Secretary's Files, box 148, Report by the Director of Defense Mobilization to the President, 1 January 1952, p. 8.

67. Rae, *Climb to Greatness*, p. 198.

68. HSTL, President's Secretary's Files, box 148, Report to the President by the Office of Defense Mobilization, 1 August 1952, p. 10.

69. PRO FO 371/90989, AU 1225/1, "Annual Report for 1950 on the US Air Force, Prepared by the Air Attache," 5 March 1951, appendix L.

70. PRO FO 371/90985, AU 1201/1, Military Attache's Annual Report for 1950, 16 February 1951, p. 17.

71. Rae, *Climb to Greatness*, p. 189.

72. Ibid., p. 188.

73. HSTL, President's Secretary's Files, box 148, Report to the President by the Director of Defense Mobilization, 1 August 1952.

74. PRO FO 371/90985, AU1201/1, Military Attache's Annual Report for 1950, 16 February 1951, p. 17.

75. HSTL, Harry S. Truman Papers, White House Central File, Confidential Files, box 16, folder on the Second Quarterly Report to the President by the Office of Defense Mobilization, preliminary draft of 20 June 1951, p. II-12.

76. Ibid., p. II-12.

77. Harry G. Summers Jr., *Korean War Almanac* (New York: Facts on File, 1990), p. 50.

78. PRO FO 371/90985, AU 1201/1, Military Attache's Annual Report for 1950, 16 February 1950, p. 13.

79. Summers, *Korean War Almanac,* p. 50.

80. Ibid., p. 50.

81. Ibid., p. 50.

82. PRO FO 371/90985, AU 1201/1, Military Attache's Annual Report for 1950, 16 February 1950, p. 13.

83. HSTL, White House Central Files: Papers of Harry S. Truman, box 16, folder on the Second Quarterly Report to the President by the Office of Defense Mobilization, preliminary draft of 20 June 1951, p. II-3.

84. Ibid., p. II-3.

85. PRO FO 371/90985, AU 1201/1, Military Attache's Annual Report for 1950, 16 February 1950, p. 12.

86. HSTL, President's Secretary's Files, box 148, Report to the President by the Office of Defense Mobilization, 1 August 1952, p. 9.

87. Ibid.

88. PRO FO 371/90985, AU 1201/1, Military Attache's Annual Report for 1950, 16 February 1950, p. 12.

89. Ibid.

90. HSTL, White House Central Files: Papers of Harry S. Truman, box 16, folder on the Second Quarterly Report to the President by the Office of Defense Mobilization, preliminary draft of 20 June 1951, p. II-10.

91. "Helicopters Again: Rescue Jobs in Korea Boom Demand For 'Flying Windmills,'" *The Wall Street Journal,* January 5, 1951, p. 1.

92. Summers, *Korean War Almanac,* pp. 136–37.

93. Ibid., p. 40.

94. "Helicopters Again," p. 1.

95. Ibid.

96. Summers, *Korean War Almanac,* p. 196.

97. A higher estimate of North Korean deaths during the strategic bombing is two million, roughly one-quarter of the North Korean population, made in Bruce Cumings, *War and Television* (London: Verso, 1992), p. 158.

98. PRO FO 371/90985, AU 1201/1, Military Attache's Annual Report for 1950, 16 February 1950, p. 12.

99. HSTL, White House Central Files: Papers of Harry S. Truman, box 16, folder on the Second Quarterly Report to the President by the Office of Defense Mobilization, preliminary draft of 20 June 1951, p. II-11.

100. PRO FO 371/90985, AU 1201/1, Military Attache's Annual Report for 1950, 16 February 1951, p. 12.

101. Ibid.

102. For Doron, see Summers, *Korean War Almanac,* p. 53.

For other products, see HSTL, White House Central Files: Papers of Harry S. Truman, box 16, folder on the Second Quarterly Report to the President by the Office of Defense Mobilization, preliminary draft of 20 June 1951, p. II-11.

103. PRO FO 371/90987, AU 1213/1, Naval Attache's Annual Report on the US Navy for the Year 1950.

104. Ibid.

105. PRO FO 371/81723, AU 12110/1, "Expansion of US Armed Forces—Testimony of Chief of Naval Operations, Admiral Sherman, Before House Armed

Services Committee on Oct. 3rd, About the Navy's Share of the Revised Programme," from Sir O. Franks, 11 Oct 1950.

106. Charles Morris, *Iron Destinies, Lost Opportunities: The Arms Race Between the USA and the USSR, 1945–1987* (New York: Harper and Row, 1988), p. 85.

107. HSTL, White House Central File, Papers of Harry S. Truman, Confidential Files; box 16, folder for the Second Quarterly Report by the Office of Defense Mobilization to the President, preliminary draft of 20 June 1951, p. II-9.

108. Hamby, *Man of the People*, p. 606.

109. PRO FO 371/90987, AU 1213/1, Naval Attache's Annual Report on the US Navy for the Year 1950.

110. Ibid.

111. Ibid.

112. Frederick Graham, "Combat Airplanes Increasing in Size," *New York Times*, 25 June 1950, p. 17.

113. PRO FO 371/90989, AU 1225/1, "Annual Report for 1950 on the US Air Force, Prepared by the Air Attache," 5 March 1951.

114. Ibid.

115. PRO FO 371/90985, AU 1201/1, Military Attache's Annual Report for 1950, p. 13.

116. Millett and Maslowski, *Common Defense*, p. 495.

117. Ibid.

118. Christopher Andrew, *For the President's Eyes Only: Secret Intelligence and the American Presidency from Washington to Bush* (New York: Harper Collins, 1995), p. 197.

119. Ibid.

120. HSTL, President's Secretary's Files, box 148, Report by the Director of Defense Mobilization to the President, 1 January 1952, p. 9; Richard Rhodes, *Dark Sun: The Making of the Hydrogen Bomb* (New York: Simon and Schuster, 1995), p. 561, claims that both the plants were gaseous diffusion plants.

121. Rhodes, *Dark Sun*, p. 561.

122. Ibid., p. 561.

123. FRUS, 1950, vol. 1, Summary Log of Atomic Energy Work, undated, pp. 580–87; Arneson to Marten, 4 December 1950, pp. 591–92; Arneson to the Secretary of State, 14 December 1950, p. 593; Millett and Maslowski, *For the Common Defense*, p. 493.

124. 1949: David Callahan, *Dangerous Capabilities: Paul Nitze and the Cold War* (New York: Harper Collins, 1990), p. 78; 1952, 1953, and 1954: David Holloway, *Stalin and the Bomb: The Soviet Union and Atomic Energy, 1939–1956* (New Haven: Yale University Press, 1994), p. 329; 1950 and 1955: Rhodes, *Dark Sun*, p. 562.

125. Rhodes, *Dark Sun*, p. 562.

126. Barry Steiner, *Bernard Brodie and the Foundations of American Nuclear Strategy* (Lawrence, Kansas: University of Kansas Press, 1991), p. 252.

127. Holloway, *Stalin and the Bomb*, p. 300.

128. Rhodes, *Dark Sun*, p. 504. The test occurred at 7:15 A.M. local time, which made it 31 October in the United States, a date used in many sources.

129. PRO FO 371/90989, AU 1225/1, "Annual Report for 1950 on the US Air Force, Prepared by the Air Attache," 5 March 1951.

130. Lawrence Freedman, *The Evolution of Nuclear Strategy* (New York: St. Martin's Press, 1983), p. 64.

131. Ibid.

132. Weinberg, *World At Arms*, p. 541.

133. Samuel F. Wells, "The First Cold War Buildup: Europe in United States Strategy and Policy, 1950–1953," *Western Security: The Formative Years; European and Atlantic Defence, 1947–53,* ed. Olav Riste (Oslo: Norwegian University Press, 1985), p. 191.

134. Freedman, *Evolution*, p. 64.

135. DDEL, Oral History with Andrew Goodpaster (OH-477), p. 4.

136. Melvyn Leffler, *A Preponderance of Power: National Security, the Truman Administration, and the Cold War* (Stanford, Calif.: Stanford University Press, 1992), p. 489.

137. Wells, "Buildup," p. 191.

138. Rhodes, *Dark Sun*, p. 562.

139. Millett and Maslowski, *Common Defense*, p. 494.

140. HSTL, President's Secretary's Files, box 148, Report by the Director of Defense Mobilization to the President, 1 January 1952, p. 9.

141. DDEL, Oral History with Andrew Goodpaster (OH-477), p. 4.

142. HSTL, President's Secretary's Files, box 148, Report to the President by the Director of Defense Mobilization, 1 August 1952.

143. DDEL, Oral History with Andrew Goodpaster (OH-477), p. 4; also Holloway, *Stalin and the Bomb*, p. 329.

144. PRO FO 371/90989, AU 1225/1, "Annual Report for 1950 on the US Air Force, Prepared by the Air Attache," 5 March 1951, appendix H.

145. Millett and Maslowski, *Common Defense*, p. 494.

146. 1951 and 1959: Rhodes, *Dark Sun*, p. 562; mid-1950s: Robert Dorr, "Thermonuclear Legacy," *Military History* (August 1995): p. 65.

147. Wells, "Buildup."

148. Robert Ferrell, "The Formation of the Alliance, 1948–1949," *American Historians and the Atlantic Alliance,* ed. Lawrence Kaplan (Kent, Ohio: Kent State University Press, 1991), p. 29.

149. SAC's powers over target selection would also grow dramatically. First the air force won the right to veto suggestions for the list of targets in the USSR to be bombed in the event of a nuclear war with the Soviet Union. Then General Curtis LeMay, chief of SAC, gradually won the ability to create his own target planning, separate from the other elements of the air force, becoming essentially autonomous by 1955. This change went against the opinion of many outside the air force who favored centralized war planning and keying all resources on agreed targets, such as particular bottlenecks in Soviet production or critical strategic locales. However, the destructive power of the United States' and Soviet Union's nuclear arsenals would become so great that each was capable of destroying thousands of sites, making nuclear targeting a less vital issue. By 1952, the air force already had plans to attack 5,000 to 6,000 sites in the event of a nuclear war with the Soviet Union. By the early 1960s, Secretary of Defense Robert MacNamara would be talking about placing ceilings on the size of the U.S. nuclear arsenal, since a stage of what he termed mutually assured destruction had been reached. Rhodes, *Dark Sun*, p. 560–61; MacNamara quote: Dorr, "Legacy."

150. Dorr, "Legacy," p. 64.

151. Rhodes, *Dark Sun*, p. 561.

152. Doris M. Condit, *The Test of War, 1950–1953*, vol. 2 of *History of the Office of Secretary of Defense* (Washington, D.C.: Office of the Secretary of Defense, 1988), see caption on last page of photo insert between pp. 418 and 419. According to James H. Hansen, *Correlation of Forces: Four Decades of Soviet Military Development* (New York: Praeger, 1987), p. 5, the United States began to study tactical nuclear weapons for use on the battlefield in 1949.

153. DDEL, Oral History with Andrew Goodpaster (OH-477), p. 3.

154. Dorr, "Legacy," p. 64.

155. PRO FO 371/90989, AU 1225/1, "Annual Report for 1950 on the US Air Force, Prepared by the Air Attache," 5 March 1951.

156. HSTL, The Papers of Matthew Connelly, Set 1: Cabinet Meetings, meeting of 21 September 1951. The new secretary of defense, Robert Lovett, mentioned this fact in a Cabinet meeting.

157. HSTL, President's Secretary's Files, box 148, Report to the President by the Director of Defense Mobilization, 1 August 1952. p. 10.

158. William Manchester, *The Glory and the Dream: A Narrative History of America, 1932–72* (New York: Bantam Books, 1990), p. 575.

159. PRO FO 371/97579, AU 1011/2, "Annual Political Review of the United States of America for the Years 1950 and 1951," 19 May 1952; Holloway, *Stalin and the Bomb*, p. 326.

160. Ike told Louis Johnson in 1949 that "I am glad you have taken the bull by the horns in your drive for real economy." DDEL, Eisenhower Pre-Presidential Papers, Box, 62, Johnson folder, memo of 16 August 1949.

161. DDEL, Personal Papers of Dwight D. Eisenhower, box 116, Truman folder, note dated 16 December 1950. It is a good thing for Eisenhower that he never sent this letter. If he had, the Democrats could have used it against him in the 1952 presidential campaign, when Eisenhower made the elimination of direct controls one of the main planks of his platform.

162. DDEL, Oral History with Andrew Goodpaster (OH-477), p. 2.

163. HSTL, Oral History #454 (Paul Nitze), p. 306.

164. DDEL, Oral History with Andrew Goodpaster (OH-477), p. 14.

165. PRO FO 371/90905, AU 1013/41, Weekly Political Summary by Ambassador Sir Oliver Franks, 15–21 September 1951.

166. John Lewis Gaddis, *We Now Know: Rethinking Cold War History* (New York: Oxford University Press, 1997), p. 100.

167. Ibid.

168. Ibid., p. 231.

169. Steiner, *Brodie*, p. 159.

170. Eisenhower threatened the use of the bomb during the armistice negotiations. After the armistice, it became American policy to plan on using atomic weapons against North Korean supply centers should the Communist forces breach the demilitarized zone in Korea, a policy to which the British government agreed. FRUS, 1952–54, vol. 5, Section 2, p. 1739.

171. Dorr, "Legacy," pp. 64–65.

172. John Lewis Gaddis, *Strategies of Containment: A Critical Appraisal of Postwar American National Security Policy* (New York: Oxford University Press, 1982), p. 121.

173. Although the idea was present earlier, Dulles didn't use the term massive retaliation until a speech in New York in January 1954.

174. The remark was made in a 16 March 1955 press conference, as quoted in Gaddis, *Strategies*, p. 149.

175. The military, however, opposed such a stance.

176. Gaddis, *Strategies*, p. 146. In The Oral History of Andrew Goodpaster (OH-477) at the Eisenhower Library, p. 13, Andrew Goodpaster defines the second group as essentially advocating a spheres of influence arrangement.

177. DDEL, Oral History with Andrew Goodpaster (OH-477), p. 14.

178. NARA record group 273, NSC-149/2, 29 April 1953.

179. This was from a total of 3,505,661. NARA, record group 273, NSC 149/2, 29 April 1953, p. 1.

180. Maxwell Taylor, *The Uncertain Trumpet* (Westport, Connecticut: Greenwood, 1974).

181. FRUS, 1952–54, vol. 15, minutes of NSC meeting of 24 June 1954, p. 694. By the 1960s, however, NATO had adopted a flexible response strategy that entailed a willingness to use any weapon available if it saw fit to do so.

182. John Lewis Gaddis, *The United States and the End of the Cold War: Implications, Reconsiderations, and Provocations* (Oxford: Oxford University Press, 1994), p. 67.

183. DDEL, Oral History with Andrew Goodpaster (OH-37). p. 97. Goodpaster, speaking in 1967, commented that the level of U.S. forces was the same then, and had been continuously, since 1951.

184. Marc Trachtenberg, The Nuclearization of NATO and U.S.-West European Relations," *History and Strategy*, ed. Marc Trachtenberg (Princeton: Princeton University Press, 1991), p. 165.

185. ACMH, file 091, folder entitled "Soviet Union," planned presentation of 4 December 1961, by Major General A. R. Fitch, Assistant Chief of Staff for Intelligence, Department of the Army, p. 1.

186. Paul Kennedy, *The Rise and Fall of the Great Powers: Economic Change and Military Conflict, 1500–2000* (London: Fontana, 1989), chart on p. 495.

187. Hansen, *Correlation*, p. 21.

188. Ibid.

189. Ibid., p. 4.

190. Holloway, *Stalin and the Bomb*, p. 299. Beria had written an order, in May 1953, to test the new weapon. Pavel Sudoplatov and Anatoli Sudoplatov, *Special Tasks: The Memoirs of an Unwanted Witness—A Soviet Spymaster* (Boston: Little, Brown and Company, 1995), p. 363.

191. Ibid., p. 307.

192. Ibid., p. 308, gives the 500-kiloton statistic. Holloway claims that it was not clear to the Americans whether it was a fusion weapon or fission weapon using a thermonuclear boost.

Rhodes, *Dark Sun*, p. 524, quotes American physicist Carson Mark, who claims that the U.S. team, after studying the fallout from the Soviet explosion (nicknamed Joe 4 by the Americans), "managed to speak of an object physically similar to what Joe 4 must have been," even reaching the accurate conclusion that the Soviet weapon had been a single-stage bomb using alternate layers of uranium and lithium deuteride, in which compression was achieved with high explosives rather than radiation.

193. Rhodes, *Dark Sun*, p. 526.

194. Holloway, *Stalin and the Bomb*, p. 322.

195. Ibid., p. 307, Rhodes, *Dark Sun*, p. 523.

196. Rhodes, *Dark Sun*, p. 541.

197. Ibid., p. 570.

198. Holloway, *Stalin and the Bomb*, p. 324.

199. Dr. Donald Steury, interview by author, CIA Historical Office, 12 September 1995.

200. Sudoplatov, *Special Tasks*, p. 363.

201. Holloway, *Stalin and the Bomb*, p. 324.

202. Harriet Fast Scott and William Scott, ed., *The Soviet Art of War; Doctrine, Strategy, and Tactics* (Boulder, Colo.: Westview Press, 1982), p. 125; Holloway, *Stalin and the Bomb*, p. 313.

203. Holloway, *Stalin and the Bomb*, p. 324.

204. Ibid., p. 323.

205. ACMH, History Resources Center, file 091, folder entitled "Soviet Union," article from the United States Naval Institute Proceedings, June 1955, by Rear Admiral E. M. Eller, entitled "Soviet Bid for the Sea," p. 623.

206. CIAH, CIA National Intelligence Estimate 11–15–82/D, "Soviet Naval Strategy and Programs Through the 1990s," March 1983, pp. 7, 8, 26, and 32.

207. Sudoplatov, *Special Tasks*, chapter 12.

208. Ibid.

CONCLUSIONS

1. James Reston, *Deadline: A Memoir* (New York: Random House, 1991), pp. 145-46.

2. Alonzo Hamby, *Man of the People: A Life of Harry S. Truman* (New York: Oxford University Press, 1995); David McCollough, *Truman* (New York: Simon and Schuster, 1992).

3. PRO FO 371/90951, AU 1104/3, Truman's mid-year Economic Report to Congress, 23 July 1951.

4. Alan R. Millett and Peter Maslowski, *For the Common Defense: A Military History of the United States of America* (New York: Free Press, 1984), pp. 496-97.

5. For a discussion of the orthodox, revisionist, and post-revisionist schools of history, see Bruce Cumings, "Revising Postrevisionism," *America in the World: The Historiography of the American Foreign Relations Since 1941*, ed. Michael Hogan (Cambridge: Cambridge University Press, 1995).

6. Matthew A. Evangelista, "Stalin's Post-War Army Reappraised," *International Security* (winter 1982/83).

7. George F. Kennan, "The Failure of Our Success," *New York Times*, 14 March 1994.

8. FRUS, 1950, vol. 1, Memorandum of National Security Council Consultants' Meeting, Thursday, 29 June 1950.

9. Vladislav Zubok and Constantine Pleshakov, *Inside the Kremlin's Cold War: From Stalin to Khrushchev* (Cambridge: Harvard University Press, 1996).

10. It was not unusual for Truman to take the lead. As political scientist Samuel Huntington has described, "virtually all the great Congressional debates on foreign policy in the Truman administration took place after the executive had committed the nation. The decisions on the Berlin Airlift, the hydrogen bomb, Formosa policy, the Korean War, the proclamation of national emergency [in December 1950], the troops to Europe, the firing of MacArthur all tended to follow this pattern." Samuel P. Huntington, *The Soldier and the State: The Theory and Politics of Civil-Military Relations* (Cambridge, Massachusetts: Belknap Press, 1957), p. 383.

11. *The New York Times*, 1–2 December 1950.

12. Melvyn Leffler, *A Preponderance of Power: National Security, the Truman Administration, and the Cold War* (Stanford, Calif.: Stanford University Press, 1992), p. 447.

Bibliography

UNPUBLISHED GOVERNMENT DOCUMENTS AND PERSONAL PAPERS

Basil Liddell Hart Center, King's College, London
  Official Conversations and Meetings of Dean Acheson
  Public Statements of the Secretaries of Defense
  Records of the Joint Chiefs of Staff, Part 2: Europe & NATO
  U.S. State Department Central Files

Churchill Archive Center, Churchill College, Cambridge
  Winston Churchill Papers

Eisenhower Presidential Library, Abilene, Kansas
  Dwight Eisenhower Pre-Presidential Papers
  Oral History of Charles Bohlen
  Oral History of General Lucius Clay
  Oral History of John McCloy
  Oral History of General Andrew Goodpaster (3)
  Oral History of Robert Donovan

National Archives and Record Administration, Washington, D.C.
  Record Group 218, Joint Chiefs of Staff
  Record Group 273, National Security Council
  Record Group 330, Office of the Secretary of Defense

Office of Secretary of Defense History Branch, The Pentagon

Oral History of Robert Lovett, parts 1 and 2
Oral History of Donald Carpenter
Oral History of General J. Lawton Collins

Public Record Office of the United Kingdom, Kew, Surrey

FO 371 Foreign Office Records
FO 800 Ernest Bevin Papers
FO 800 Herbert Morrison Papers

Roosevelt Presidential Library, Hyde Park, New York

Map Room Papers
Adolph Berle Papers
Alexander Sachs Papers
Harold Smith Papers

Truman Presidential Library, Independence, Missouri

Dean Acheson Papers
Eben Ayers Papers
Clark Clifford Papers
Connelly Papers (Cabinet Minutes)
George Elsey Papers
Robert Goodwin Papers
Leon Keyserling Papers
Daniel Kimball Papers
Frederick Lawton Papers
David Lloyd Papers
Francis Matthews Papers
Charles Murphy Papers
Frank Pace Jr. Papers
John Snyder Papers
Stephen Springarn Papers
W. Stuart Symington Papers
Harry Truman Papers
James E. Webb Papers
White House Central Files
Oral History of Eben Ayers
Oral History of Clark Clifford

Oral History of Loy Henderson
Oral History of Leon Keyserling
Oral History of Robert Lovett
Oral History of Paul Nitze
Oral History of Edwin Nourse

United States Army Center of Military History, Washington, D.C.

Senior Officer Debriefing of General Maxwell Taylor
Senior Officer Debriefing of General Matthew Ridgway
Senior Officer Debriefing of General Mark Clark
Senior Officer Debriefing of Army Secretary Frank Pace

PUBLISHED GOVERNMENT DOCUMENTS

Central Intelligence Agency. *Estimates on Soviet Military Power 1954 to 1984*. Washington, D.C.: 1994.
Central Intelligence Agency. *Selected Estimates On the Soviet Union, 1950–1959*. Washington, D.C.: 1993.
Department of State. *Foreign Relations of the United States,* selected volumes 1948–1952. (Washington, D.C.)
Ovendale, Ritchie.*Documents in Contemporary History: British Defence Policy Since 1945*. Manchester: Manchester University Press, 1994.
Woodrow Wilson International Center for Scholars. Documents From The Russian Archives, *Cold War International History Project Bulletin* (fall 1993, fall 1994, spring 1995, winter 1995/96).

PUBLISHED PERSONAL PAPERS

Eisenhower, Dwight. *The Papers of Dwight David D. Eisenhower,* ed. Louis Galambos. Baltimore: The Johns Hopkins University Press, 1984.
Truman, Harry S. *Public Papers of the Presidents of the United States: Harry S. Truman, 1950*. Washington, D.C.: GPO, 1965.
Vandenberg, Arthur, Jr. *The Private Papers of Senator Vandenberg.* Boston: Houghton Mifflin, 1952.

NEWSPAPERS AND PERIODICALS, 1949–51

The *Current Digest of the Soviet Press*
The *Economist*
The *Los Angeles Times*
The *New York Times*
Newsweek
Time
The *Times* (London)
The *Wall Street Journal*
The *Washington Post*

MEMOIRS AND PERSONAL ACCOUNTS

Acheson, Dean. *Present at the Creation: My Years at the State Department*. New York: W. W. Norton, 1969.

———. *The Korean War*. New York: W. W. Norton, 1971.

Bohlen, Charles E. *Witness to History, 1929–1969*. New York: W. W. Norton, 1973.

Bradley, Omar Nelson. *A General's Life: An Autobiography*. New York: Simon and Schuster, 1983.

Cline, Ray. *Secrets, Spies, and Scholars: Blueprint of the Essential CIA*. Washington, D.C.: Acropolis Books, 1976.

Eden, Anthony. "Britain in World Strategy." *Foreign Affairs* (January 1951): p.   .

Eisenhower, Dwight. *Mandate for Change, 1953–1956*. Garden City, N.Y.: Doubleday, 1963.

Kennan, George F. *Memoirs 1925–1950*. Boston: Little, Brown, 1967.

———. *Memoirs, 1950–63*. Boston: Little, Brown, 1972.

Kent, Sherman. *Sherman Kent and the Board of National Estimates: Collected Essays*. Ed. Donald Steury. Washington, D.C.: Central Intelligence Agency, 1994.

Khrushchev, Nikita. *Khrushchev Remembers*. Trans. Strobe Talbott. Boston: Little Brown, 1970.

Lilienthal, David E. *The Atomic Energy Years, 1945–1950*. Vol. 2, *The Journals of David E. Lilienthal*. New York: Harper and Row, 1964.

———. *The Venturesome Years, 1950–1955*. Vol. 3, *The Journals of David E. Lilienthal*. New York: Harper and Row, 1966.

Nitze, Paul H. *From Hiroshima to Glasnost*. London: Weidenfield and Nicholson, 1989.

———. "The Development of NSC #68." *International Security* (spring 1980).

Nourse, Edwin. *Economics in the Public Service*. New York: Harcourt Brace & Co., 1953.

Reston, James. *Deadline: A Memoir*. New York: Random House, 1991.

Ridgway, Matthew Bunker. *Soldier: The Memoirs of Matthew B. Ridgway*, as told to Harold H. Martin. New York: Harper, 1956.

———. *The Korean War*. New York: DaCapo, 1967.

Rusk, Dean, and Richard Rusk. *As I Saw It*. New York: Penguin, 1990.

Sudoplatov, Pavel, and Anatoli Sudoplatov. *Special Tasks: The Memoirs of an Unwanted Witness—A Soviet Spymaster*. Boston: Little, Brown and Company: 1995.

Taylor, Maxwell. *Uncertain Trumpet*. Westport, Conn.: Greenwood, 1974.

Truman, Harry. *Memoirs: 1945, Year of Decisions*. New York: Signet, 1955.

———. *Memoirs: Years of Trial and Hope, 1946–1952*. New York: Signet, 1956.

———. *Plain Speaking: An Oral Biography of Harry S Truman*, co-written with Merle Miller. London: Victor Gollancz, 1974.

NATO AND U.S. GOVERNMENT BOOKS

Central Intelligence Agency. *The CIA Under Harry Truman*. Washington, D.C.: 1994.

Congressional Service Quarterly. *Congress and the Nation, 1945–64*. Washington, D.C.: 1965.

Department of Defense. *Semiannual Report of the Secretary of Defense, July 1 to December 31, 1950*. Washington, D.C.: GPO, 1951.

NATO Information Service. *NATO: Facts and Figures*. Brussels: 1971.

President's Air Policy Commission. *Survival in the Air Age*. Washington, D.C.: 1948.

SECONDARY BOOKS

Abramson, Rudy. *Spanning the Century: The Life of W. Averell Harriman, 1891–1986*. New York: William Morrow, 1992.

Adair, Paul. *Hitler's Greatest Defeat: The Collapse of Army Group Centre, June 1944*. London: Brockhampton Press, 1996.

Adler, Selig. *The Isolationist Impulse: Its Twentieth Century Reaction*. London: Abelard-Schuman, 1957.

Albright, Joseph, and Marcia Kunstel. *Bombshell: The Secret Story of America's Unknown Atomic Spy Conspiracy*. New York: Times Books, 1997.

Ambrose, Stephen. *Eisenhower: Soldier and President*. New York: Simon and Schuster, 1990.

———. *Rise to Globalism: American Foreign Policy Since 1938*. New York: Penguin Books, 1988.

Andrew, Christopher. *For the President's Eyes Only: Secret Intelligence and the American Presidency from Washington to Bush*. New York: Harper Collins, 1995.

Appleman, Roy E. *South to the Naktong, North to the Yalu: The United States Army in the Korean War*. Washington, D.C.: Department of the Army, 1960.

Barker, Elisabeth. *Britain in a Divided Europe, 1945–70*. London: Weidenfield and Nicholson, 1971.

Barnett, Corelli. *The Lost Victory: British Dreams, British Realities, 1945–1950*. London: MacMillan, 1996.

Bartlett, C. J. *The Global Conflict: The International Rivalry of the Great Powers, 1880–1970*. Harlow, Essex: Longman Group, 1984.

Blair, Clay. *The Forgotten War*. New York: Times Books, 1987.

Botting, Douglas. *In the Ruins of the Reich*. London: Grafton Books, 1985.

Boyd, Alexander. *The Soviet Air Force Since 1918*. London: MacDonald and Jane's, 1977.

Boyer, Paul. *By the Bomb's Early Light: American Thought and Culture at the Dawn of the Atomic Age*. New York: Pantheon, 1985.

Brinkly, Douglas. *Dean Acheson: The Cold War Years, 1953–71*. New Haven: Yale University Press, 1992.

Bullock, Alan. *Foreign Secretary*. Vol. 3, *Ernest Bevin*. New York: Norton, 1983.

Callahan, David. *Dangerous Capabilities: Paul Nitze and the Cold War*. New York: Harper Collins, 1990.

Caridi, Ronald J. *The Korean War and American Politics: The Republican Party as a Case Study*. Philadelphia: University of Pennsylvania Press, 1969.

Catudal, Honore M. *Soviet Nuclear Strategy from Stalin to Gorbachev: A Revolution in Soviet Military and Political Thinking*. London: Mansell Publishing, 1988.

Coblenz, Constance, Morton Kaplan, and William Reitzel. *United States Foreign Policy, 1945–1955*. Washington, D.C.: The Brookings Institution, 1956.

Codevilla, Angelo. *Informing Statecraft: Intelligence for a New Century*. New York: The Free Press, 1992.

Cogan, Charles G. *Oldest Allies, Guarded Friends: The United States and France Since 1940*. Westport, Conn.: Praeger, 1994.

Cohen, Warren I. *America in the Age of Soviet Power, 1945–1991*. Vol. 4, *The Cambridge History of American Foreign Relations*. Cambridge: Cambridge University Press, 1993.

Condit, Doris M. *The Test of War, 1950–1953*. Vol. 2, *History of the Office of Secretary of Defense*. Washington, D.C.: Office of the Secretary of Defense, 1988.

Condit, Kenneth W. *The Joint Chiefs of Staff and National Policy, 1947–1949*. Vol. 2, *The History of the Joint Chiefs of Staff*. Wilmington, Delaware: Michael Glazier, 1979.

Cook, Chris, and John Stevenson. *The Atlas of Modern Warfare*. London: Weidenfeld and Nicolson, 1978.

Cook, Don. *Forging the Alliance: NATO, 1945–50*. London: Secker and Warburg, 1989.

Crankshaw, Edward. *The New Cold War: Moscow v. Peking*. Harmondsworth, Middlesex: Penguin, 1963.

Cray, Ed. *General of the Army: George C. Marshall, Soldier and Statesman*. New York: Norton, 1990.

Crockatt, Richard. *The Fifty Years War: The United States and the Soviet Union in World Politics, 1941–91*. London: Routledge, 1995.

Cumings, Bruce. *The Roaring of the Cataract*. Vol. 2, *The Origins of the Korean War*. Princeton: Princeton University Press, 1990.

———. *War and Television*. London: Verso, 1992.

Cumings, Bruce, and Jon Halliday. *Korea: The Unknown War*. London: Viking, 1988.

Darby, Phillip. *British Defence Policy East of Suez, 1947–1968*. London: Oxford University Press, 1973.

Darling, Arthur. *The Central Intelligence Agency: An Instrument of Government, to 1950*. University Park: Pennsylvania University Press, 1990.

Deighton, Anne, ed. *Britain and the First Cold War*. London: MacMillan Press, 1990.

DePorte, A. W. *Europe Between the Superpowers: The Enduring Balance*. New Haven: Yale University Press, 1979.

Donovan, Robert J. *Tumultuous Years: The Presidency of Harry S. Truman, 1949–53*. New York: W. W. Norton, 1982.

Erickson, John, Lynn Hansen, and William Schneider. *Soviet Ground Forces: An Operational Assessment*. Boulder, Colo.: Westview Press, 1986.

Farrar-Hockley, Anthony. *The British Part in the Korean War*. London: Her Majesty's Stationary Office, 1990.

Ferrell, Robert H. *Truman: A Centenary Remembrance*. New York: Viking Press, 1984.

Foot, Rosemary. *The Wrong War: American Policy and the Dimensions of the Korean Conflict, 1950–1953*. Ithaca, N.Y.: Cornell University Press, 1985.

Freedman, Lawrence. *The Evolution of Nuclear Strategy*. New York: St. Martin's Press, 1983.

Fursdon, Edward. *The European Defense Community: A History*. London: MacMillan, 1980.

Gaddis, John Lewis. *Strategies of Containment: A Critical Appraisal of Postwar American National Security Policy*. New York: Oxford University Press, 1982.

———. *The Long Peace: Inquiries into the History of the Cold War*. New York: Oxford University Press, 1987.

————. *The United States and the End of the Cold War: Implications, Reconsiderations, and Provocations.* Oxford: Oxford University Press, 1994.

————. *We Now Know: Rethinking Cold War History.* New York: Oxford University Press, 1997.

Gallup, George H. *The Gallup Poll: Public Opinion, 1935–71.* New York: Random House, 1972.

Garder, Michel. *A History of the Soviet Army.* London: Pall Mall Press, 1966.

Gentry, Curt. *J. Edgar Hoover: The Man and His Secrets.* New York: Plume, 1991.

Goncharov, Sergei, John Lewis, and Xue Litai. *Uncertain Partners: Stalin, Mao, and the Korean War.* Stanford: Stanford University Press, 1993.

Gorodetsky, Gabriel. *Soviet Foreign Policy, 1917–1991.* London: Frank Cass, 1994.

Gough, Terrence J. *US Army Mobilization and Logistics in the Korean War: A Research Approach.* Washington, D.C.: Army Center of Military History, 1987.

Grove, Eric J. *Vanguard to Trident: British Naval Policy Since World War II.* London: The Bodley Head, 1987.

Hamby, Alonzo. *Beyond the New Deal: Harry S. Truman and American Liberalism.* New York: Columbia University Press, 1973.

————. *Man of the People: A Life of Harry S. Truman.* New York: Oxford University Press, 1995.

Hansen, James H. *Correlation of Forces: Four Decades of Soviet Military Development.* New York: Praeger, 1987.

Hastings, Max. *The Korean War.* New York: Simon and Schuster, 1987.

Heller, Michel, and Aleksandr Nekrich. *Utopia in Power: A History of the USSR From 1917 to the Present.* Trans. Phyllis Carlos. London: Hutchinson, 1985.

Helmreich, Jonathan. *Belgium and Europe: A Study in Small Power Diplomacy.* The Hague: Mouton, 1976.

Herken, Gregg. *Cardinal Choices: Presidential Science Advising from the Atomic Bomb to SDI.* New York: Oxford University Press, 1992.

Herring, George. *America's Longest War: The United States and Vietnam, 1950–75.* New York: John Wiley & Sons, 1979.

Hershberg, James. *James B. Conant.* New York: Knopf, 1993.

Hilsman, Roger. *The Politics of Policy Making in Defense and Foreign Affairs.* New York: Harper and Row, 1971.

Hogan, Michael J. *A Cross of Iron: Harry S. Truman and the Origins of the National Security State, 1945–1954.* Cambridge: Cambridge University Press, 1998.

Holloway, David. *Stalin and the Bomb: The Soviet Union and Atomic Energy, 1939–56.* New Haven: Yale University Press, 1994.

Huizinga, J. H. *Mr. Europe: A Political Biography of Paul Henri Spaak.* London: Weidenfield and Nicholson, 1961.

Hunt, Michael. *Ideology and US Foreign Policy.* New Haven: Yale University Press, 1987.

Huntington, Samuel P. *The Soldier and the State: The Theory and Politics of Civil-Military Relations.* Cambridge, Mass.: Belknap Press, 1957.

————. *Common Defense: Strategic Programs in National Politics.* New York: Columbia University Press, 1961.

Huston, James A. *Outposts and Allies: U.S. Army Logistics in the Cold War, 1945–53.* Cranbury, N.J.: Associated University Presses, 1988.

Inglis, Fred. *The Cruel Peace: Everyday Life and the Cold War.* New York: Basic Books, 1991.

Isaacson, Walter, and Evan Thomas. *The Wise Men: Six Friends and the World They Made*. London: Faber and Faber, 1986.

Ismay, Hastings L. *NATO: The First Five Years, 1949–54*. New York: NATO, 1955.

James, D. Clayton, with Anne Sharp Wells. *Refighting the Last War: Command and Crisis in Korea, 1950–1953*. New York: The Free Press, 1993.

Jentleson, Bruce, and Thomas Paterson, ed. *Encyclopedia of U.S. Foreign Relations*. New York: Oxford University Press, 1997.

Jonas, Manfred. *The United States and Germany: A Diplomatic History*. London: Cornell University Press, 1984.

Kaplan, Lawrence. *NATO and the United States: The Enduring Alliance*. Boston: Twayne Publishers, 1988.

Keegan, John. *A History of Warfare*. New York: Vintage Books, 1993.

Kennedy, Paul. *The Rise and Fall of the Great Powers: Economic Change and Military Conflict, 1500–2000*. London: Fontana, 1989.

Kepley, David R. *The Collapse of the Middle Way: Senate Republicans and the Bipartisan Foreign Policy, 1948–52*. New York: Greenwood, 1988.

Kilmarx, Robert A. *A History of Soviet Air Power*. London: Faber and Faber, 1962.

Kofsky, Frank. *Harry S. Truman and the War Scare of 1948: A Successful Campaign to Deceive the Nation*. New York: St. Martin's Press, 1993.

Koistinen, Paul A. C. *The Military Industrial Complex: A Historical Perspective*. New York: Praeger, 1980.

Kolko, Gabriel. *The Roots of American Foreign Policy*. Boston: Beacon Press, 1969.

Lacouture, Jean. *De Gaulle: The Ruler, 1945–1970*. London: Harvill, 1992.

LaFeber, Walter. *America, Russia, and the Cold War, 1945–1980*. New York: Wiley and Sons, 1980.

———. *The American Age: United States Foreign Policy at Home and Abroad, 1750 to the Present*. New York: W. W. Norton, 1994.

Larson, Deborah Welch. *Origins of Containment: A Psychological Explanation*. Princeton: Princeton University Press, 1995.

Lee, William T., and Richard Staar. *Soviet Military Policy Since World War II*. Stanford: Hoover Institution Press, 1986.

Leffler, Melvyn. *A Preponderance of Power: National Security, the Truman Administration, and the Cold War*. Stanford, Calif.: Stanford University Press, 1992.

———. *The Specter of Communism: The United States and the Origins of the Cold War, 1917–1953*. New York: Hill and Wang, 1994.

Mackintosh, Malcolm. *Juggernaut: A History of the Soviet Armed Forces*. New York: Macmillan, 1967.

MacMillan, Margaret O., and David S. Sorenson. *Canada and NATO: Uneasy Past, Uncertain Future*. Waterloo, Ontario: University of Waterloo Press, 1990.

Manchester, William. *The Glory and the Dream: A Narrative History of America, 1932–72*. New York: Bantam Books, 1990.

Martin, David. *Wilderness of Mirrors*. New York: Ballantine Books, 1980.

Mastny, Vojtech. *Russia's Road to the Cold War: Diplomacy, Warfare, and the Politics of Communism, 1941–1945*. New York: Columbia University Press, 1979.

McCollough, David. *Truman*. New York: Simon and Schuster, 1992.

Medvedev, Roy A. *Khrushchev*. Trans. Brian Pearce. Oxford: Basil Blackwell, 1982.

Melanson, Richard, and David Mayers, ed. *Reevaluating Eisenhower: American Foreign Policy in the 1950's*. Urbana, Ill.: University of Illinois Press, 1987.

Millett, Allan R., and Peter Maslowski. *For the Common Defense: A Military History of the United States of America.* New York: Free Press, 1984.

Moorhead, Caroline. *Troublesome People: Enemies of War: 1916–1986.* London: Hamish Hamilton, 1987.

Morgan, Kenneth O. *The People's Peace: British History, 1945–89.* Oxford: Oxford University Press, 1990.

Morris, Charles R. *Iron Destinies, Lost Opportunities: The Arms Race Between the USA and the USSR, 1945–1987.* New York: Harper and Row, 1988.

Naimark, Norman. *The Russians in Germany: A History of the Soviet Zone of Occupation, 1945–1949.* Cambridge, Mass.: Belknap Press, 1995.

O'Neill, William. *American High: The Years of Confidence, 1945–1960.* New York: Macmillan, 1986.

Pach, Chester, Jr. *Arming the Free World: The Origins of the United States Military Assistance Program, 1945–1950.* Chapel Hill: University of North Carolina Press, 1991.

Parmet, Herbert S. *The Democrats: The Years After FDR.* New York: Oxford University Press, 1976.

Patterson, James T. *Grand Expectations: The United States, 1945–1974.* New York: Oxford University Press, 1996.

Perrett, Geoffrey. *A Dream of Greatness.* New York: Coward, McCann, and Geoghegan, 1979.

Pogue, Forrest C. *George C. Marshall: Statesman, 1945–1959.* New York: Viking Press, 1987.

Poole, Walter S. *The Joint Chiefs of Staff and National Policy, 1950–1952.* Vol. 4, *The History of the Joint Chiefs of Staff.* Wilmington, Del.: Michael Glazier, 1980.

Porter, Bruce. *The USSR In Third World Conflicts: Soviet Arms and Diplomacy in Local Wars, 1945–1980.* Cambridge: Cambridge University Press, 1984.

Postan, M. M. *An Economic History of Western Europe, 1945–64.* London: Cambridge University Press, 1967.

Powaski, Ronald E. *The Entangling Alliance: The United States and European Security, 1950–1993.* Westport, Conn.: Greenwood Press, 1994.

Rae, John. *Climb to Greatness: The American Aircraft Industry, 1920–1960.* Cambridge: MIT Press, 1968.

Rearden, Stephen L. *History of the Office of Secretary of Defense: The Formative Years, 1947–1950.* Washington, D.C.: Historical Office, Office of the Secretary of Defense, 1984.

Rhodes, Richard. *Dark Sun: The Making of the Hydrogen Bomb.* New York: Simon and Schuster, 1995.

Richelson, Jeffrey. *A Century of Spies: Intelligence in the Twentieth Century.* New York: Oxford University Press, 1995.

Rogow, Arnold. *James Forrestal: A Study of Personality, Politics, and Policy.* New York: MacMillan, 1963.

Rose, Lisle A. *Roots of Tragedy: the United States and the Struggle for Asia, 1945–53.* Westport, Conn.: Greenwood Press, 1976.

Schnabel, James F., and Robert Watson. *The Joint Chiefs of Staff and National Policy, The Korean War, Part I.* Vol. 2, *The History of the Joint Chiefs of Staff.* Wilmington, Del.: Michael Glazier, 1979.

Schulzinger, Robert D. *American Diplomacy in the Twentieth Century*. 3d ed. New York: Oxford University Press, 1995.

Schwartz, Thomas A. *America's Germany: John J. McCloy and the Federal Republic of Germany*. Cambridge: Harvard University Press, 1991.

Scott, Harriet Fast, and William F. Scott, ed. *The Soviet Art of War: Doctrine, Strategy, and Tactics*. Boulder, Colo.: Westview Press, 1982.

Seaton, Albert, and Joan Seaton. *The Soviet Army: 1918 to the Present*. London: The Bodley Head, 1986.

Slowe, Peter. *Manny Shinwell: An Authorized Biography*. London: Pluto Press, 1993.

Smith, Gaddis. *Dean Acheson*. New York: Cooper Square, 1972.

Smith, Richard Norton. *Thomas E. Dewey and His Times*. New York: Simon and Schuster, 1984.

Snyder, William P. *The Politics of British Defense Policy, 1945–1962*. Columbus, Ohio: Ohio State University Press, 1964.

Steiner, Barry. *Bernard Brodie and the Foundations of American Nuclear Strategy*. Lawrence, Kans.: University of Kansas Press, 1991.

Stueck, William. *The Korean War: An International History*. Princeton: Princeton University Press, 1995.

Summers, Harry G., Jr. *Korean War Almanac*. New York: Facts on File, 1990.

Swomley, John. *The Military Establishment*. Boston: Beacon Press, 1964.

Theoharis, Athan. *Seeds of Repression: Harry S. Truman and the Origins of McCarthyism*. Chicago: Quadrangle, 1971.

Ulam, Adam. *The Rivals*. New York: Viking, 1971.

———. *Stalin: The Man and His Era*. New York: Viking, 1973.

———. *Expansion and Coexistence: Soviet Foreign Policy 1917–1973*. 2d ed. New York: Holt, Reinhart, and Winston, 1974.

Urwin, Derek W. *Western Europe Since 1945: A Political History*. London: Longman, 1991.

Vigor, P. H. *Soviet Blitzkrieg Theory*. London: MacMillan, 1983.

Volkogonov, Dimitri. *Stalin: Triumph and Tragedy*. New York: Grove Weidenfield, 1992.

Walker, J. Samuel. *Henry A. Wallace and American Foreign Policy*. Westport, Conn.: Greenwood Press, 1976.

Walker, Martin. *The Cold War and the Making of the Modern World*. London: Vintage, 1994.

Warren, Sidney. *The President as World Leader*. New York: McGraw Hill, 1964.

Weigley, Russell F. *History of the United States Army*. London: B. T. Batsford, 1967.

Weinberg, Gerhard. *A World At Arms: A Global History of World War Two*. Cambridge: Cambridge University Press, 1994.

Westerfield, H. Bradford. *Foreign Policy and Party Politics: Pearl Harbor to Korea*. New Haven: Yale University Press, 1955.

———. *The Instrument of America's Foreign Policy*. Westport, Conn.: Greenwood Press, 1980.

Whelan, Richard. *Drawing the Line: The Korean War, 1950–1953*. London: Faber and Faber, 1990.

Whiting, Allan S. *China Crosses the Yalu*. Stanford: Stanford University Press, 1960.

Williams, Phil. *The Senate and US Troops in Europe*. London: Macmillan, 1985.

Williams, William Appleman. *The Tragedy of American Diplomacy*. 2d. rev. ed. New York: Dell Publishing, 1972.

Yergin, Daniel. *Shattered Peace: The Origins of the Cold War and the National Security State*. Boston: Houghton Mifflin Press, 1977.

————. *The Prize*. New York: Simon and Schuster, 1991.

Young, John W. *Britain, France, and the Unity of Europe, 1945–1951*. Leicester: Leicester University Press, 1984.

Zametica, John, ed. *British Officials and British Foreign Policy, 1945–50*. Leicester: Leicester University Press, 1990.

Ziemke, Earl, and Magna Bauer. *Moscow to Stalingrad: Decision in the East*. New York: Military Heritage Press, 1988.

Zubok, Vladislav, and Constantine Pleshakov. *Inside the Kremlin's Cold War: From Stalin to Khrushchev*. Cambridge: Harvard University Press, 1996.

HISTORY ARTICLES

Adams, Gordon, and Randal Humm. "The US Military-Industrial Complex and National Strategy." In *Strategic Power: USA/USSR*, ed. Carl G. Jacobsen. London: Macmillan, 1990.

Almond, Gabriel. "The Elites and Foreign Policy." In *Readings in the Making of American Foreign Policy*, ed. Andrew Scott and Raymond Dawson. New York: Macmillan, 1965.

Bernhard, Nancy E. "Clearer Than Truth: Public Affairs Television and the State Department Domestic Information Campaigns, 1947–1952." *Diplomatic History* (Fall 1997).

Bernstein, Barton J. "The Truman Administration and the Korean War." In *The Truman Presidency*, ed. Michael Lacy. Cambridge: Cambridge University Press, 1989.

Booth, Ken. "US Perceptions of Soviet Threat: Prudence and Paranoia." In *Strategic Power: USA/USSR*, ed. Carl G. Jacobsen. London: Macmillan, 1990.

————. "American Strategy: The Myths Revisited." In *American Thinking About Peace and War*, ed. Ken Booth and Moorhead Wright. Sussex: Harvester Press, 1978.

Buhite, Russell, and W. Christopher Hamel. "War for Peace: The Question of an American Preventive War Against the Soviet Union, 1945–55." *Diplomatic History* (summer 1990).

Carpenter, Ted Galen. "U.S. and NATO Policy at the Crossroads: The Great Debate of 1950–51." *International History Review* (August 1986).

Clifford, J. Garry. "Bureaucratic Politics." *Journal of American History* (June 1990).

Combs, Jerald A. "The Compromise That Never Was: George Kennan, Paul Nitze, and the Issue of Conventional Deterrence in Europe, 1949–1952," *Diplomatic History* (Summer 1991).

Costigliola, Frank. "The Nuclear Family: Tropes of Gender and Pathology in the Western Alliance." *Diplomatic History* (Spring 1997).

Cumings, Bruce. " 'Revising Postrevisionism,' Or, The Poverty of Theory in Diplomatic History." In *America in the World: The Historiography of American Foreign Relations Since 1941*, ed. Michael Hogan. Cambridge: Cambridge University Press, 1995.

Cunningham, William Glenn, "Postwar Developments and the Location of the

Aircraft Industry in 1950." In *The History of the American Aircraft Industry: An Anthology*, ed. G. R. Simonson. Cambridge: MIT Press, 1968.

Day, John. "The Korean War Expansion." In *The History of the American Aircraft Industry: An Anthology*, ed. G. R. Simonson. Cambridge: MIT Press, 1968.

Door, Robert. "Thermonuclear Legacy." *Military History* (August 1995).

Evangelista, Matthew A. "Stalin's Post-War Army Reappraised." *International Security* (winter 1982/83).

Ferrell, Robert. "The Formation of the Alliance, 1948–1949," In *American Historians and the Atlantic Alliance*, ed. Lawrence Kaplan. Kent, Ohio: Kent State University Press, 1991.

Foot, Rosemary. "Making Known The Unknown War: Policy Analysis of the Korean Conflict Since the Early 1980s." In *America in the World: The Historiography of American Foreign Relations Since 1941*, ed. Michael Hogan. Cambridge: Cambridge University Press, 1995.

Friedberg, Aaron. "Why Didn't the United States Become a Garrison State?" *International Security* (spring 1992).

Gaddis, John Lewis. "NSC 68 and the Problem of Ends and Means." *International Security* (spring 1990).

———. "The Insecurities of Victory: the United States and the Perception of the Soviet Threat After World War II." In *The Truman Presidency*, ed. Michael Lacy. Cambridge: Cambridge University Press, 1989.

Gardner, Lloyd. "From Liberation to Containment, 1945–53." In *From Colony to Empire: Essays in the History of American Foreign Relations*, ed. William Appleman Williams. New York: John Wiley and Sons, 1972.

———. "Gardner's Commentary." *American Cold War Strategy: Interpreting NSC 68*, ed. Ernest May. Boston: Bedford Books, 1993.

Greiner, Christian. "The Defence of Western Europe and the Rearmament of West Germany, 1947–50." In *Western Security: The Formative Years; Atlantic and European Defence, 1947–1953*, ed. Olav Riste. Oslo: Norwegian University Press, 1985.

Griffith, Robert. "Old Progressives and the Cold War." *Journal of American History* (September 1979).

Gutman, Jon, "Almost 43 Years After the End of the Korean War, the Debate Continues Over Who Won." *Military History* (April 1996).

Hammond, Paul Y. "Super Carriers and B-36 Bombers: Appropriations, Strategy, and Politics." *American Civil Military Decisions*, ed. Harold Stein. Birmingham, Ala.: University of Alabama Press, 1963.

———. "NSC-68: Prologue to Rearmament." *Strategy, Politics, and Defense Budgets*, ed. Warner Schilling, Paul Hammond, and Glenn Snyder. New York: Columbia University Press, 1966.

Higgins, Andrew. "Secret Plot That Led to Korean War", *The Guardian*, April 13, 1996, page 15.

Hogan, Michael. "American Marshall Planners and the Search for a European Neocapitalism." *The American Historical Review* (February 1985).

Iriye, Akira. "Culture." *Journal of American History* (June 1990).

Jacob, Ian. "Principles of British Military Thought." *Foreign Affairs* (January 1951).

Jacobsen, Carl G. "The Impact of Neighbors and Allies: the Soviet Case." In *Strategic Power USA/USSR*, ed. Carl G. Jacobsen. London: Macmillan, 1990.

Kaplan, Lawrence S. "An Unequal Triad: The United States, Western Union, and NATO." In *Western Security: The Formative Years; European and Atlantic Defence, 1947–53*, ed. Olav Riste. Oslo: Norwegian University Press, 1985.

Kornienko, Georgi M. "Kornienko's Commentary." In *American Cold War Strategy: Interpreting NSC 68*, ed. Ernest May. Boston: Bedford Books, 1993.

LaFeber, Walter. "NATO and the Korean War: A Context." *Diplomatic History* (fall 1989).

Leffler, Melvyn. "National Security." *Journal of American History* (June 1990).

———. "New Approaches, Old Interpretations, and Prospective Reconfigurations." In *America in the World: The Historiography of American Foreign Relations Since 1941*, ed. Michael Hogan. Cambridge: Cambridge University Press, 1995.

———. "The Interpretive Wars Over the Cold War, 1945–1960." In *American Foreign Relations Reconsidered, 1890–1993*, ed. Gordon Martel. London: Routledge, 1994.

———. "Strategy, Diplomacy, and the Cold War: The United States, Turkey, and NATO, 1945–1952." *Journal of American History* (March 1985).

Maier, Charles S. "Alliance and Autonomy: European Identity and US Foreign Policy Objectives in the Truman Years." In *The Truman Presidency*, ed. Michael Lacy. Cambridge: Cambridge University Press, 1989.

Mark, Eduard. "The War Scare of 1946 and Its Consequences." *Diplomatic History* (summer 1997).

Matray, James I. "Truman's Plan for Victory: National Self-Determination and the Thirty-Eight Parallel Decision in Korea." *Journal of American History* (September 1979).

May, Ernest R. "The American Commitment to Germany, 1949–55." *Diplomatic History* (Fall 1989).

———. "NSC 68: The Theory and Politics of Strategy." In *American Cold War Strategy: Interpreting NSC 68*, ed. Ernest R. May. Boston: Bedford Books, 1993.

McLachlan, Donald. "Rearmament and European Integration." *Foreign Affairs* (January 1951).

McMahon, Robert J. "Credibility and World Power: Exploring the Psychological Dimension in Postwar American Diplomacy." *Diplomatic History* (fall 1991).

Miller, Steven. "The US Navy in the Nuclear Age." In *Strategic Power: USA/USSR*, ed. Carl G. Jacobsen. London: Macmillan, 1990.

Millis, Walter. "Sea Power: Abstraction or Asset?" *Foreign Affairs* (January 1951).

Mossman, B.C. "Peace Becomes Cold War, 1945–1950." In *American Military History; Volume Two: 1902–1996*, ed. Maurice Matloff. Conshohocken, Penn.: Combined Books, 1996.

Nelson, Anna Kasten. "President Truman and the Evolution of the National Security Council." *Journal of American History* (September 1985).

Norris, Robert, and William Akin. "Nuclear Notebook: Estimated US and Soviet/ Russian Nuclear Stockpile, 1945–94." *Bulletin of the Atomic Scientists* (November/December 1994).

Rearden, Steven L. "Congress and the National Defense, 1945–1950." In *The United States Military Under the Constitution of the United States, 1789–1989*, ed. Richard Kohn. New York: New York University Press, 1991.

Roman, Peter J. "Curtis LeMay and the Origins of NATO Atomic Targeting." *The Journal of Strategic Studies* (March 1993).

Rosenberg, David Alan. "American Atomic Strategy and the Hydrogen Bomb Decision." *Journal of American History* (June 1979).

Rosenberg, Emily. "Rosenberg's Commentary." In *American Cold War Strategy: Interpreting NSC 68*, ed. Ernest May. Boston: Bedford Books, 1993.

Siracusa, Joseph M. "Paul H. Nitze, NSC 68, and the Soviet Union." In *Essays in Twentieth Century American Diplomatic History Dedicated to Professor Daniel M. Smith*. Washington, D.C.: University Press of America, 1982.

Summers, Harry G., Jr. "The Korean War: A Fresh Perspective." *Military History* (April 1996).

Swartz, Thomas A. "The 'Skeleton Key'—American Foreign Policy, European Unity, and German Rearmament, 1949–54." *Central European History* (December 1986).

Trachtenberg, Marc. "A Wasting Asset: American Strategy and the Shifting Nuclear Balance, 1949–1954." In *History and Strategy*, ed. Marc Trachtenberg. Princeton: Princeton University Press, 1991.

———. "The Nuclearization of NATO and U.S.-West European Relations." In *History and Strategy*, ed. Marc Trachtenberg. Princeton: Princeton University Press, 1991.

———. "American Thinking on Nuclear War." In *Strategic Power: USA/USSR*, ed. Carl G. Jacobsen. London: Macmillan, 1990.

van der Harst, Jan. "From Neutrality to Alignment: Dutch Defense Policy, 1945–1951." In *NATO: The Founding of the Atlantic Alliance and the Integration of Europe*, ed. Francis Heller and John Gillingham. London: St. Martin's Press, 1992.

Walker, J. Samuel. "Historians and Cold War Origins." In *Major Problems in American Foreign Policy, Volume 2: Since 1914*, ed. Thomas G. Paterson. Lexington, Mass.: D.C. Heath and Company, 1984.

Watson, S. J. "A Comparison of the Russian, American and British Field Armies." *The Army Quarterly 60* (April-July 1950).

Weathersby, Kathryn. "Korea, 1949–50: To Attack or Not to Attack? Stalin, Kim Il-Sung and the Prelude to War." *Cold War International History Project Bulletin* (spring 1995).

———. "New Findings on the Korean War." *Cold War International History Project Bulletin* (fall 1993).

———. "New Russian Documents on the Korean War." *Cold War International History Project Bulletin* (winter 1995/96).

Wells, Samuel F. "The Origins of Massive Retaliation." *Political Science Quarterly* (spring 1981): pp. 31–52.

———. "Sounding the Tocsin: NSC 68 and the Soviet Threat." *International Security* (fall 1979): pp. 116–48.

———. "The First Cold War Buildup: Europe in United States Strategy and Policy, 1950–1953." In *Western Security: The Formative Years; European and Atlantic Defence, 1947–53*, ed. Olav Riste. Oslo: Norwegian University Press, 1985.

Wettig, Gerhard. "The Soviet Union and Germany in the Late Stalin Period, 1950–53." In *The Soviet Union and Europe in the Cold War, 1943–53*, ed. Francesca Gori and Silvio Pons. London: Macmillan, 1996.

Wyndham, E. H. "The Military Situation in Europe." *The Army Quarterly 60* (April-July 1950).

DOCTORAL DISSERTATIONS

Elzy, Martin Ivan. "The Origins of American Military Policy, 1945–50." Ph.D. diss., Miami University, 1975.

Patterson, Thomas. "The Economic Cold War: American Business and Economic Foreign Policy, 1945–50." Ph.D. diss., University of California, Berkeley, 1968.

Rosenberg, David Alan. *"The Development of American Nuclear Strategy, 1945–1961."* Ph.D. diss., University of Chicago, 1983.

TELEVISION PROGRAM

The Discovery Channel, "Korean War Duel." *Wings Over the Red Star Series,* 25 August 1997.

UNPUBLISHED CONFERENCE PAPERS

Arakawa, K. "The Cold War and the Foundation of the Japanese Self Defense Force." Paper presented at the Army Center of Military History Conference, Arlington, Va., June 1996.

Kaplan, Lawrence. "The Office of the Secretary of Defense and NATO, 1948–1951." Paper presented at the Army Center of Military History Conference, Arlington, Va., June 1996.

Soffer, Jonathan. "The Moral Economy of Military Keynesianism." Paper presented at the American Historical Association Conference, New York, January 1997.

Index

Acheson, Dean, 25, 47, 49–56, 59–61,
  63–64, 66–71, 73–78, 82–83, 89–90,
  100, 104, 108, 111, 117, 120–22, 154;
  case for increase in spending/
  military build-up, 49–56;
  conventional arms build-up, 59–61;
  opposition to Kennan, 55–56
Adenauer, Conrad, 110, 112–14
Airborne operations, 139; landings,
  25, 47; VTA, 38
Aircraft carriers, 8, 14, 19, 28, 49, 76,
  93, 141, 152
Algeria, 23
Alsop, Joseph and Stewart, 73
Alvarez, Luis, 59
American Legion, 47
American Telephone and Telegraph
  (AT&T), 95
Anti-tank warfare, 21, 31, 140
ANZUS Security Treaty, 124
Arctic ocean, 3
Argentina, 25
Army: Czech, 39, 127; German, East,
  108; German, Pre-1945, 32, 37;
  German, West, 110, 111; NATO
  forces, 107, 114–15, 122; North
  Korean, 85; pan-European, 40, 110,
112–14; Polish, 39; Soviet, 9, 10, 25,
  29, 31–32, 34, 36–42, 51, 55, 97, 108,
  126–27, 150–51, 155; U.S., 6, 7, 8,
  14, 17, 18–21, 26–29, 32–33, 44, 48,
  49, 61, 76, 78–80, 87, 90, 92
Army Air Corps, 7–8
Army Ordnance Tank and
  Automotive Center, 133
Asia-first strategy, 52
Atlas Corporation, 49
Atomic Energy Commission (AEC),
  49, 57–59, 61–62, 80, 91, 94, 102–3,
  116, 126
Atomic weapons, 2, 11, 14, 20, 34, 55,
  57, 59–60, 62–63, 86, 90, 92, 94,
  143–46, 151; atomic bombs, 14, 19,
  28, 33–34, 49, 54, 57–62, 77, 81, 83,
  93, 102, 108; cry for use in Korea,
  116, 144–45, 150; U.S. atomic
  monopoly, 5–6, 9, 14, 24–25, 42, 67,
  146–47
Auriol, Vincent, 115
Australia, 4, 11, 25, 124
Austria, U.S. Occupation, 8, 30; Soviet
  start of anti-aircraft bases in
  Austria, 42, 70, 86
Automotive industry, 134

Aviation industry, 133, 138–39;
    German, 36; U.S., 133, 138
Azores, 19, 123

Barents Sea, 40
Baruch, Bernard, 64
Belgium, 23–24, 33, 115
Beria, Laventri, 57–58, 150
Berlin blockade, 2, 22–23, 34, 77, 156
Bevin, Ernest, 23–24, 112
Biological warfare, 31, 38
Black Sea, 38, 40
Bohlen, Charles, 1, 56, 74, 78, 91, 96,
    109
Bombers: Soviet, 31, 36, 127, 141; U.S.,
    2, 8, 14, 20–23, 28, 49, 61, 117,
    142–45
Boosted fission weapons, 62, 143
Bowles, Chester, 18, 131
Bradley, Omar, 14, 27, 58, 61, 72, 87,
    90, 95, 102, 109
Brewster, Owen, 116
Bridges, Styles, 122
BROILER, 14, 22
Bulganin, Nikolai, 40, 149
Bulgaria, 89, 97
Bureau of the Budget, 6, 15, 27–28,
    74–75, 79, 91, 99–101, 105
Burma, 51, 89, 125
Burns, James, 52, 64–65
Byrd, Harry, 121

Canada, 25, 32, 114, 141–42
Cannon, Clarence, 80
Caribbean Sea, 18
Caspian Sea, 40
Central Intelligence Agency (CIA), 30,
    43–44, 54, 67, 89, 91, 97, 117, 125;
    lack of reliable intelligence on
    USSR, 43–45
Chemical warfare, 38
China, 2, 10, 18, 32, 34, 51, 63, 66, 76,
    77, 83, 86, 89, 92, 97–98, 101–2, 105,
    112–13, 119–24, 126–28, 147;
    Chinese nationalist resistance, Civil
    war, 2–3, 17–18, 32, 34, 66, 77, 86;
    and Korean War, 2, 76, 86, 89,
    97–98, 101–2, 105, 112–13, 119–24,

126–28, 147; Sino-Soviet alliance, 2,
    77, 83, 86, 147; and Tibet, 2
China Lobby, 83, 102, 120
Churchill, Winston, 33, 42, 105, 154
Coast Guard, 102
Cold war, 3, 14, 17, 22–23, 54, 71–73,
    94, 124, 126, 157, 159
Collins, Lawton, 34
Colonialism, 5, 24, 25, 32, 51, 67, 92,
    123
Communism, 1, 8–9,10, 17, 21, 23,
    33–34, 38–39, 41, 44, 51, 53, 57, 60,
    66–72, 82–84, 86, 93, 97, 108–9, 113,
    116–17, 120, 123–24, 126–27, 131,
    137, 154–59; anti-Communism, 18,
    34, 44, 66, 70, 72, 83, 89, 116–17,
    120, 154, 157; in China, 17, 34, 86,
    89, 93, 113, 126; in Czechoslovakia,
    21, 23, 39; in East Germany, 108; in
    Korea, 108–9, 113; in NSC-68,
    66–67; in Poland, 39, 44; in
    Philippines, 124; in Romania, 39; in
    U.S. during Korean war, 116–57
Congressional Aviation Policy
    Board, 21
Connally, Thomas, 84
Containment, 1, 17, 19, 53–54, 71–72,
    74, 79, 96, 98, 120–21, 123, 125,
    147–48, 153, 156; coined by
    Kennan, 53
Coudert, Frederic, 121
Council of Economic Advisors, 90
Council of European Economic
    Cooperation (CEEC), 8
Cuban missile crisis, 102
Czechoslovakia, 14, 21, 23–24, 39, 53,
    127

Daughters of the American
    Revolution, 48
Dean, Gordon, 90
Dean, William, 93
Debt, 5–6, 8–9, 13–16, 28, 71, 82, 129,
    133
Defense Production Act, 132
Democratic Party/Democrats, 7, 8, 16,
    48, 50, 121, 130, 136
Denfeld, Louis, 27, 49

Department of Defense, 2, 6, 21, 26–27, 52, 54, 61, 79, 94, 99–100, 103, 105, 132, 138, 145
de Silva, Peer, 43
Dewey, Thomas, 17, 50, 81, 121
Distant Early Warning (DEW) System, 2, 142
Dulles, John Foster, 17, 81, 84, 121, 147–48

Early, Stephen, 48
Economic Stabilization Agency (ESA), 131–32
Egypt, 23
Eisenhower, Dwight, 2, 5, 27–29, 79–80, 114–15, 117–18, 122, 145–49, 158
Elections, 6–7, 17, 99, 117, 158
Elsey, George, 75, 88
Estonia, 10
European Coal and Steel Community, 115
European Defense Community (EDC), 114

Fair Deal, 16, 28, 129–30
Fermi, Enrico, 62
Finletter, Thomas, 80, 95, 146
Foreign Aid, 28, 50, 71, 82, 100; mark of U.S. as global power, 124, 153
Foreign Office (U.K.), 107, 112, 126, 135
Forrestal, James, 17, 22–23, 27, 47–48, 60, 103, 141
France, 5, 9, 14, 23–24, 33, 51, 111, 113, 115, 124, 136; demobilization, 5; economy, 5, 8–9; and German rearmament, 51, 110–15
Freedom and Independence Movement (Poland), 44
Free trade, 10, 119
Fuchs, Klaus, 83

Gehlen, Reinhard, 43
General Motors, 95, 134
George, Walter, 78, 121
Germany: catalyst for change in U.S. political philosophy, 19; change in balance of power, 96–97; demilitarized, 5; French opposition to rearmament, 110; German economy, 22, 110; paramilitary strength, 96; rearmament, 51, 107; Soviet occupation of East Germany, 42; Soviet use of German scientific/ military knowledge, 35–37
Gold, Harry, 83
Goodpaster, Andrew, 146
Gray, Gordon, 49
Great Debate, 119–23, 130, 154
Greece, 2, 3, 10, 17, 26, 29, 42, 53, 84, 123
Greenland, 19
Gross National Product (GNP), 6, 7, 9, 14, 16, 24, 28–29, 82, 94, 132
Groves, Leslie, 57
Gruenther, Alfred, 27
Guam, 76
Guomindang Party, 34, 83

Harmon Report, 60
Harriman, Averell, 50, 52
Helicopters, 133, 140–41
Hillenkoetter, Roscoe, 89
Hiroshima, 11, 14, 34, 58, 62, 143
Hiss, Alger, 83
Hitler, Adolph, 14
Hong Kong, 33, 55, 89
Hoover, Herbert, 84; sparks debate on foreign policy, 118–21, 142
House of Representatives, 7, 49, 80, 95, 100, 106, 130
Huk insurgency, 124
Hull, John, 58, 61
Hungary, 66, 97, 148
Hydrogen weapons, H-bombs, 57, 59, 62–64, 118, 142–43, 145, 150–51

Iceland, 19, 111, 123
India, 25, 51, 124
Indochina, 9, 24, 51–52, 87, 89, 109, 125, 147
Indonesia, 24–25, 33, 125
Inflation, 71, 95, 105, 130–35
International Ruhr Authority, 110
Iran, 2, 8, 10, 17, 34, 53, 89, 98

Isolationism, 6, 18, 25, 68–69, 72, 83–84, 87, 119–20

Japan, 1–3, 6, 8–10, 13–14, 18–19, 25, 28, 38, 40, 42–43, 53, 66, 70, 76, 81, 84, 92, 96, 124, 153; Japanese Peace Treaty, 96; U.S. occupation, 8, 18
Jenner, William, 82
Johnson, Louis, 27, 40; case for reduced military spending, 47–49, 63–80, 87, 89, 91, 93–94, 99, 101, 103–4, 111
Johnson, Lyndon, 116
Johnston, Olin, 121
Joint Chiefs of Staff (JCS), 26–34, 49, 56, 59, 61, 64–67, 72–73, 75–76, 79, 88, 90, 93–95, 101, 103–5, 126, 147, 149

Kennan, George, 53–56, 58, 60, 62, 64, 72, 74, 89, 148, 155; case against build-up, 53–58; opposition to first-use, 53–58
Keynesian economic theory, 15, 71
Keyserling, Leon, 15
Khariton, Yuri, 57
Khrushchev, Nikita, 39, 150
Knowland, William, 121
Kohler, Foy, 34
Korea/Korean War: expansion of American Influence, in alliances, 123–24; intervention of China, 98, 101, 105; in military aid, 124–25; North Korean Attack of South Korea, 85; phases of the war, 97; turning point in arms race, 88–97; U.S. participation indirect war with Soviets, 106
Krock, Arthur, 75, 120
Kuznetsov, Nikolai, 40

Labor, 16, 92, 134, 136
Labrador, 19
Landon, Truman, 64–65
Latvia, 10
Lawrence, Ernest, 59
Lawton, Frederick, 75, 99–100
LeMay, Curtis, 146

Lend-Lease (lend-lease payments), 30
Libya, 23, 123; organized labor, 16, 136
Lilienthal, David, 59, 61–64, 116
Lindley, Ernest, 76–77
Linse, Walter, 44
Lippman, Walter, 53, 120
Lithuania, 10–11, 41
Lodge, Henry Cabot, Jr., 121
London Conference of 1947, 9
Long, Russell, 121
Long Range Detection Program (LRDP), 57
Lovett, Robert, 102, 104–5
Lunn, Arnold, 119
Luxembourg, 23, 112

Macao, 89
MacArthur, Douglas, 6, 89, 92, 96–97, 103, 116, 125, 158
Maclean, Donald, 11, 126–27
Malaya, 33, 51
Manchuria, 38, 43, 87
Manhattan Project, 57, 83, 95
Marine Corps, 7, 54, 79, 101, 104
Marshall, George, 21, 47, 50, 102, 104, 111, 122
Marshall Plan (European Recovery Program), 8, 54, 78, 80, 84, 125, 156
Massive Retaliation, 147–49
McCarthy, Joseph, 77, 83–84, 117
McClellan, John, 121
McCloy, John, 109
McMahon, Brien, 48, 78, 94, 146
Mediterranean, 17, 28, 42, 51; eastern Mediterranean, 17, 51; western Mediterranean, 28
Mexico, 18
MGB, 37–38
Mig-15, 36
Millikin, Eugene, 87
Mitchell, Billy, 20
Moch, Jules, 111
Montgomery, Bernard, 33
Morgenstierne, Wilhelm, 108–9
Morocco, 23, 123
Murray, Phillip, 136
Murrow, Edward R., 64

Mutual Defense Assistance Program
   (MDAP), 26
Mutual Security Program, 125

Nagasaki, 14, 34, 146
National Advisory Board on
   Mobilization Policy, 131
National Assembly (France), 114
National Guard, 91, 94
National Press Club, 117
National Security Act of 1947, 43
National Security Agency (NSA), 142
National Security Council (NSC), 2,
   42, 50, 56, 59, 62–80, 84–85, 87–91,
   93–94, 97, 105, 131–32, 147–48. *See
   also* NSC-68
National Security Resources Board
   (NSRB), 89, 116, 131–32
National War College, 148
NATO, 3, 26, 32, 48, 51–52, 103,
   107–16, 121–24, 131, 148–49, 151,
   154
Navy, 1, 8, 17, 19–20, 27–28, 49, 60, 76,
   79–80, 93, 100–102, 104, 123,
   138–41, 144, 150–51
Nerve gas, 38
Netherlands, 5, 9, 23–24
New Deal, 15, 18, 81, 129, 132
New Look, 78, 146, 149
New Zealand, 3, 26, 124
Nitze, Paul, 51, 56, 59–61, 63–66,
   71–78, 87, 104
Norstad, Lauris, 30, 58
North Atlantic Council, 26, 111
North Atlantic Treaty, 1, 3, 19, 23–24,
   26, 29–33, 51, 53, 77, 82, 84, 96, 110,
   120–22
Norway, 24, 32
Nourse, Edwin, 16, 28
NSC-68, 64–80, 84, 86, 89, 91, 96, 98,
   103–5, 113, 118, 122, 146, 157
Nuclear power, 3, 145, 148, 151
Nuclear weapons, 1, 3, 13–14, 19–20,
   22, 29, 37, 42, 48–49, 58, 60–61, 63,
   72, 78, 90, 92, 108, 122, 127, 142–43,
   146–52. *See also* Thermonuclear
   weapons

Office of Defense Mobilization
   (ODM), 131–32, 138, 143
Office of Price Stabilization (OPS), 132
OFFTACKLE, 28–29
Okinawa, 14, 19, 76
Old Guard, 72, 77, 81–84, 88, 120–23,
   146
Operation Barbarossa, 37
Operation CHROMITE, 93
Oppenheimer, J. Robert, 57, 62, 71

Pace, Frank, 28, 87–88, 101, 111
Pakistan, 25, 124
Palestine, 51
Pearson, Drew, 64
Perkins, George, 74
Philby, Kim, 43–44, 126
Philippines, 1, 18–19, 34, 76, 87,
   124–25
Pleven, Rene, 112–14
Plutonium, 34, 59
Point Four, 124
Poland, 10
Polls: election, 6; German
   rearmament, 110; H-bomb, 64;
   Korean war, 88; price controls, 71;
   Truman popularity, 132, 158;
   UMT, 21; Whermacht Generals, 32;
   WWI, 18
Potsdam Conference, 10, 113
Price controls, 71, 82, 130–31, 134
Pyrenees, 33

Quemoy and Matsu, 123, 147

Rabi, Isador, 59
Radar, 2, 36, 133, 138, 141–42, 151
Radar Defense Organization (RDO),
   141
Republican Party/Republicans, 7, 16,
   81–83, 87, 95, 116–17, 121–22, 130,
   131, 146, 158
Rockets, 36, 127, 145, 151
Romania, 41
Roosevelt, Franklin, 6, 15, 47, 49–50,
   81, 83, 97
Royall, Kenneth, 49

Saudi Arabia, 1, 19, 123, 125
Schaub, William, 74
Schuman, Robert, 112, 115
Securities and Exchange Commission
    (SEC), 133
Selective Service Act, 22, 79
Senate, U.S., 16, 25, 77, 78, 80, 83–84,
    87, 100, 106, 117, 120–22, 132
Sherman, Forest, 76, 92, 139
Shinwell, Manny, 40, 111
Slack, Alfred, 83
Smith, Harold, 6
Smith, Margaret Chase, 88
Smith, Walter Bedell, 30, 43, 90
Sonar, 141
Soong, T. V., 42
Souers, Sidney, 62
South Africa, 142
South East Asian Treaty Organization
    (SEATO), 124
Soviet air force, 31, 35–36; VTA, 38
Soviet army, 9, 25, 28–32, 34, 37,
    39–41, 51, 55, 97, 108, 127, 155; use
    of German Scientists, 34–39
Soviet navy, 40, 151
Spaak, Paul Henri, 23
Stalin, Josef, 2–3, 10–11, 22, 37–38,
    40–42, 45, 53, 57–58, 68, 84, 96, 98,
    113, 117, 126–28, 149–51, 155–56
Standard Oil of New Jersey, 95
Stassen, Howard, 121
State-Defense Policy Review
    Group, 65
State Department, 34, 50–51, 53, 56,
    58–59, 63, 65, 73–74, 83–84, 86, 88,
    109, 118, 136
Steel industry, 136–37
Stikker, Dirk, 109
Stimson, Henry, 47
Strategic Air Command (SAC), 2, 20,
    123, 143–44, 146
Strategic bombing, 8–9, 13–14, 19–22,
    28–29, 32, 36, 41, 55, 60, 80, 101,
    140, 143, 144
Strategic nuclear bombing, 19–20, 25,
    27–28

Submarines, 3, 20, 40, 74, 80, 140–41,
    145, 151
Subversive Activities Control Board,
    102
Sullivan, John, 49
Symington, Stuart, 49, 80, 91, 116, 132

Tactical Air Command, 20, 134
Tactical bombing, 14, 20, 92
Taft, Robert, 81–82, 87, 99, 120–22,
    136, 146, 158
Taiwan, 3, 76, 83–84, 87, 89, 123–24,
    159
Tanks, 12, 23, 37–38, 85, 92, 125, 133,
    138–40, 146–47
Taxes, 6, 15–16, 18, 28, 71, 78, 81–82,
    99, 121, 129, 135
Taylor, Maxwell, 148
Teller, Edward, 62
Thailand, 124–25
Thermonuclear weapons, 2, 62, 64,
    149–50
Third World, 124
Thompson, Llewellyn, 74
Tibet, 2, 89
Treaty of Brussels, 24
Treaty of Dunkirk, 23
TROJAN, 14
Truman Doctrine, 17, 78
Truman, Harry: budgeting and debt-
    reduction, 14–17, 21, 26, 18–29,
    47–48; budgeting and financing
    increases, 91, 129; decision to send
    forces into Korea, 86–88; distrust of
    professional corps, 100; domestic
    popularity decline, 116; estimations
    of Soviet military, 34–36, 40, 57;
    limited intelligence on Soviets,
    43–45; opposition by Old Guard,
    82–83; response to Soviet atomic
    bomb, 58–64; turning point in
    foreign affairs, 118
Tudeh Party, 89
Turkey, 2–3, 10, 17, 26, 29, 34, 42, 84,
    96, 123
Tydings, Millard, 78, 83

Ulbricht, Walter, 108
UN forces, 92–93, 97
United Kingdom (U.K.), 5, 10–11, 14, 19, 22–25, 28, 32–33, 36–37, 39–40, 42, 51, 66, 71, 81–83, 94, 97, 104, 107, 109–13, 115, 119, 123, 124, 126, 135; economy, 5, 8–9
United Nations (UN), 58, 70, 84, 87, 92–93, 97, 107, 113, 139, 158
United States Steel, 95
Universal Military Training (UMT), 21
Uranium, 62, 142
U.S. Air Force, 7–8, 14, 42, 44, 57, 95, 125
U.S. Economy, 6, 15–16, 41, 48, 71, 74, 80–82, 90, 108, 132–37
USSR, 1, 5, 9–12, 14, 19–22, 25, 28, 30–31, 34–36, 38, 41–45, 50, 53–56, 61, 67–72, 88–89, 92, 98, 103, 108, 113, 116, 125–28, 157–58; ability to evade U.S. intelligence, 43–45; appropriation of German military knowledge, 36–38; atomic program, 57; conventional superiority, 30–31; initiation of arms build-up, 126; partial demobilization, 9–12; Soviet economy, 11, 30, 41, 68; U.S. analysis of intent of USSR, 34–36

Vandenberg, Arthur, 17, 81
Vandenderg, Hoyt, 22, 27
van Zandt, Charles, 49
Vinson, Fred, 137
Voice of America, 103
von Neumann, John, 150

Wage controls, 1, 100
Wage Stabilization Board, 132, 136
Walters, Vernon, 86
Warren, Earl, 121
Webb, Jim, 15, 86, 91
Wehrmacht, 32, 37
Western European Union, 23–26, 29
Wherry, Kenneth, 81, 84, 121–22
Wilson, Charles, 131
World War II, 1–2, 5–11, 15–16, 18–20, 36–40, 43–44, 50, 60, 62, 72, 75–76, 82–83, 92, 129, 132–33, 138–39, 143, 152, 157

Yalta Conference, 70
Yugoslavia, 32, 43, 88–89, 98, 124

Zhukov, Giorgi, 40, 149